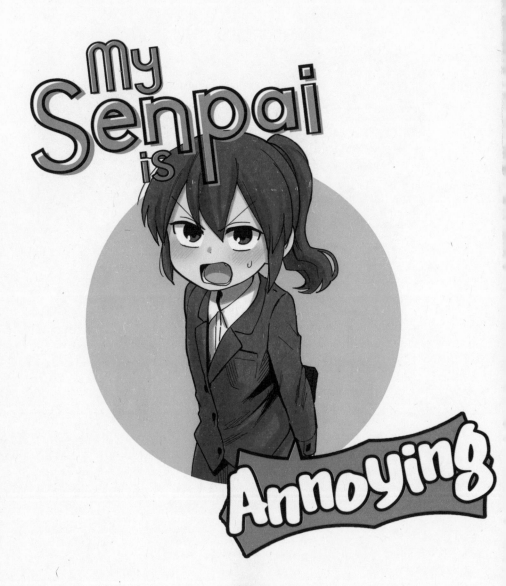

My Senpai is Annoying

2

Story & Art by
SHIROMANTA

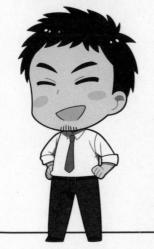

A senpai whose junior employee thinks he's annoying. Favorite drink: green tea.

Takeda Harumi

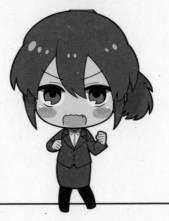

A junior employee who thinks her senpai is annoying. Favorite drink: oshiruko.

Igarashi Futaba

My Senpai is Annoying **CHARACTERS**

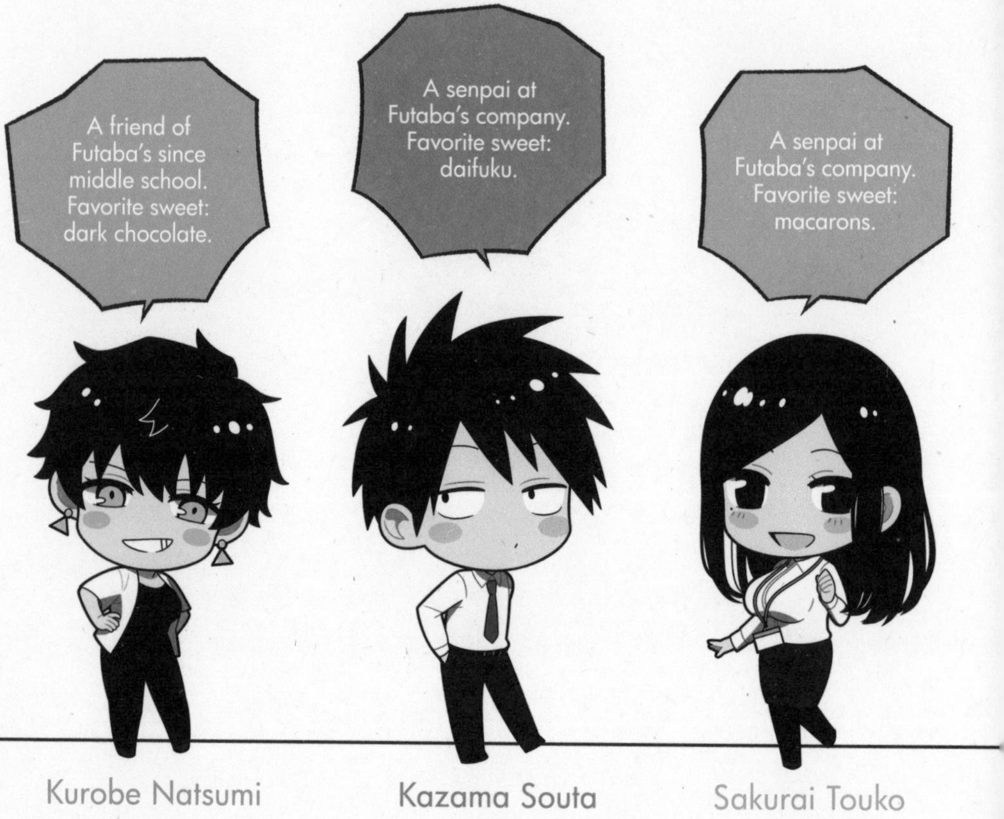
A senpai at Futaba's company. Favorite sweet: macarons.
Sakurai Touko
A senpai at Futaba's company. Favorite sweet: daifuku.
Kazama Souta
A friend of Futaba's since middle school. Favorite sweet: dark chocolate.
Kurobe Natsumi

👉 START⌐_____

ANNOYING!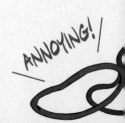

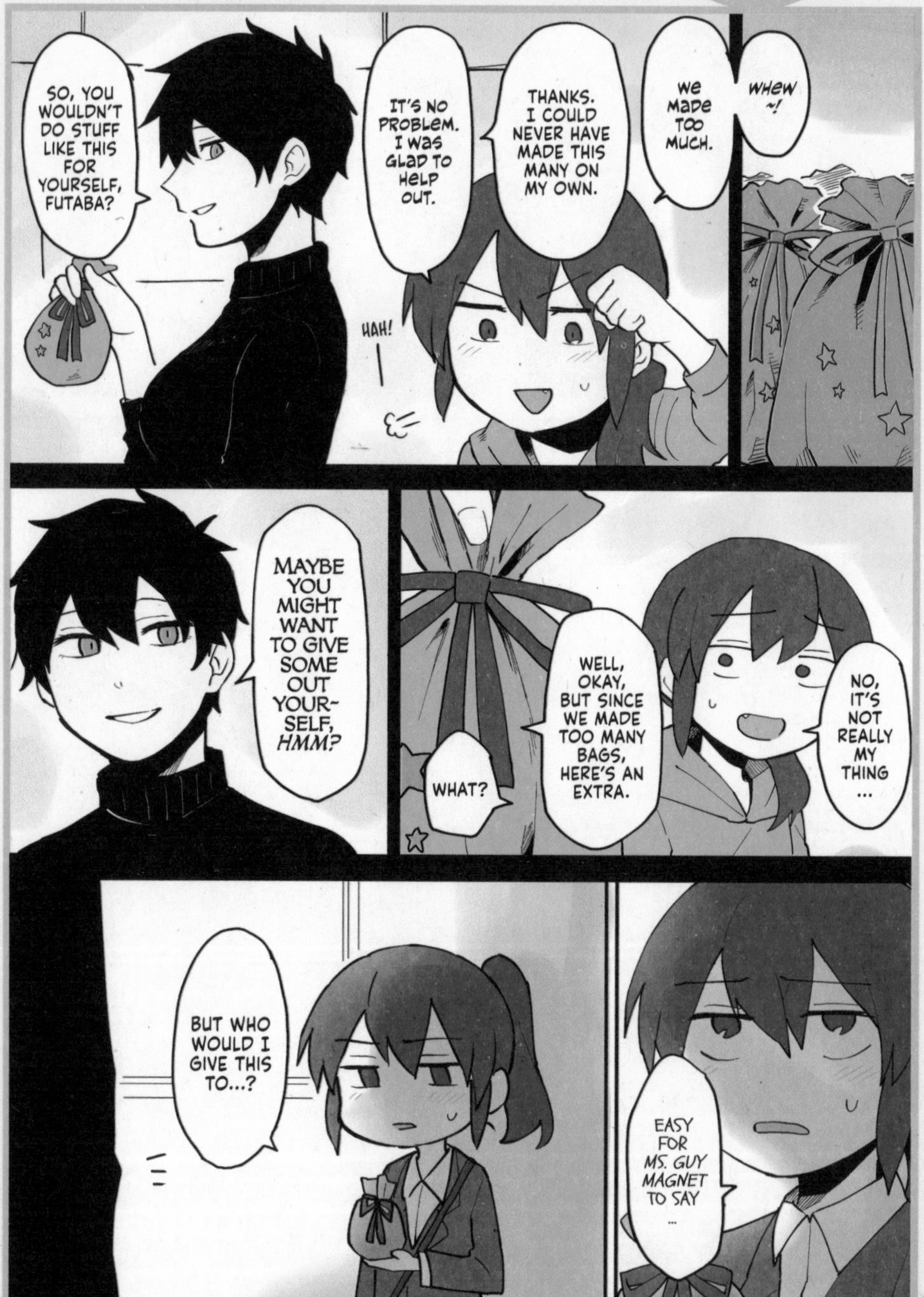
WHEW ~!
WE MADE TOO MUCH.
THANKS. I COULD NEVER HAVE MADE THIS MANY ON MY OWN.
IT'S NO PROBLEM. I WAS GLAD TO HELP OUT.
HAH!
SO, YOU WOULDN'T DO STUFF LIKE THIS FOR YOURSELF, FUTABA?
NO, IT'S NOT REALLY MY THING ...
WELL, OKAY, BUT SINCE WE MADE TOO MANY BAGS, HERE'S AN EXTRA.
WHAT?
MAYBE YOU MIGHT WANT TO GIVE SOME OUT YOURSELF, *HMM?*
EASY FOR MS. GUY MAGNET TO SAY ...
BUT WHO WOULD I GIVE THIS TO...?

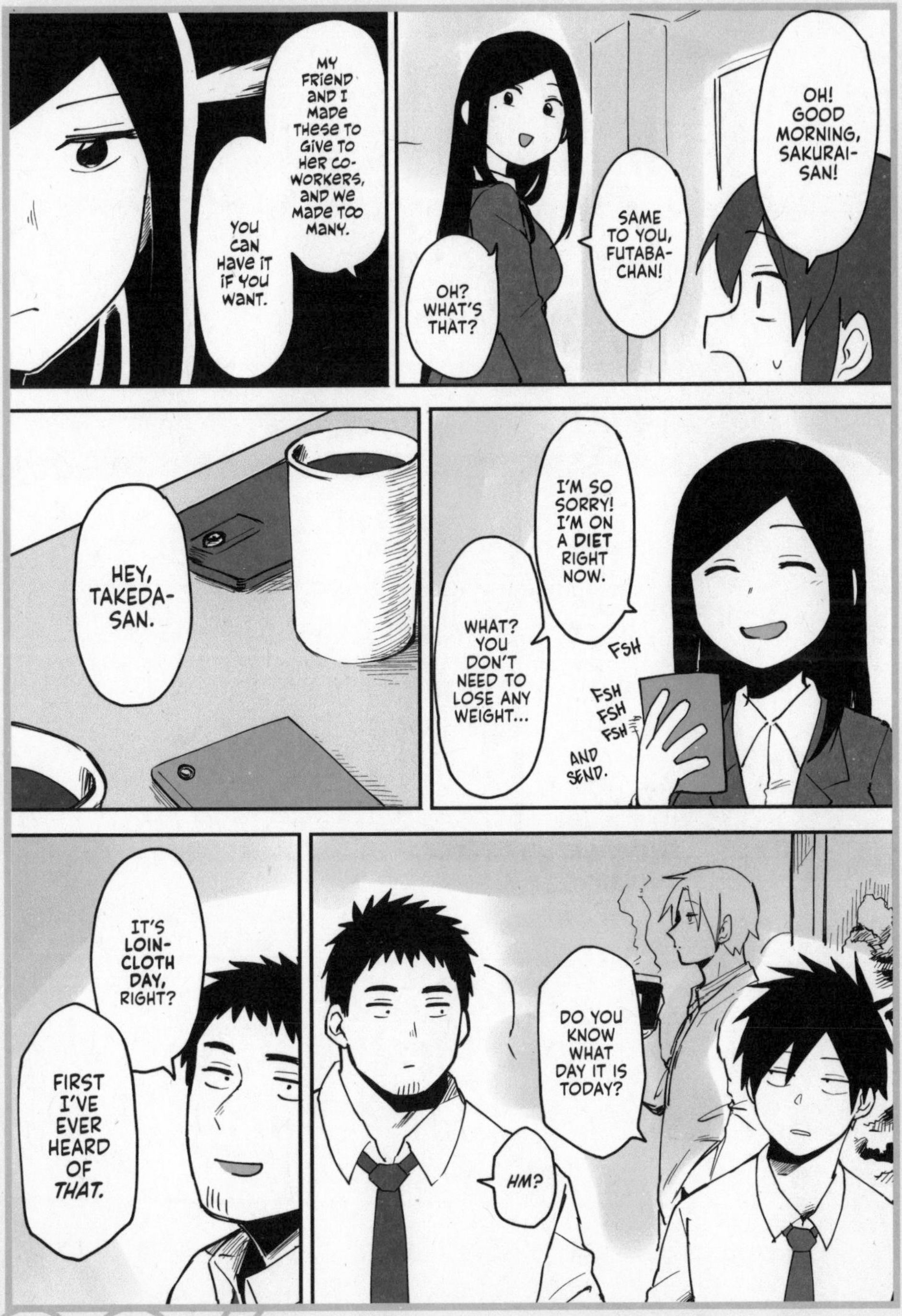
OH! GOOD MORNING, SAKURAI-SAN!
SAME TO YOU, FUTABA-CHAN!
OH? WHAT'S THAT?
MY FRIEND AND I MADE THESE TO GIVE TO HER CO-WORKERS, AND WE MADE TOO MANY.
YOU CAN HAVE IT IF YOU WANT.
I'M SO SORRY! I'M ON A **DIET** RIGHT NOW.
WHAT? YOU DON'T NEED TO LOSE ANY WEIGHT...
FSH
FSH FSH FSH
AND SEND.
HEY, TAKEDA-SAN.
DO YOU KNOW WHAT DAY IT IS TODAY?
HM?
IT'S LOIN-CLOTH DAY, RIGHT?
FIRST I'VE EVER HEARD OF *THAT.*

006

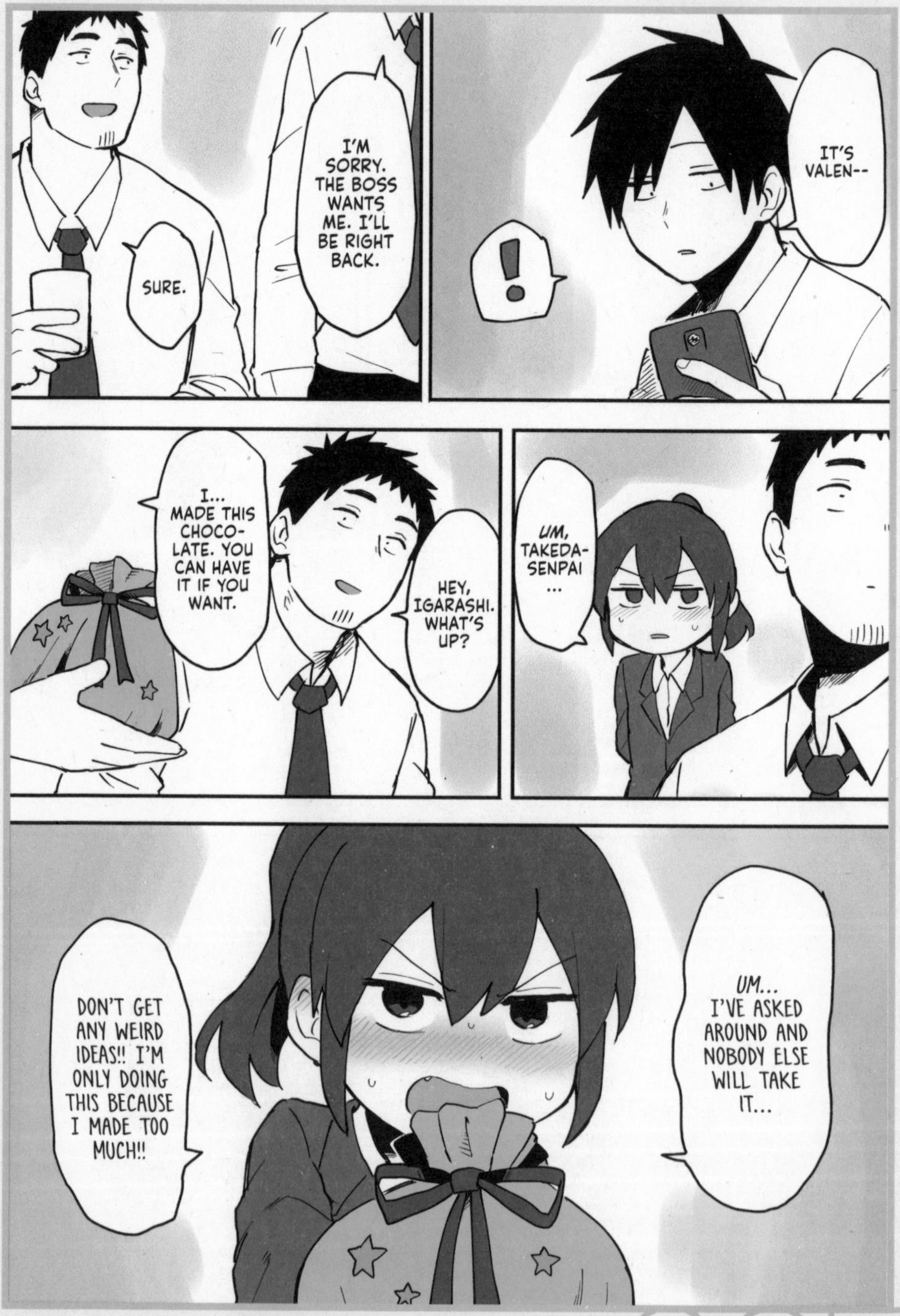
IT'S VALEN--
!
I'M SORRY. THE BOSS WANTS ME. I'LL BE RIGHT BACK.
SURE.
UM, TAKEDA-SENPAI ...
HEY, IGARASHI. WHAT'S UP?
I... MADE THIS CHOCO-LATE. YOU CAN HAVE IT IF YOU WANT.
UM... I'VE ASKED AROUND AND NOBODY ELSE WILL TAKE IT...
DON'T GET ANY WEIRD IDEAS!! I'M ONLY DOING THIS BECAUSE I MADE TOO MUCH!!

007

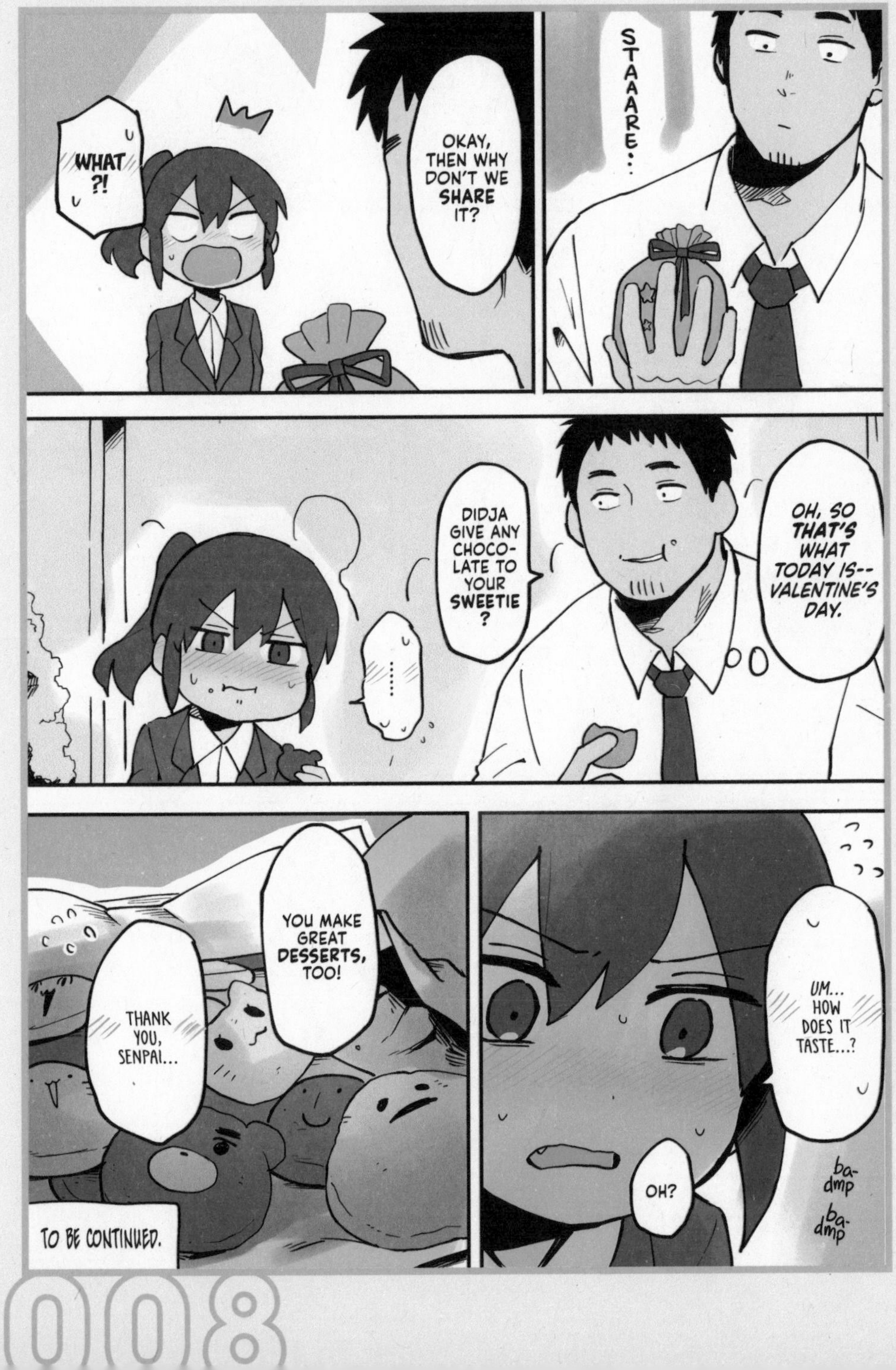
STAAAARE...
OKAY, THEN WHY DON'T WE SHARE IT?
WHAT?!
OH, SO THAT'S WHAT TODAY IS-- VALENTINE'S DAY.
DIDJA GIVE ANY CHOCO-LATE TO YOUR SWEETIE?
......
UM... HOW DOES IT TASTE...?
ba-dmp
ba-dmp
OH?
YOU MAKE GREAT DESSERTS, TOO!
THANK YOU, SENPAI...
TO BE CONTINUED.

008

Chapter 22

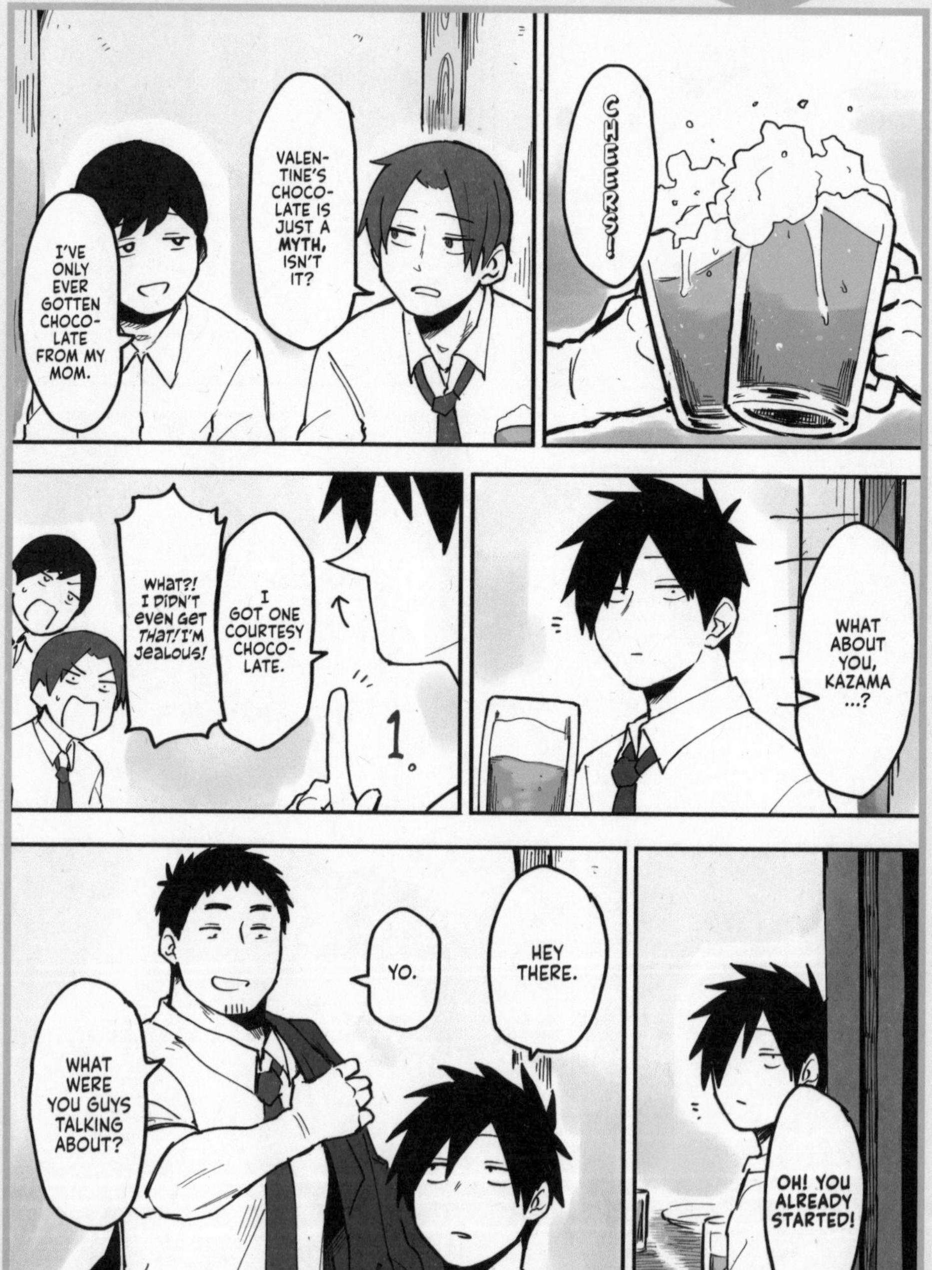
CHEERS!
VALENTINE'S CHOCOLATE IS JUST A MYTH, ISN'T IT?
I'VE ONLY EVER GOTTEN CHOCOLATE FROM MY MOM.
WHAT ABOUT YOU, KAZAMA ...?
I GOT ONE COURTESY CHOCOLATE.
1.
WHAT?! I DIDN'T even GET THAT! I'M jealous!
OH! YOU ALREADY STARTED!
HEY THERE.
YO.
WHAT WERE YOU GUYS TALKING ABOUT?

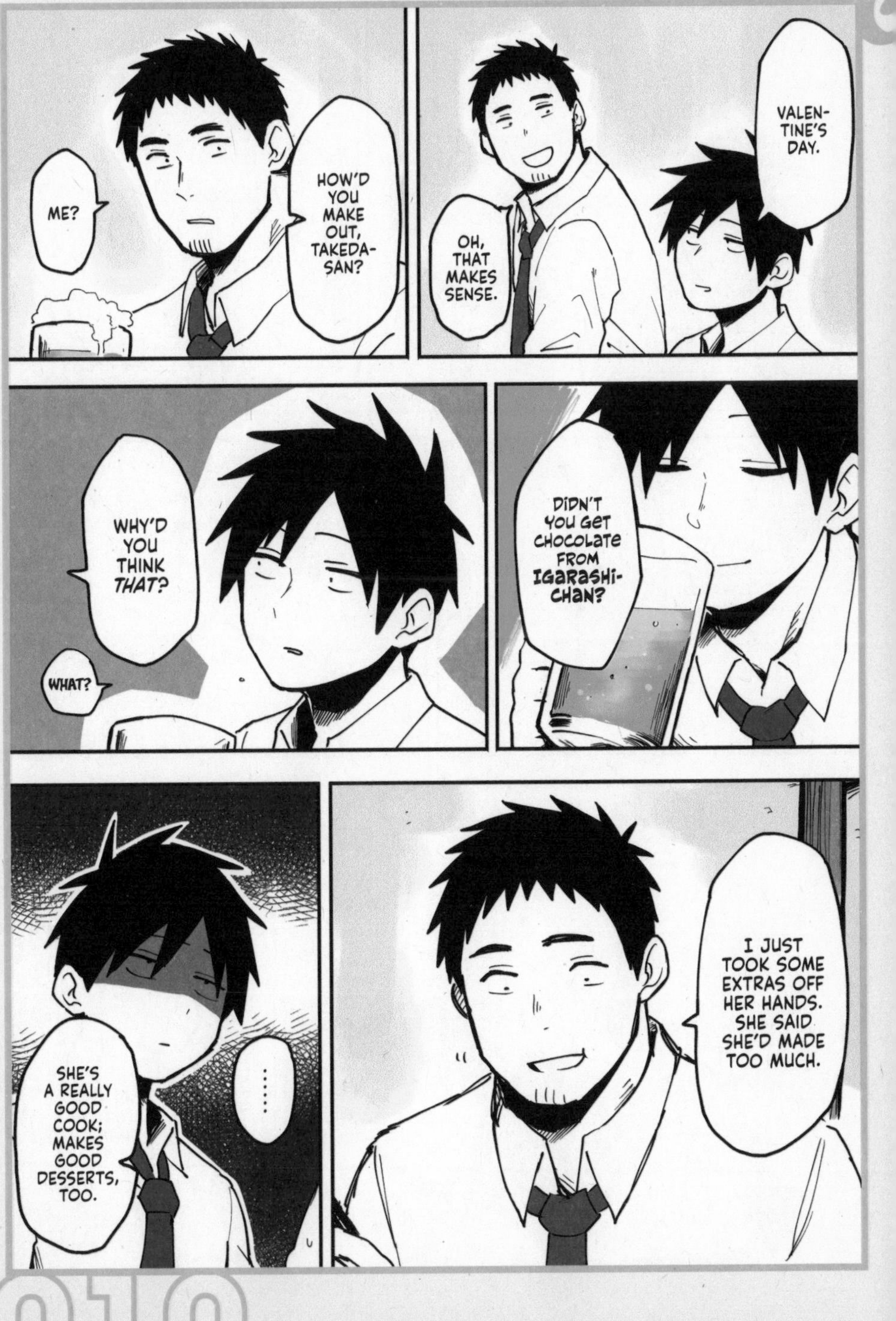
VALENTINE'S DAY.
OH, THAT MAKES SENSE.
HOW'D YOU MAKE OUT, TAKEDA-SAN?
ME?
DIDN'T YOU GET CHOCOLATE FROM IGARASHI-CHAN?
WHY'D YOU THINK *THAT*?
WHAT?
I JUST TOOK SOME EXTRAS OFF HER HANDS. SHE SAID SHE'D MADE TOO MUCH.
......
SHE'S A REALLY GOOD COOK; MAKES GOOD DESSERTS, TOO.

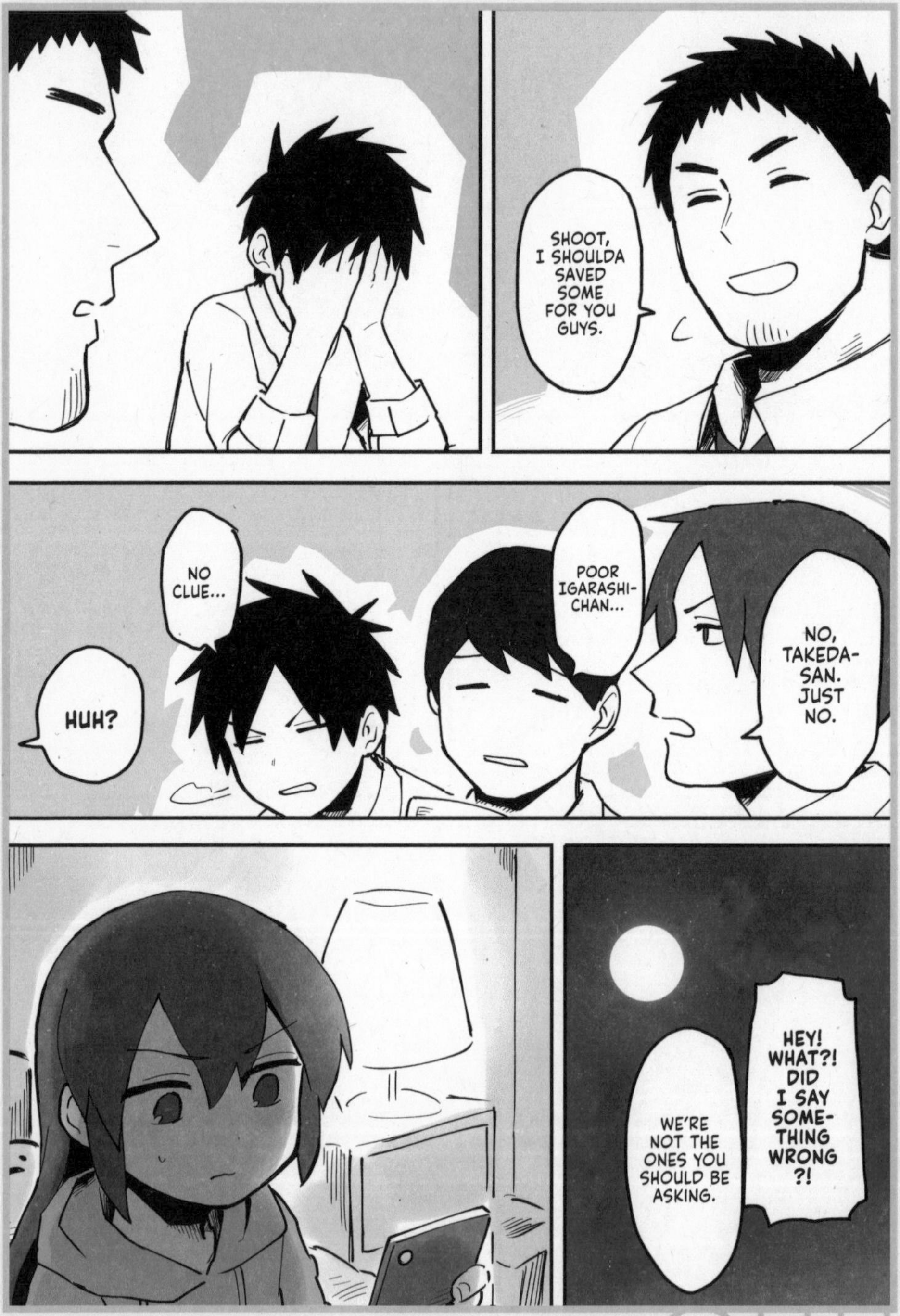
SHOOT, I SHOULDA SAVED SOME FOR YOU GUYS.
NO, TAKEDA-SAN. JUST NO.
POOR IGARASHI-CHAN...
NO CLUE...
HUH?
HEY! WHAT?! DID I SAY SOME-THING WRONG?!
WE'RE NOT THE ONES YOU SHOULD BE ASKING.

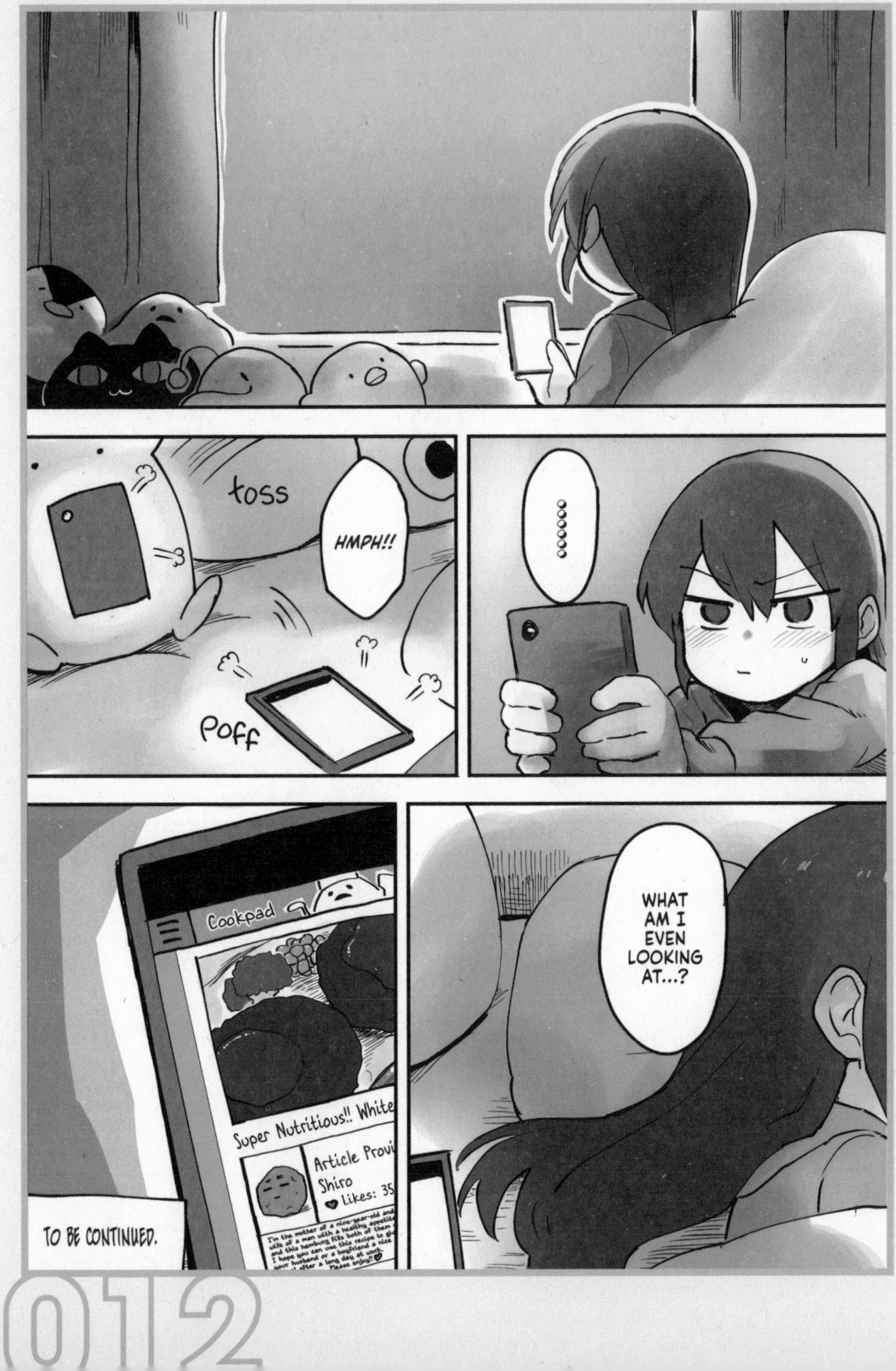
......
HMPH!!
toss
Poff
WHAT AM I EVEN LOOKING AT...?
Cookpad
Super Nutritious!! White
Article Provi
Shiro
Likes: 35
TO BE CONTINUED.

012

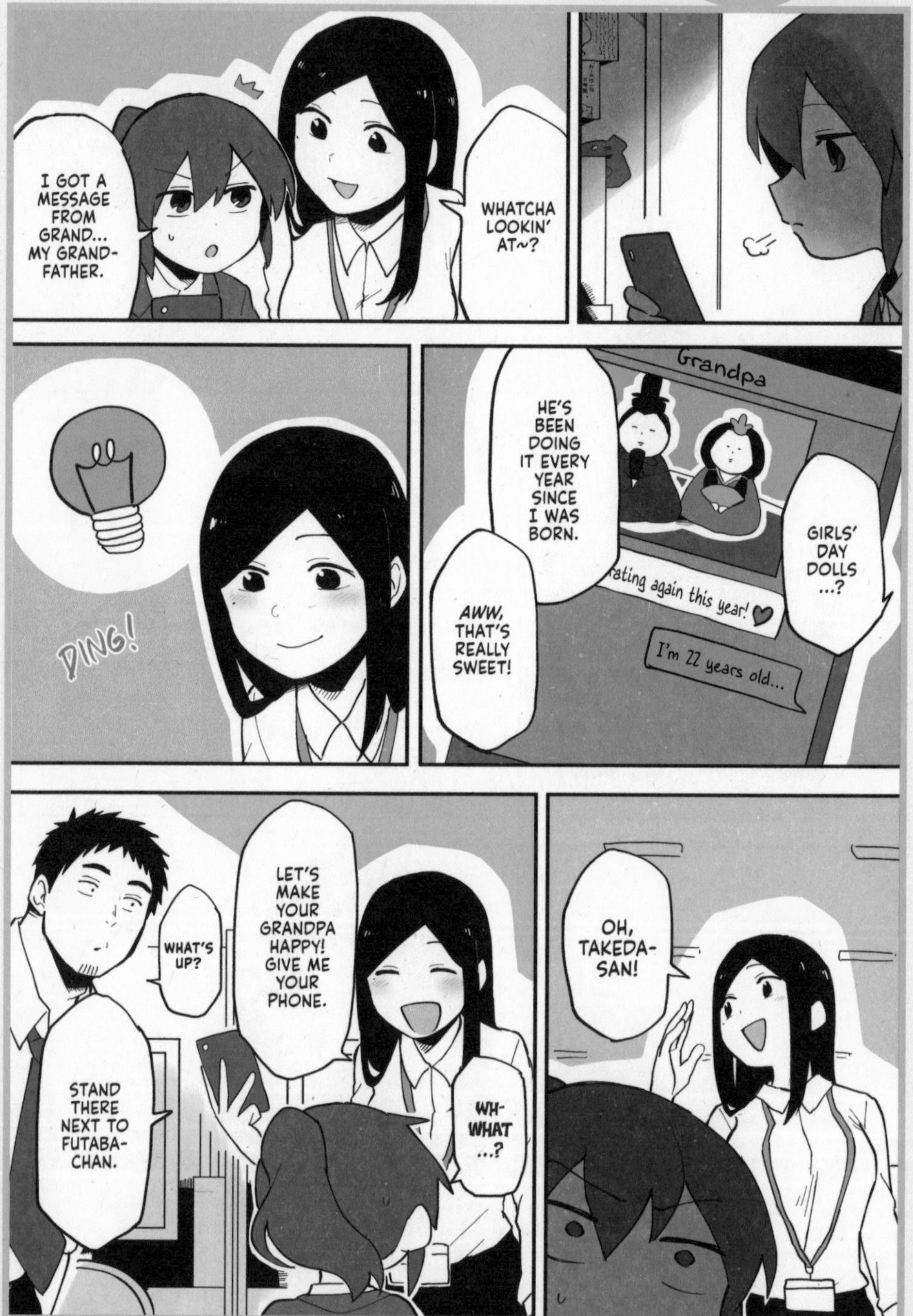
WHATCHA LOOKIN' AT~?
I GOT A MESSAGE FROM GRAND... MY GRANDFATHER.
Grandpa
rating again this year! ♥
I'm 22 years old...
GIRLS' DAY DOLLS ...?
HE'S BEEN DOING IT EVERY YEAR SINCE I WAS BORN.
AWW, THAT'S REALLY SWEET!
DING!
OH, TAKEDA-SAN!
LET'S MAKE YOUR GRANDPA HAPPY! GIVE ME YOUR PHONE.
WH-WHAT ...?
WHAT'S UP?
STAND THERE NEXT TO FUTABA-CHAN.

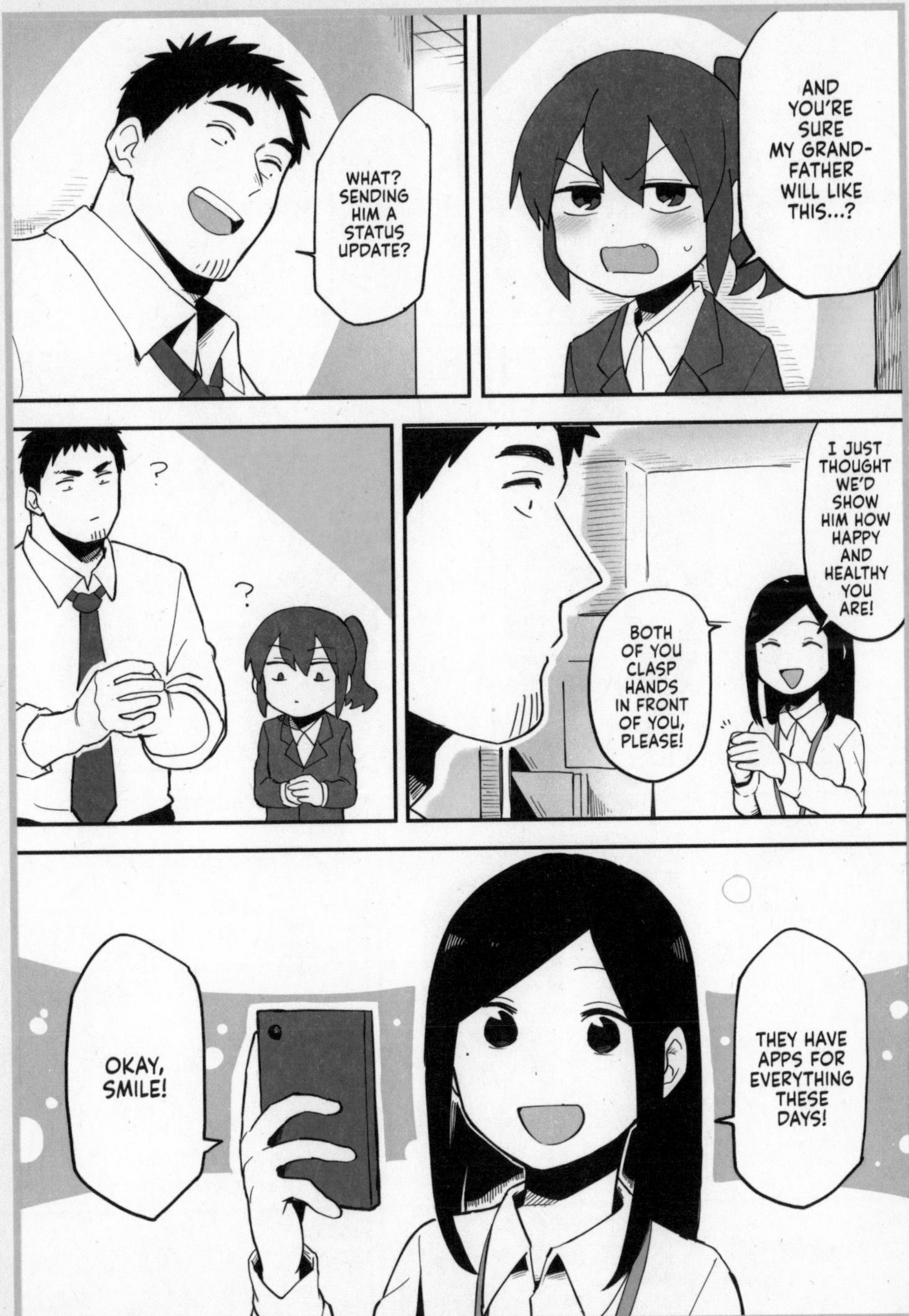
AND YOU'RE SURE MY GRAND-FATHER WILL LIKE THIS...?
WHAT? SENDING HIM A STATUS UPDATE?
I JUST THOUGHT WE'D SHOW HIM HOW HAPPY AND HEALTHY YOU ARE!
BOTH OF YOU CLASP HANDS IN FRONT OF YOU, PLEASE!
?
?
THEY HAVE APPS FOR EVERYTHING THESE DAYS!
OKAY, SMILE!

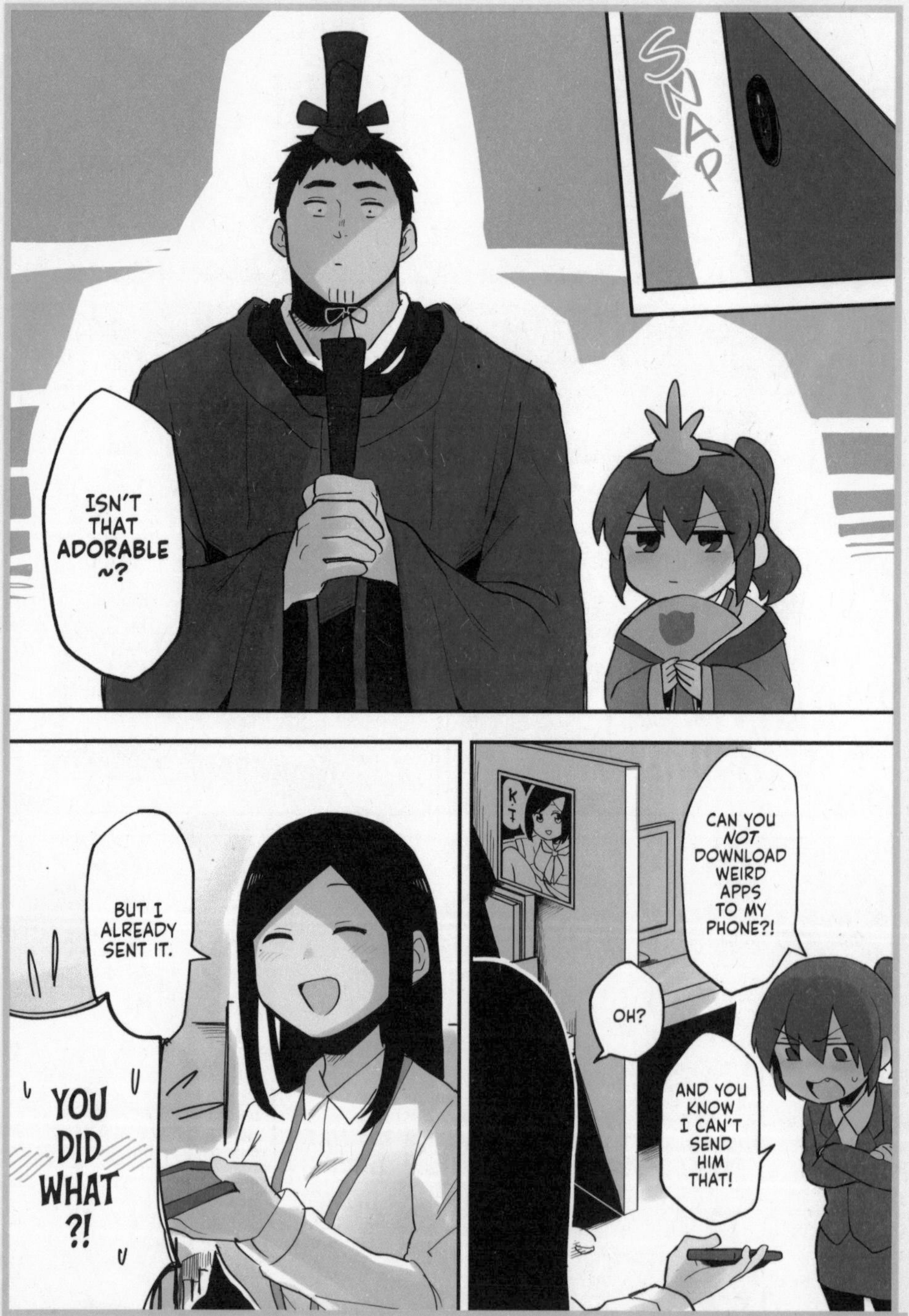
SNAP
ISN'T THAT ADORABLE ~?
CAN YOU NOT DOWNLOAD WEIRD APPS TO MY PHONE?!
OH?
AND YOU KNOW I CAN'T SEND HIM THAT!
BUT I ALREADY SENT IT.
YOU DID WHAT ?!

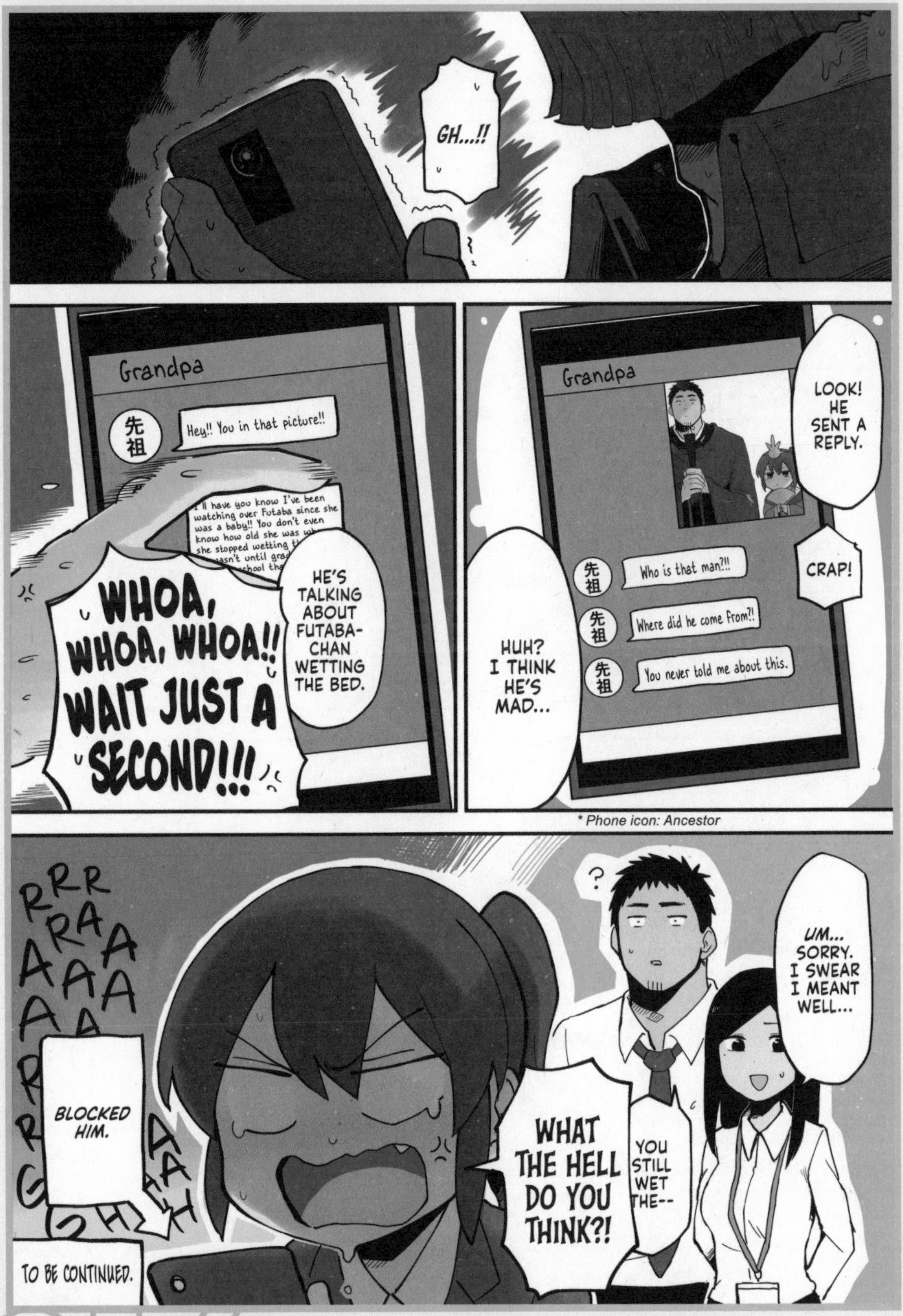
GH...!!
LOOK! HE SENT A REPLY.
Grandpa
先祖
Who is that man?!!
Where did he come from?!
You never told me about this.
CRAP!
HUH? I THINK HE'S MAD...
Grandpa
先祖
Hey!! You in that picture!!
I'll have you know I've been watching over Futaba since she was a baby!! You don't even know how old she was
HE'S TALKING ABOUT FUTABA-CHAN WETTING THE BED.
WHOA, WHOA, WHOA!! WAIT JUST A SECOND!!!
* Phone icon: Ancestor
UM... SORRY. I SWEAR I MEANT WELL...
YOU STILL WET THE--
WHAT THE HELL DO YOU THINK?!
BLOCKED HIM.
TO BE CONTINUED.

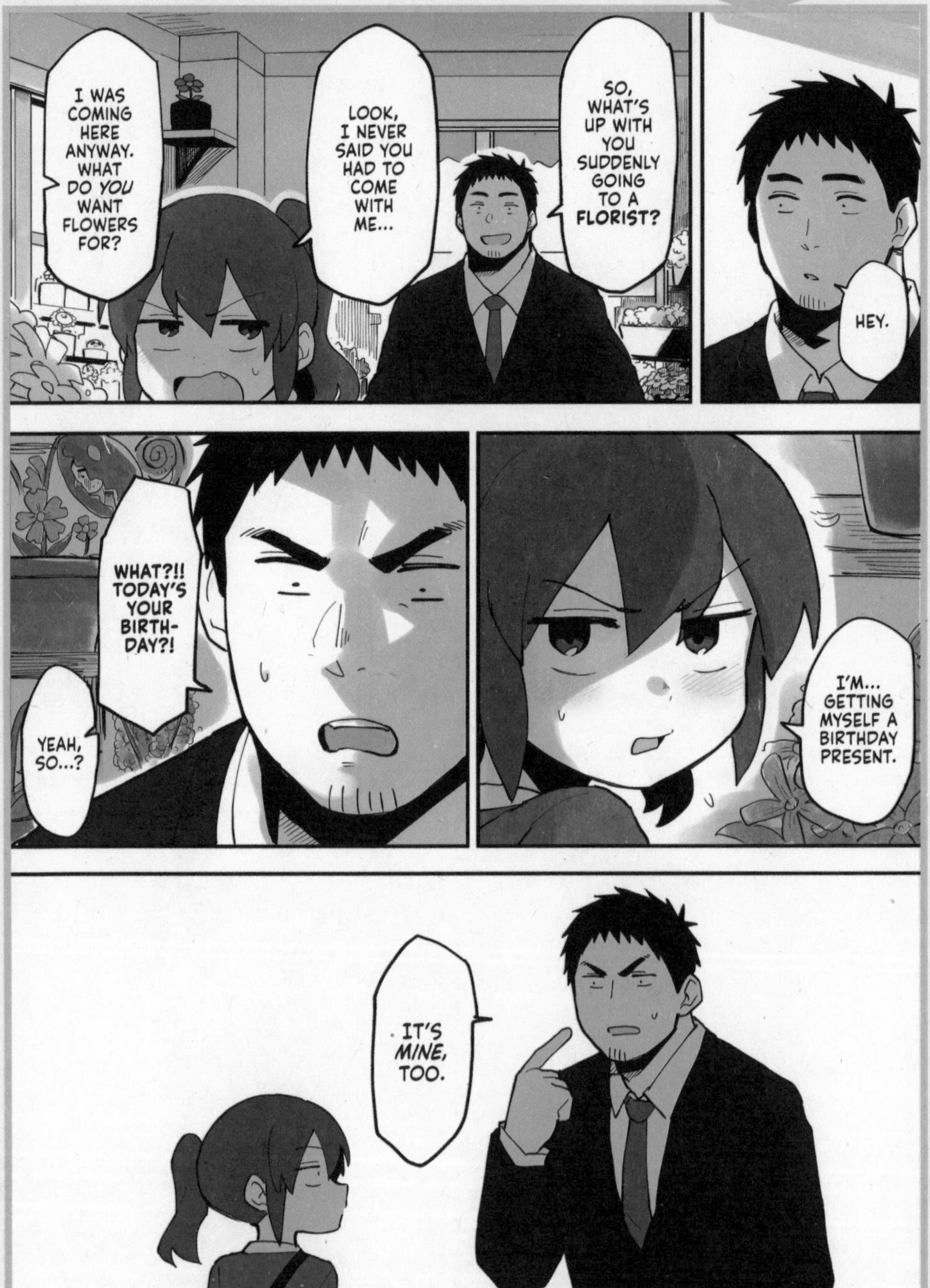
HEY.
SO, WHAT'S UP WITH YOU SUDDENLY GOING TO A FLORIST?
LOOK, I NEVER SAID YOU HAD TO COME WITH ME...
I WAS COMING HERE ANYWAY. WHAT DO *YOU* WANT FLOWERS FOR?
I'M... GETTING MYSELF A BIRTHDAY PRESENT.
WHAT?!! TODAY'S YOUR BIRTHDAY?!
YEAH, SO...?
IT'S *MINE*, TOO.

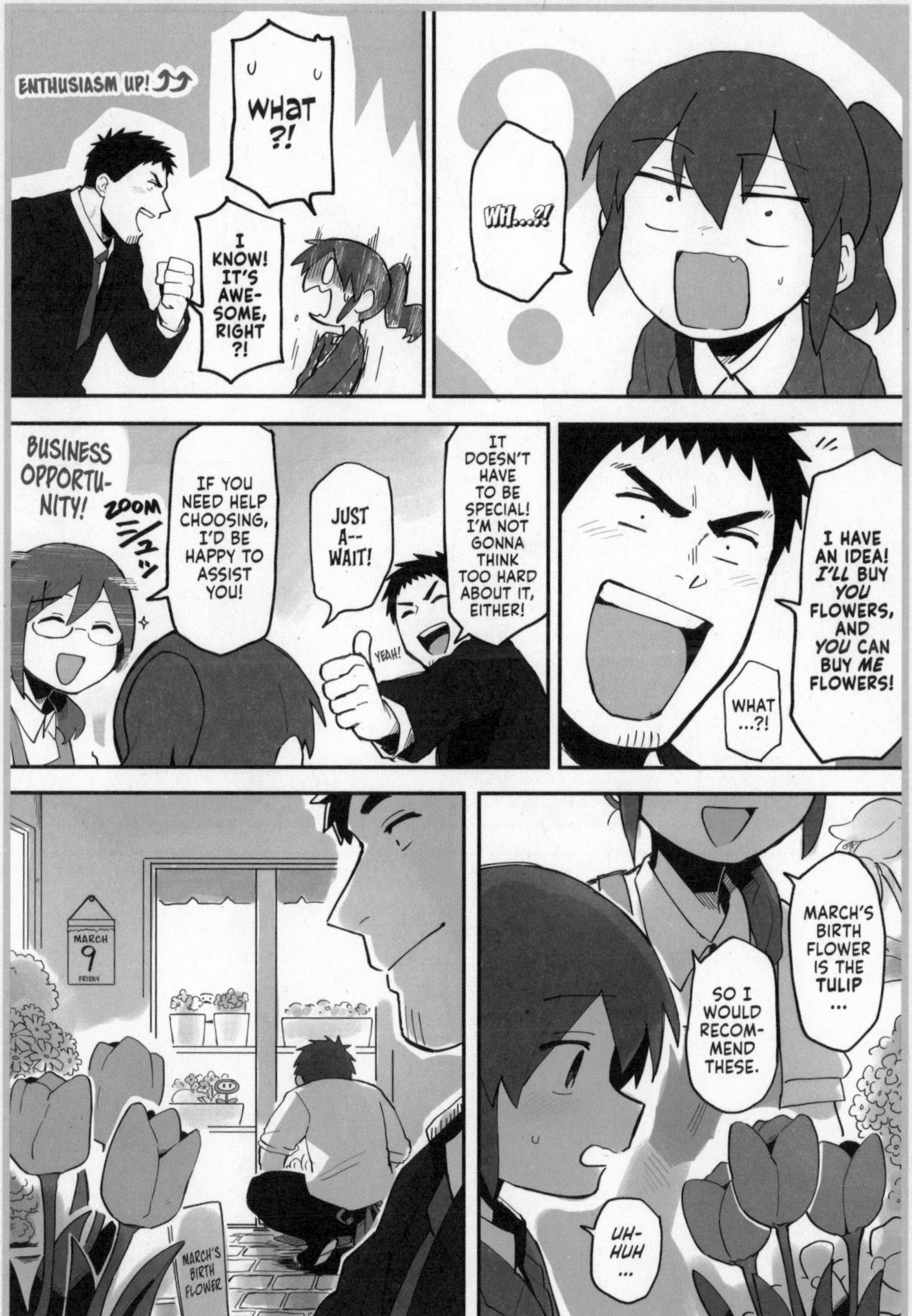
WH...?!
WHAT ?!
ENTHUSIASM UP!
I KNOW! IT'S AWESOME, RIGHT ?!
I HAVE AN IDEA! I'LL BUY YOU FLOWERS, AND YOU CAN BUY ME FLOWERS!
WHAT ...?!
IT DOESN'T HAVE TO BE SPECIAL! I'M NOT GONNA THINK TOO HARD ABOUT IT, EITHER!
JUST A-- WAIT!
YEAH!
IF YOU NEED HELP CHOOSING, I'D BE HAPPY TO ASSIST YOU!
BUSINESS OPPORTUNITY!
ZOOM
MARCH'S BIRTH FLOWER IS THE TULIP ...
SO I WOULD RECOMMEND THESE.
UH-HUH ...
MARCH
9
FRIDAY
MARCH'S BIRTH FLOWER

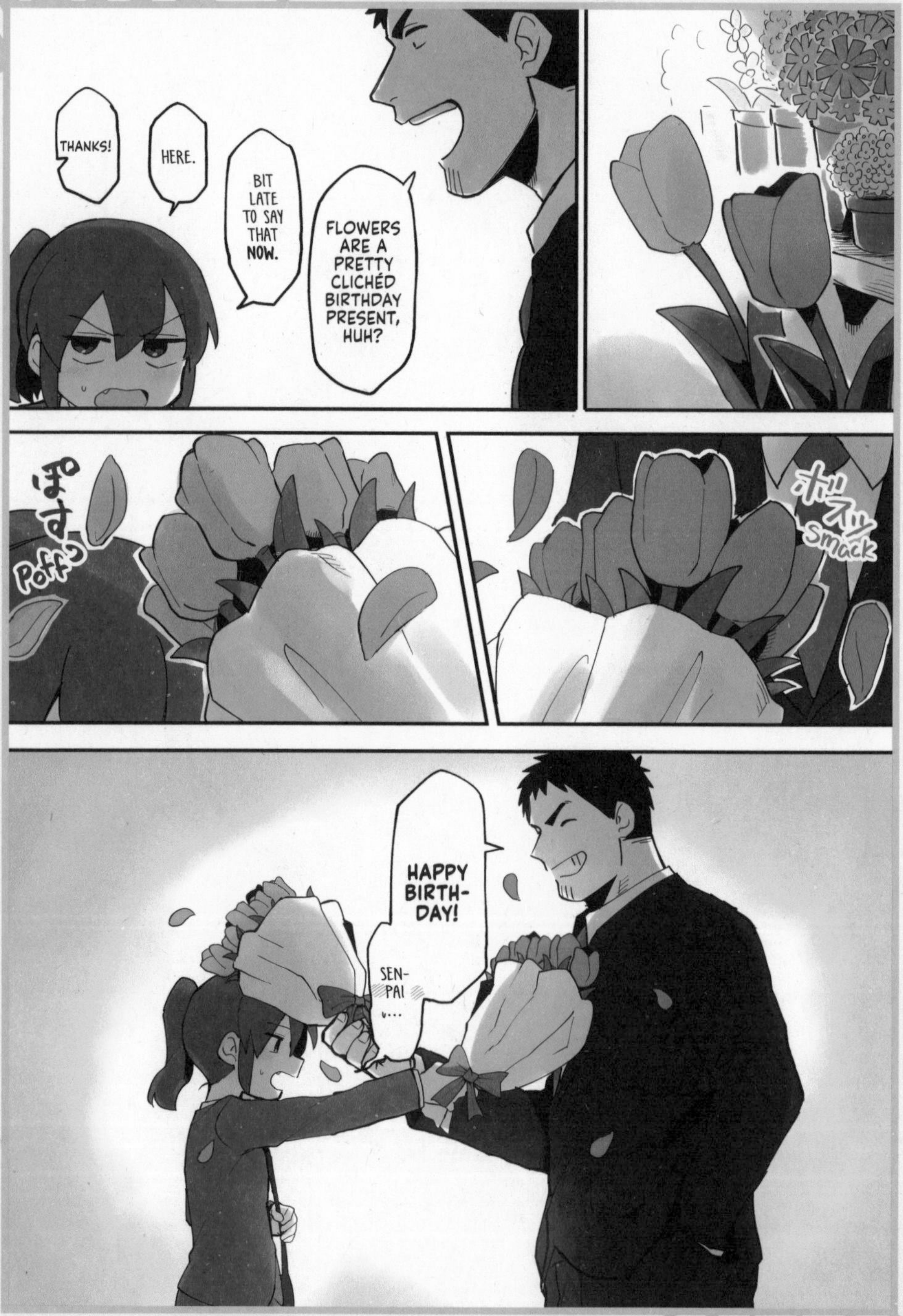

FLOWERS ARE A PRETTY CLICHÉD BIRTHDAY PRESENT, HUH?
BIT LATE TO SAY THAT NOW.
HERE.
THANKS!
ボスッ
Smack
ぽすっ
Poff
HAPPY BIRTH-DAY!
SEN-PAI...

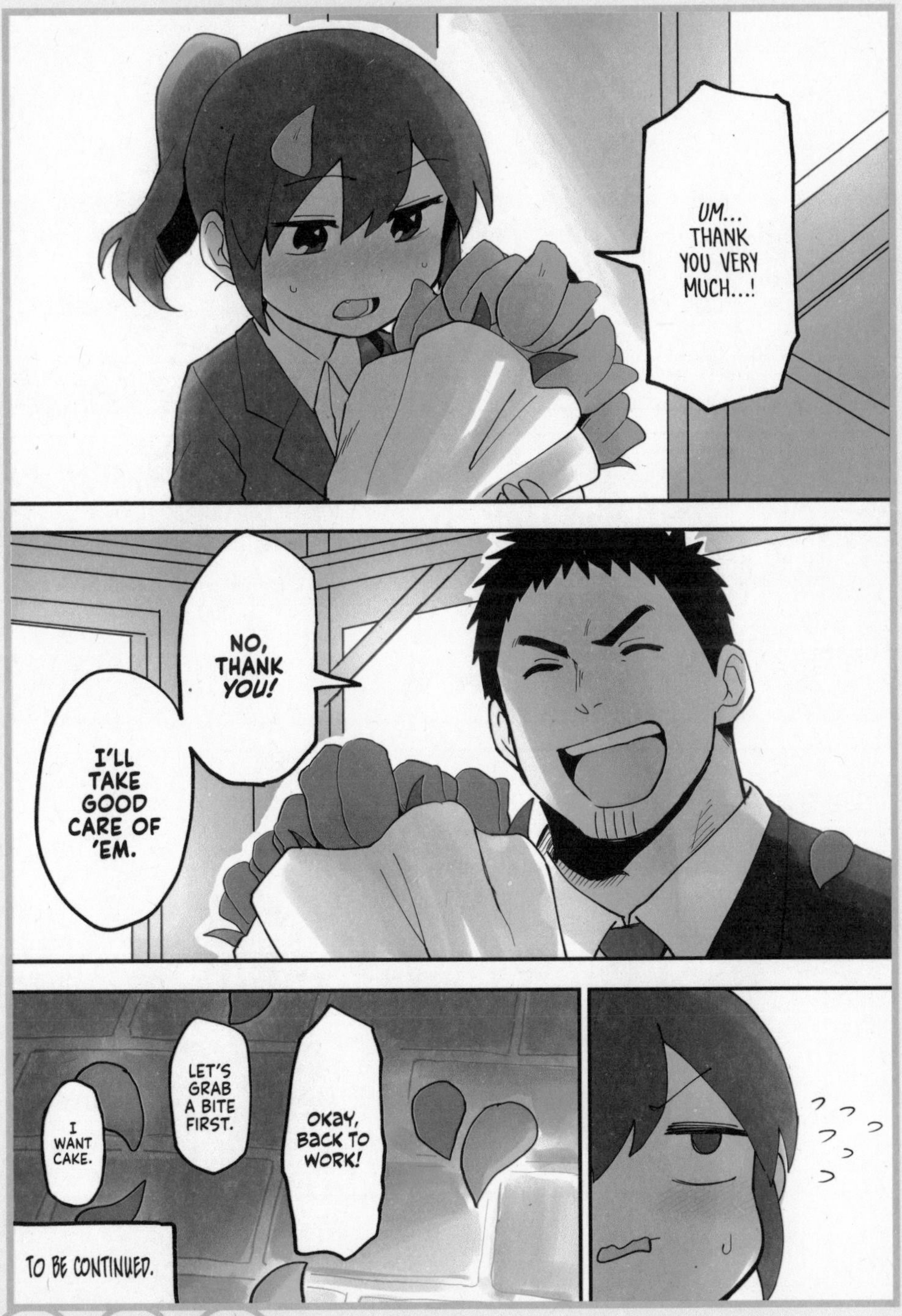
UM... THANK YOU VERY MUCH...!
NO, THANK YOU!
I'LL TAKE GOOD CARE OF 'EM.
OKAY, BACK TO WORK!
LET'S GRAB A BITE FIRST.
I WANT CAKE.
TO BE CONTINUED.

Chapter 25

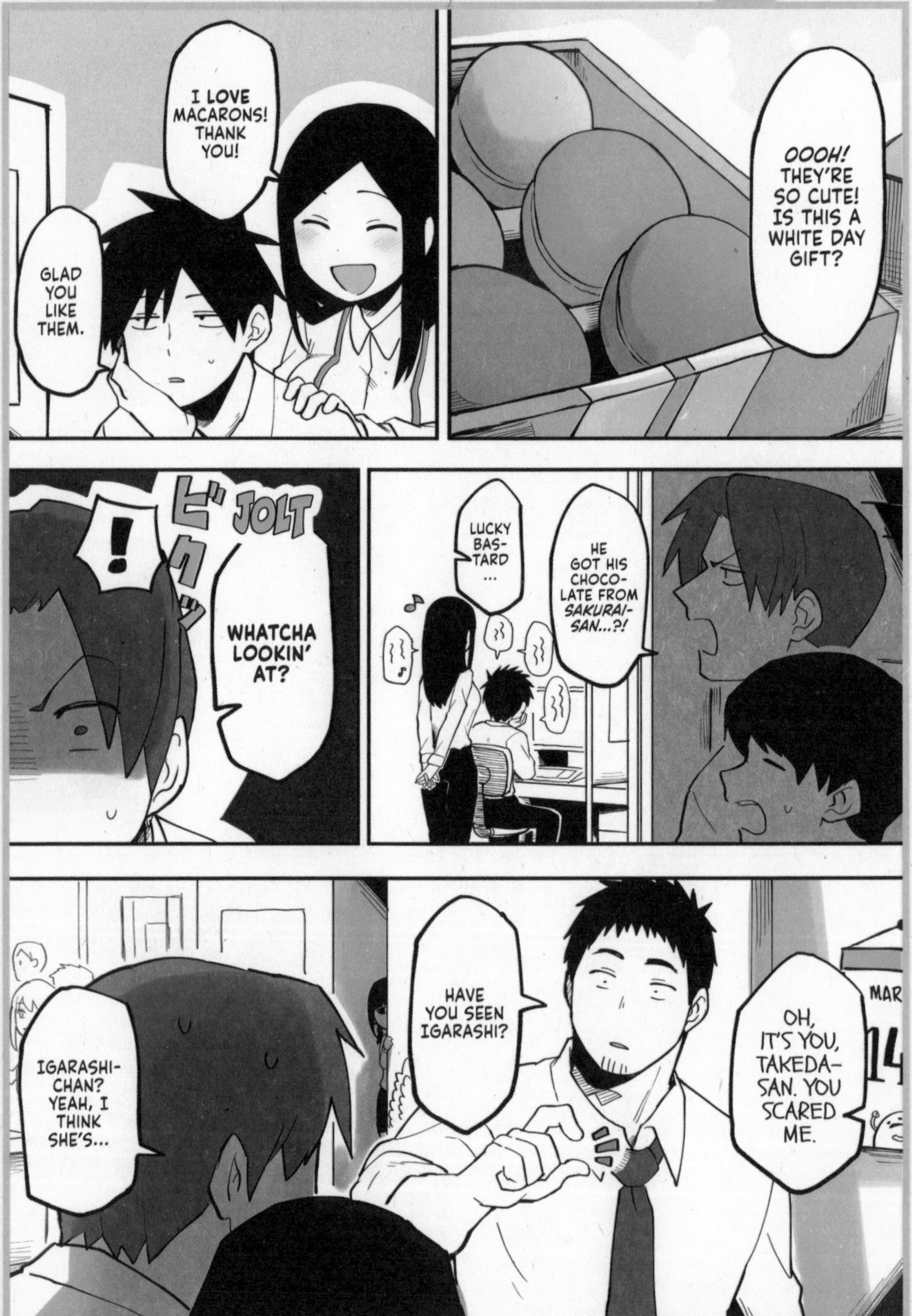
OOOH! THEY'RE SO CUTE! IS THIS A WHITE DAY GIFT?
I LOVE MACARONS! THANK YOU!
GLAD YOU LIKE THEM.
HE GOT HIS CHOCOLATE FROM SAKURAI-SAN...?!
LUCKY BASTARD...
JOLT
!
WHATCHA LOOKIN' AT?
OH, IT'S YOU, TAKEDA-SAN. YOU SCARED ME.
HAVE YOU SEEN IGARASHI?
IGARASHI-CHAN? YEAH, I THINK SHE'S...

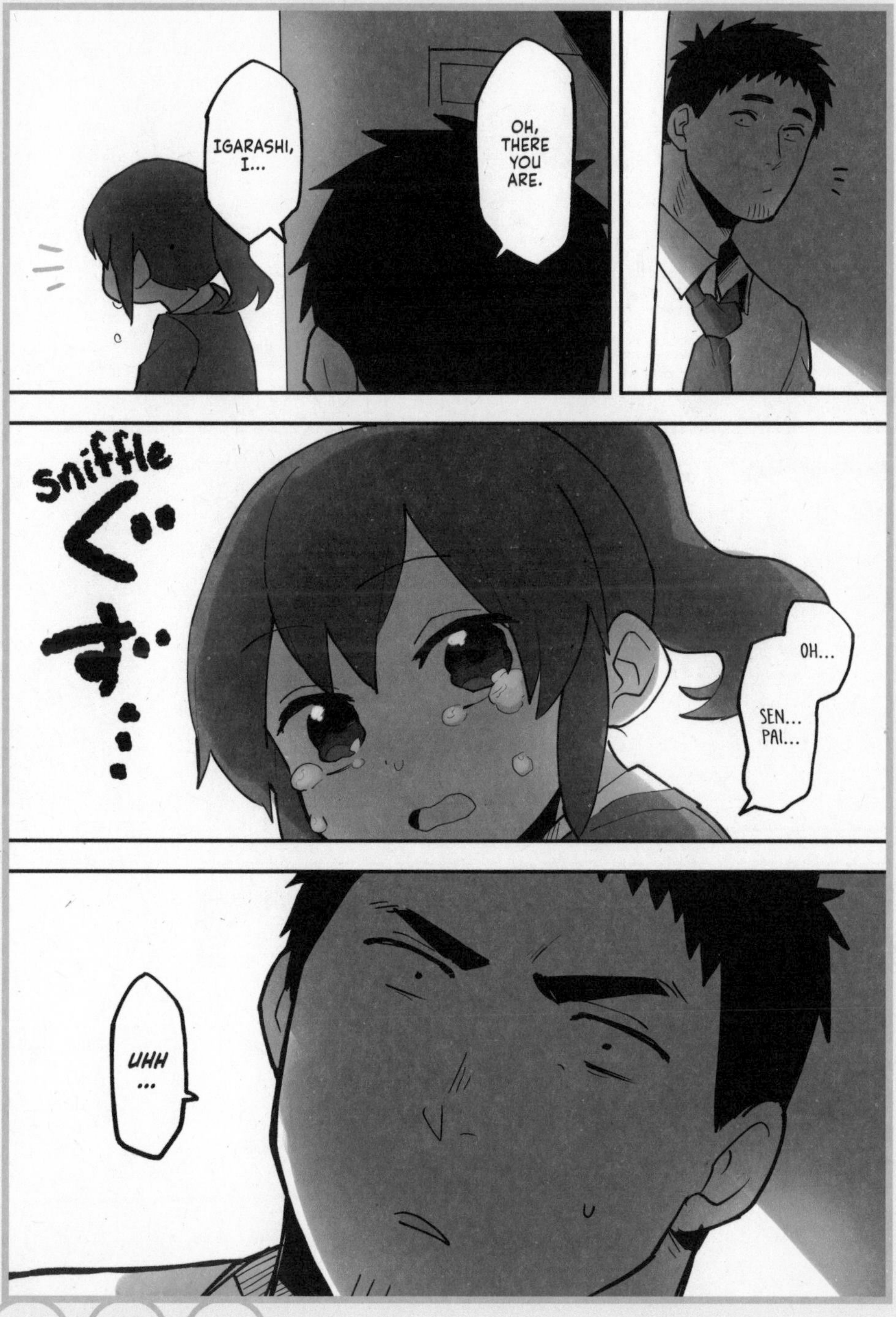
OH, THERE YOU ARE.
IGARASHI, I...
OH... SEN... PAI...
Sniffle
ぐず…
UHH ...

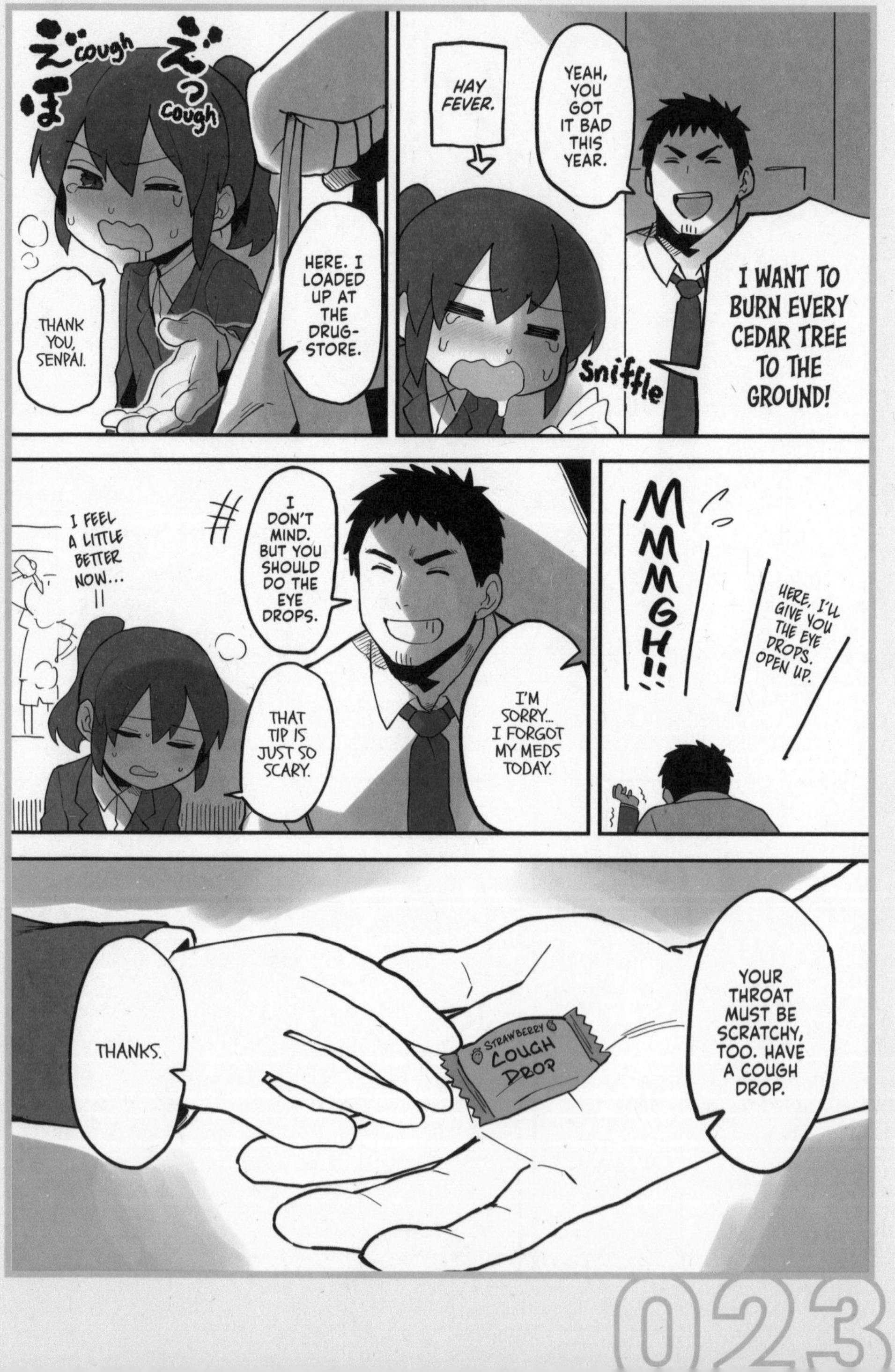
YEAH, YOU GOT IT BAD THIS YEAR.
HAY FEVER.
I WANT TO BURN EVERY CEDAR TREE TO THE GROUND!
Sniffle
cough
cough
HERE. I LOADED UP AT THE DRUG-STORE.
THANK YOU, SENPAI.
HERE, I'LL GIVE YOU THE EYE DROPS. OPEN UP.
MMMGH!!
I'M SORRY... I FORGOT MY MEDS TODAY.
I DON'T MIND. BUT YOU SHOULD DO THE EYE DROPS.
THAT TIP IS JUST SO SCARY.
I FEEL A LITTLE BETTER NOW...
YOUR THROAT MUST BE SCRATCHY, TOO. HAVE A COUGH DROP.
STRAWBERRY
COUGH DROP
THANKS.

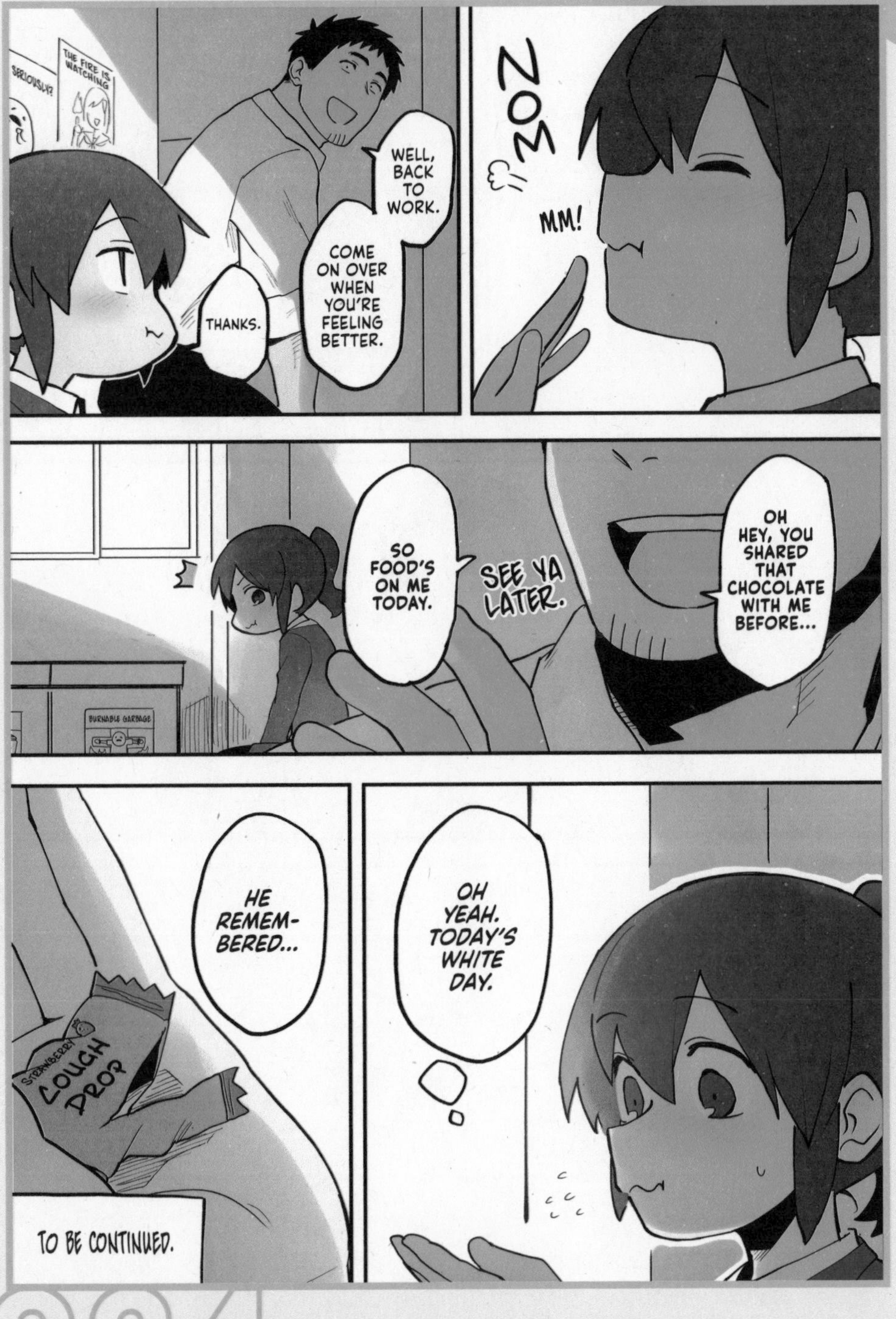
NOM
MM!
THE FIRE IS WATCHING
SERIOUSLY?
WELL, BACK TO WORK.
COME ON OVER WHEN YOU'RE FEELING BETTER.
THANKS.
OH HEY, YOU SHARED THAT CHOCOLATE WITH ME BEFORE...
SEE YA LATER.
SO FOOD'S ON ME TODAY.
BURNABLE GARBAGE
OH YEAH. TODAY'S WHITE DAY.
HE REMEMBERED...
STRAWBERRY COUGH DROP
TO BE CONTINUED.

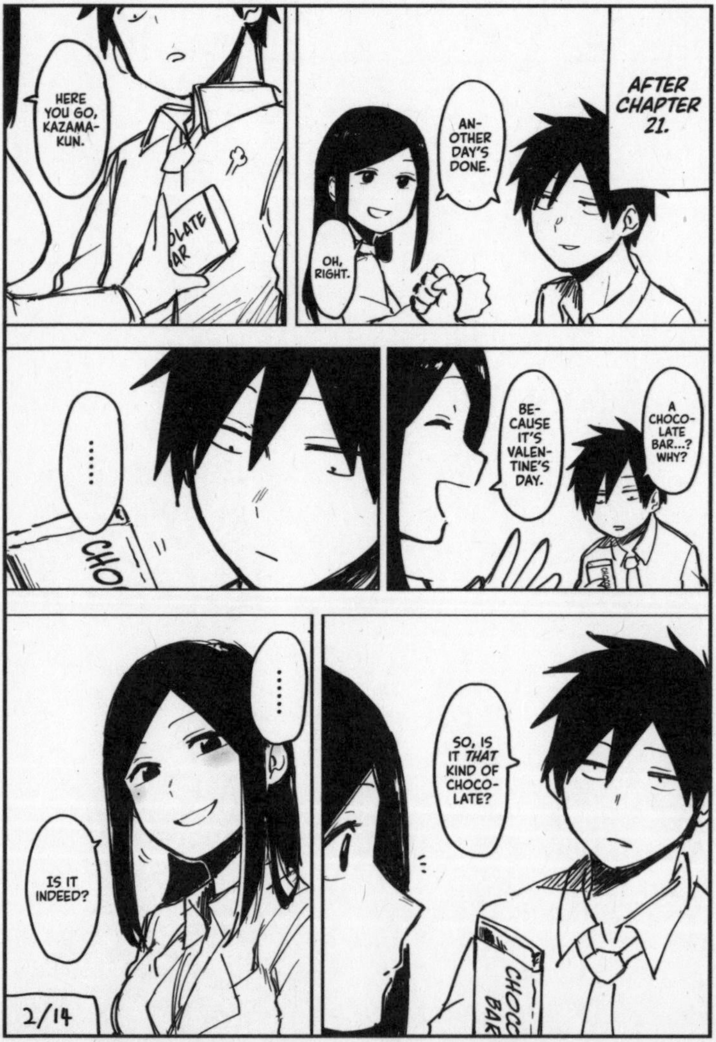
AFTER CHAPTER 21.
ANOTHER DAY'S DONE.
OH, RIGHT.
HERE YOU GO, KAZAMA-KUN.
A CHOCOLATE BAR...? WHY?
BECAUSE IT'S VALENTINE'S DAY.
......
SO, IS IT *THAT* KIND OF CHOCOLATE?
......
IS IT INDEED?
2/14

P. 6, panel 6 - Loincloth Day
One way to pronounce the numbers in February 14 (2/14)
in Japanese is *fun-do-shi,* which is also the word for a
traditional Japanese loincloth.

P. 18, panel 6 - Birth Flowers
Japan has different birth month flowers from the West,
so March's flower is the tulip, not the daffodil.

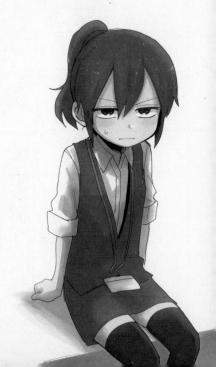

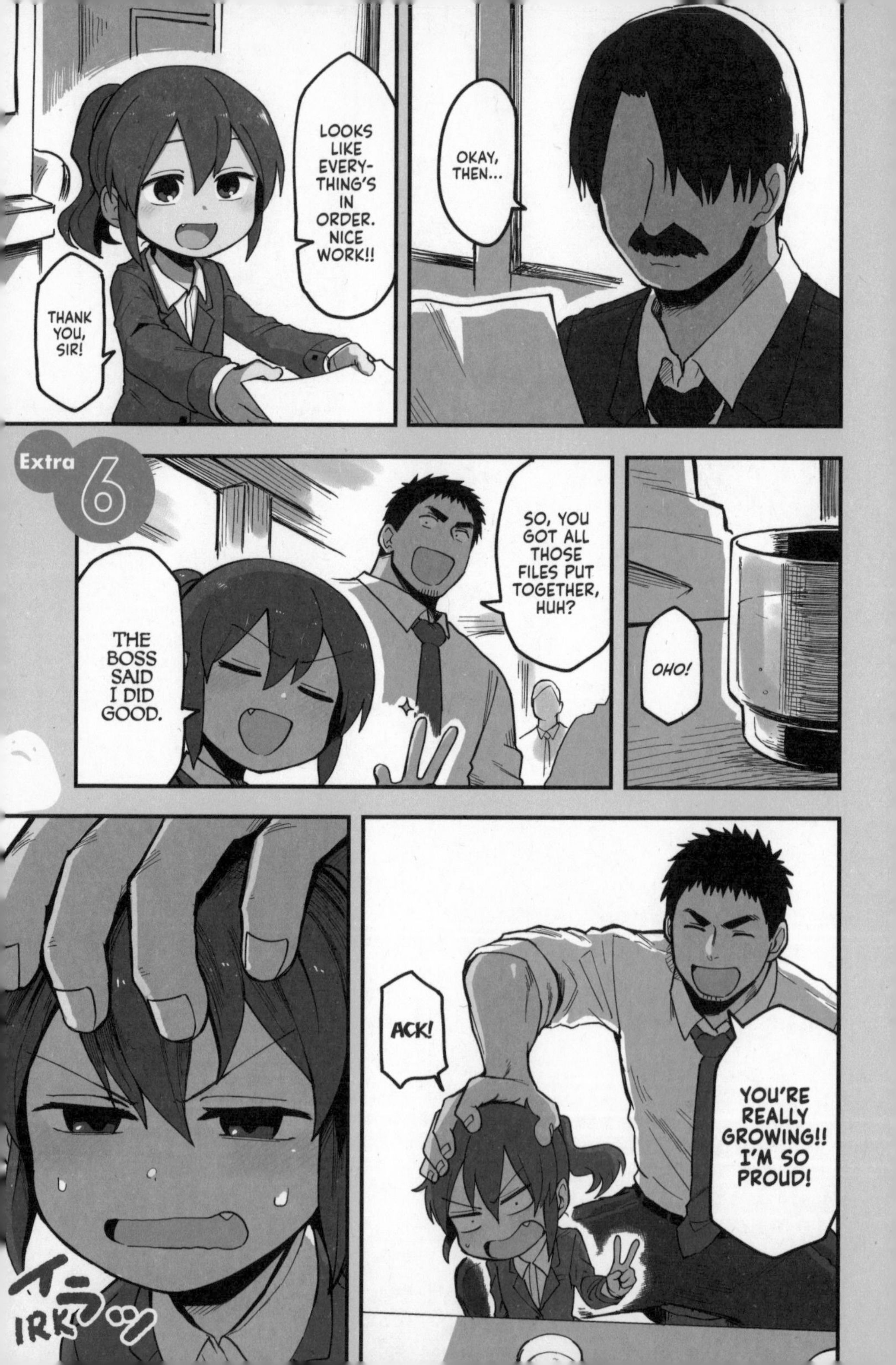
OKAY, THEN...
LOOKS LIKE EVERY-THING'S IN ORDER. NICE WORK!!
THANK YOU, SIR!
Extra 6
OHO!
SO, YOU GOT ALL THOSE FILES PUT TOGETHER, HUH?
THE BOSS SAID I DID GOOD.
ACK!
YOU'RE REALLY GROWING!! I'M SO PROUD!
イラッ
IRK

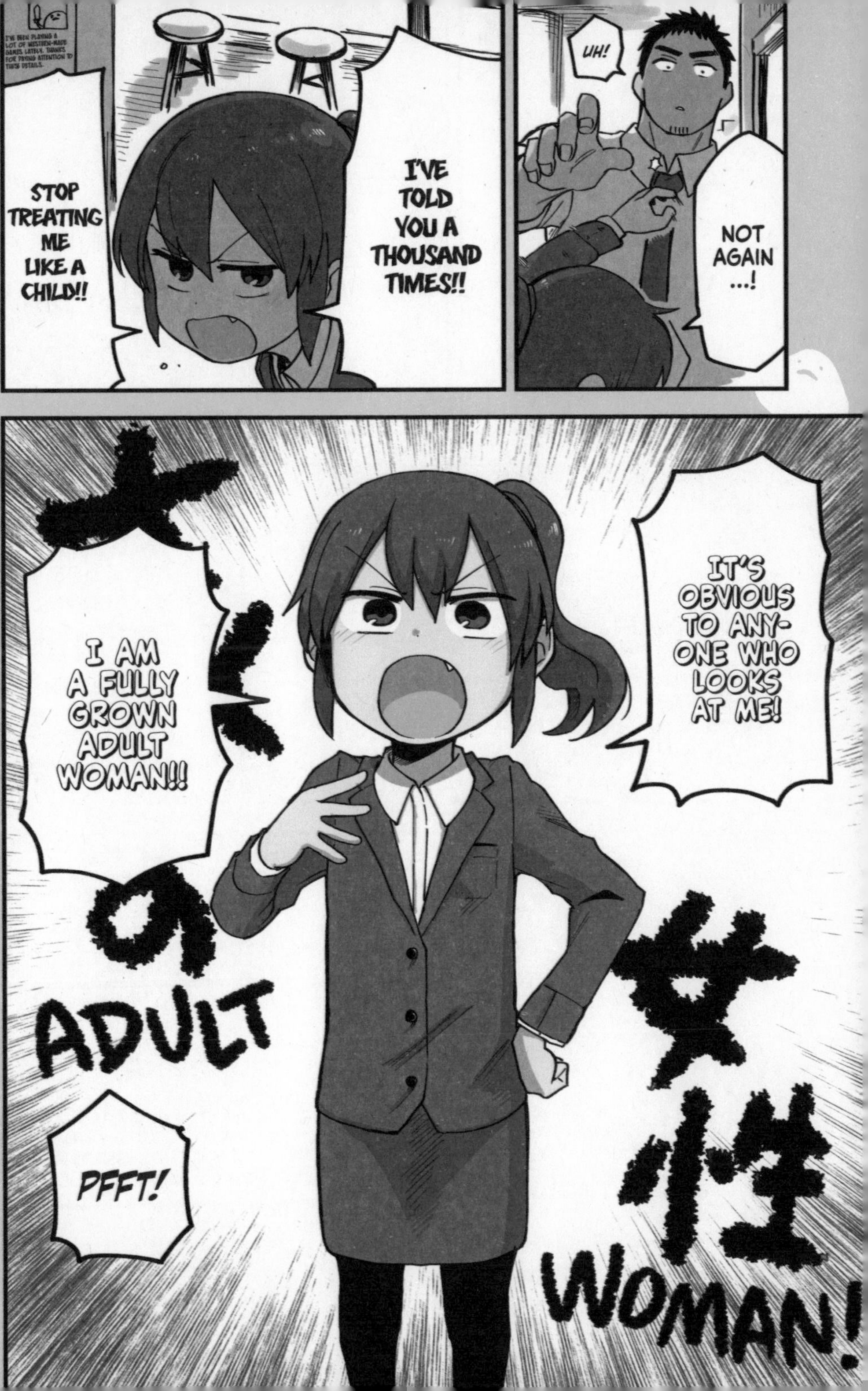
UH!
NOT AGAIN ...!
I'VE TOLD YOU A THOUSAND TIMES!!
STOP TREATING ME LIKE A CHILD!!
I'VE BEEN PLAYING A LOT OF WESTERN-MADE GAMES LATELY. THANKS FOR PAYING ATTENTION TO THESE DETAILS.
IT'S OBVIOUS TO ANY-ONE WHO LOOKS AT ME!
I AM A FULLY GROWN ADULT WOMAN!!
大人
ADULT
女性
WOMAN!
PFFT!

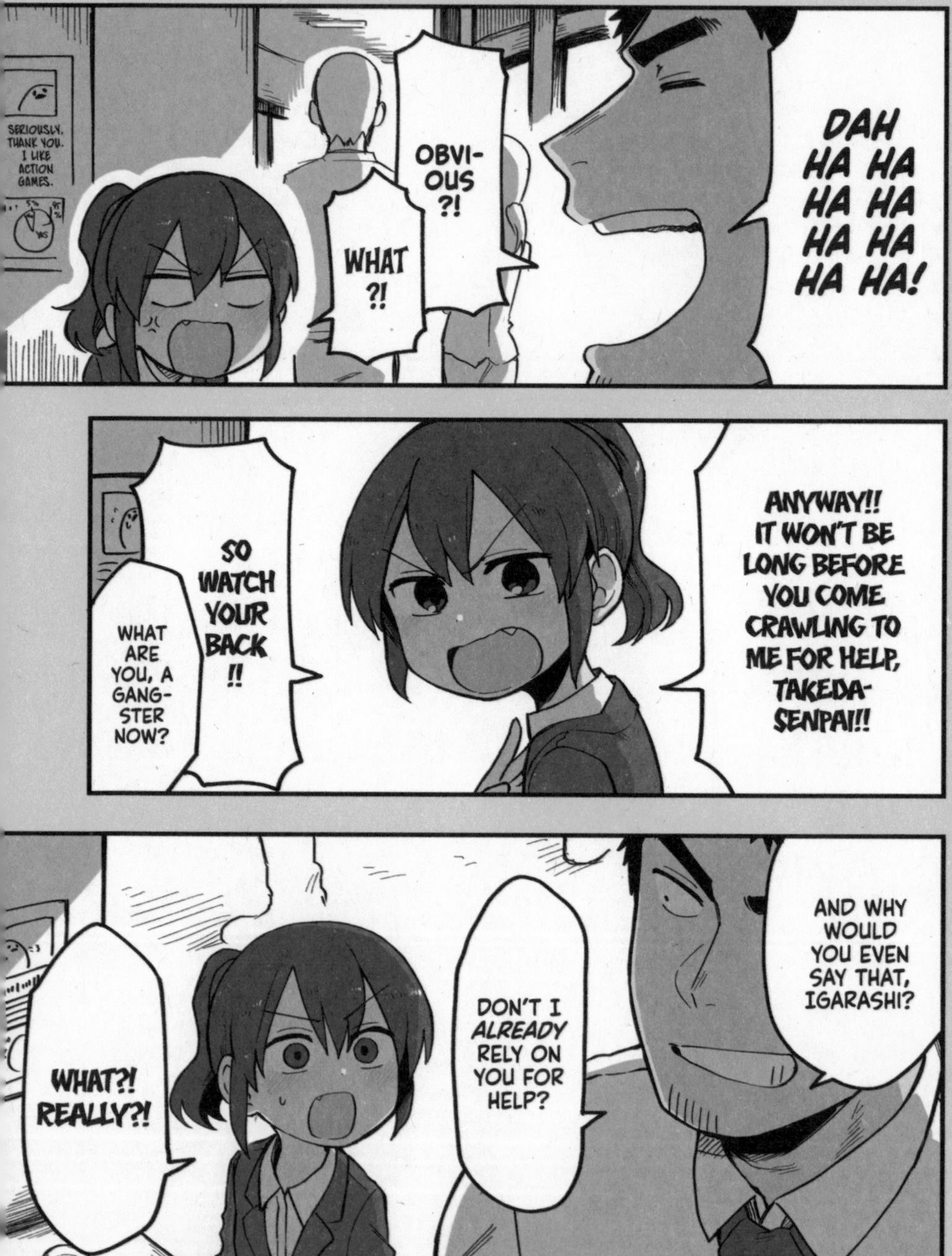
DAH HA HA HA HA HA HA HA HA!
OBVIOUS?!
WHAT?!
SERIOUSLY. THANK YOU. I LIKE ACTION GAMES.
ANYWAY!! IT WON'T BE LONG BEFORE YOU COME CRAWLING TO ME FOR HELP, TAKEDA-SENPAI!!
SO WATCH YOUR BACK!!
WHAT ARE YOU, A GANGSTER NOW?
AND WHY WOULD YOU EVEN SAY THAT, IGARASHI?
DON'T I *ALREADY* RELY ON YOU FOR HELP?
WHAT?! REALLY?!

029

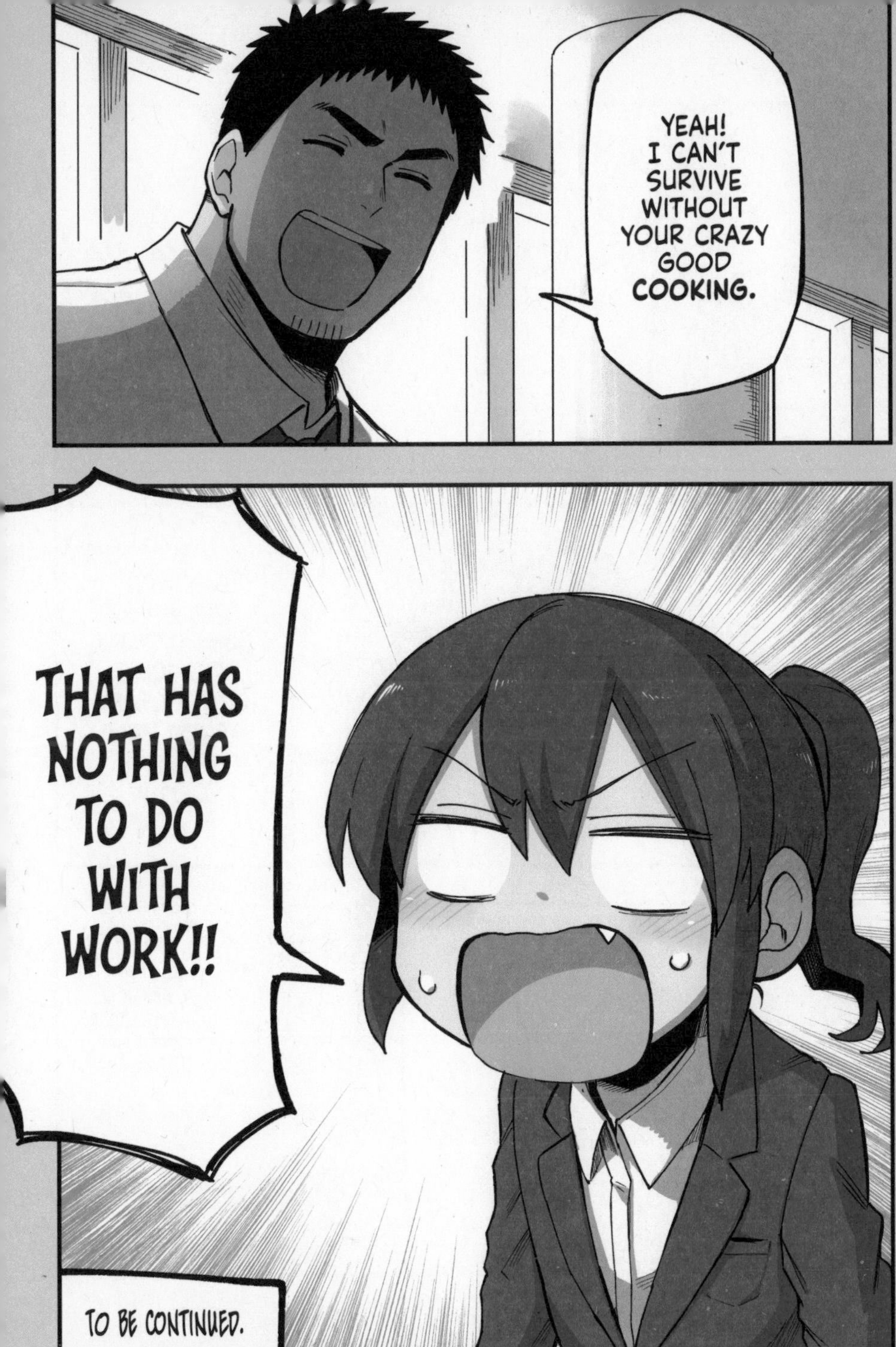
YEAH! I CAN'T SURVIVE WITHOUT YOUR CRAZY GOOD COOKING.
THAT HAS NOTHING TO DO WITH WORK!!
TO BE CONTINUED.

Chapter 26

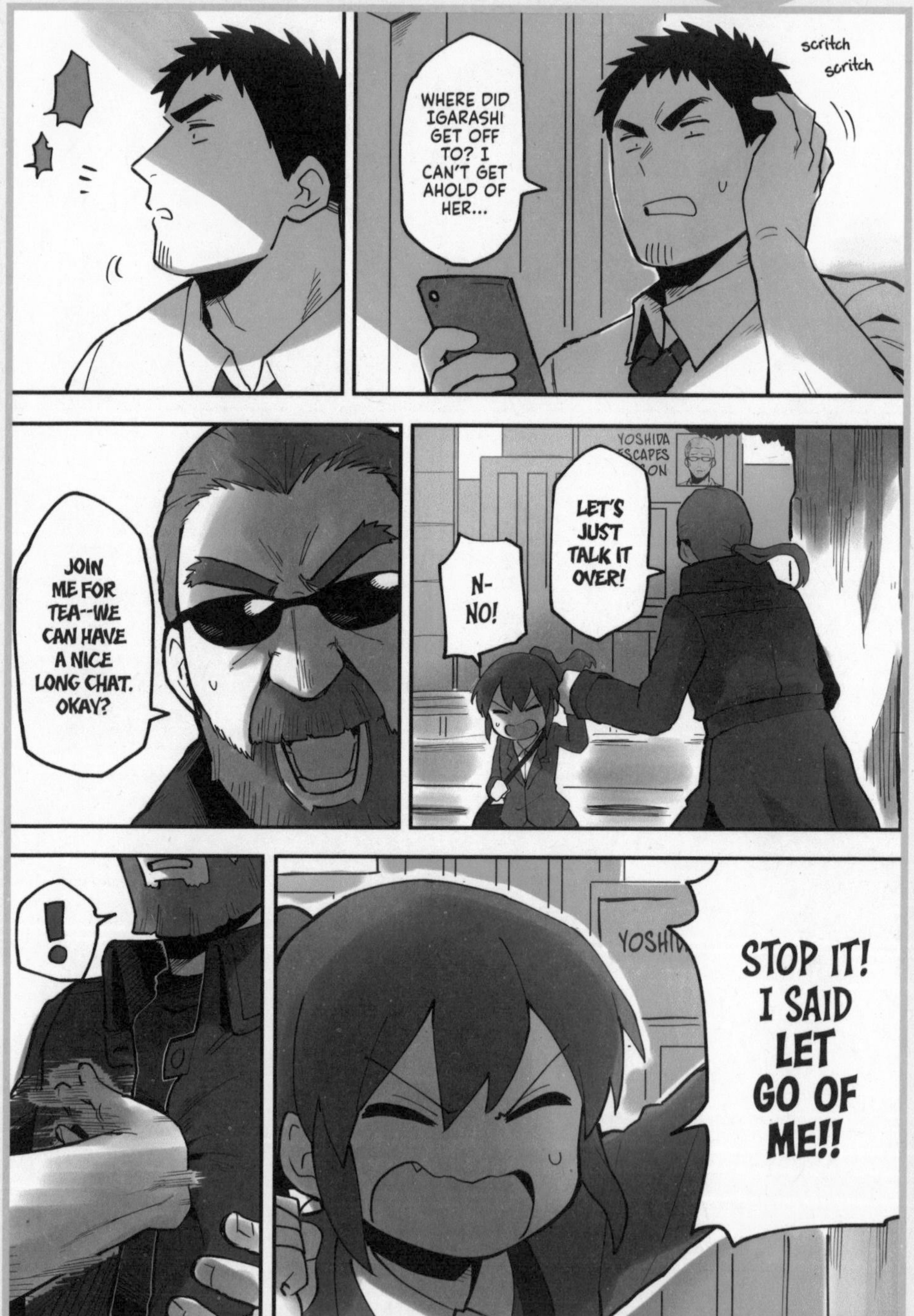
scritch scritch
WHERE DID IGARASHI GET OFF TO? I CAN'T GET AHOLD OF HER...
YOSHIDA ESCAPES
LET'S JUST TALK IT OVER!
N-NO!
JOIN ME FOR TEA--WE CAN HAVE A NICE LONG CHAT. OKAY?
YOSHIDA
STOP IT! I SAID LET GO OF ME!!
!

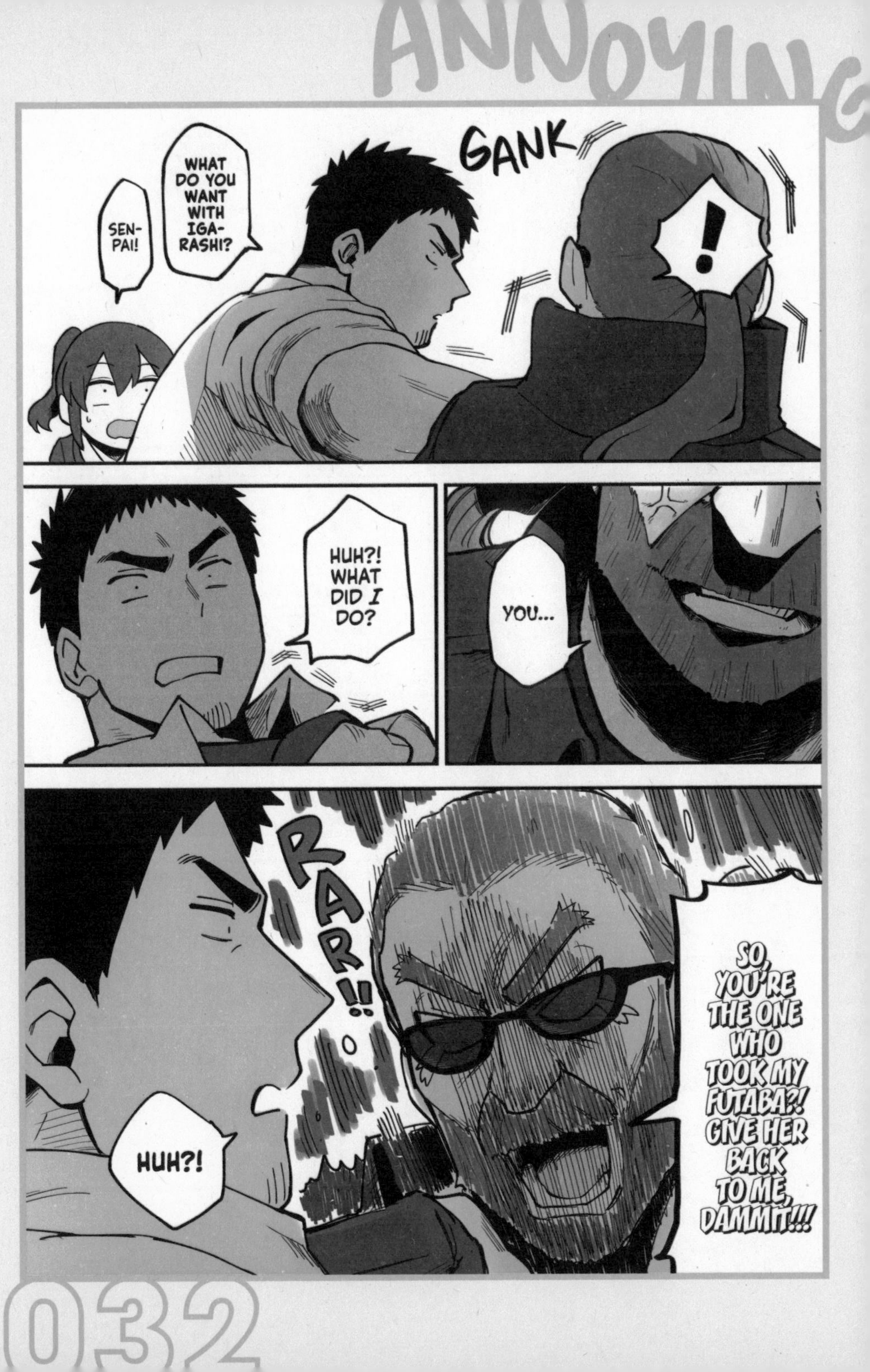
GANK
!
WHAT DO YOU WANT WITH IGA-RASHI?
SEN-PAI!
YOU...
HUH?! WHAT DID I DO?
RAR!!
SO, YOU'RE THE ONE WHO TOOK MY FUTABA?! GIVE HER BACK TO ME, DAMMIT!!!
HUH?!

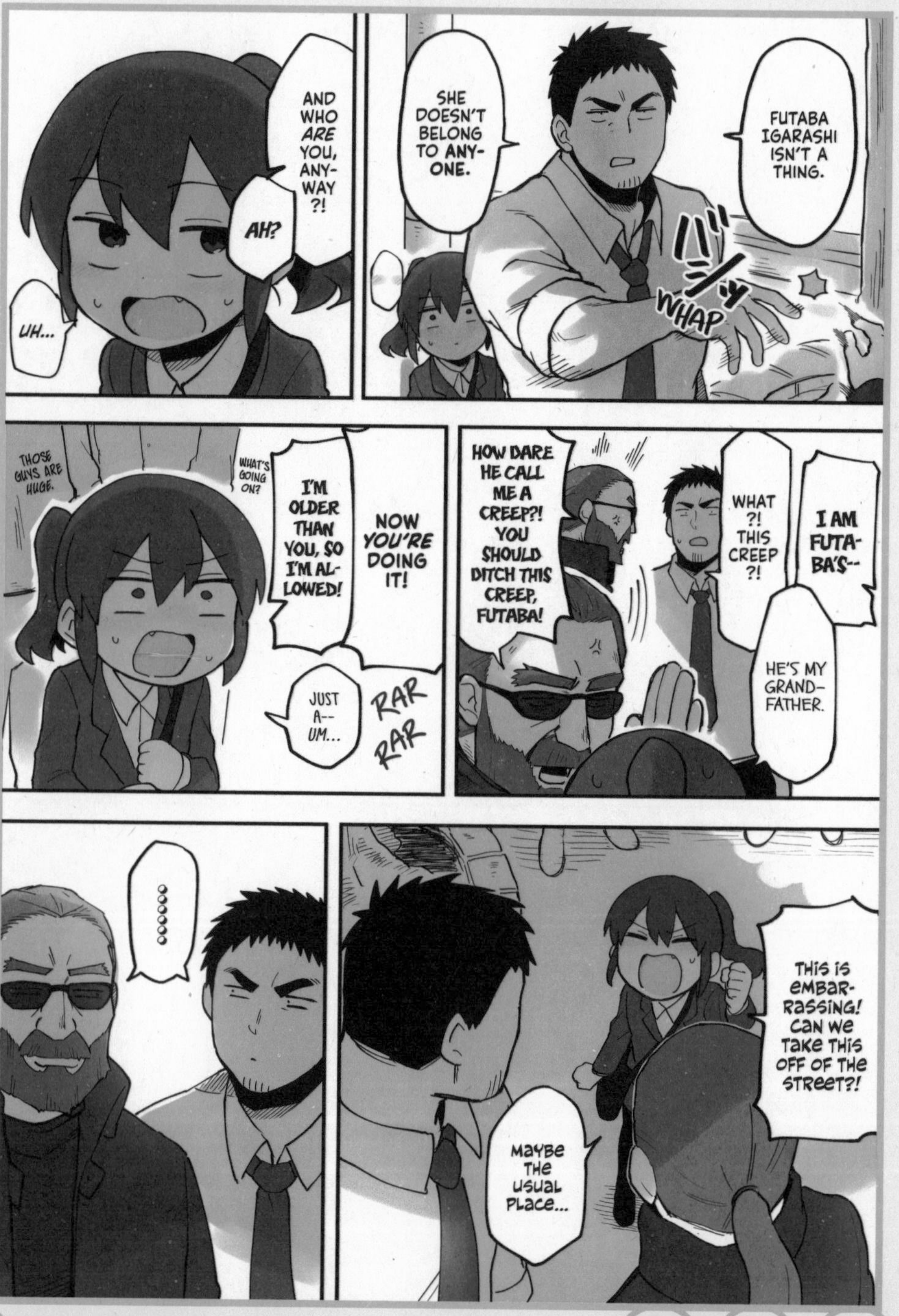
FUTABA IGARASHI ISN'T A THING.
SHE DOESN'T BELONG TO ANY-ONE.
WHAP
AND WHO *ARE* YOU, ANY-WAY?!
AH?
UH...
I AM FUTA-BA'S--
WHAT?! THIS CREEP?!
HE'S MY GRAND-FATHER.
HOW DARE HE CALL ME A CREEP?! YOU SHOULD DITCH THIS CREEP, FUTABA!
NOW *YOU'RE* DOING IT!
I'M OLDER THAN YOU, SO I'M AL-LOWED!
RAR RAR
JUST A-- UM...
WHAT'S GOING ON?
THOSE GUYS ARE HUGE.
This is embar-rassing! Can we take this off of the street?!
Maybe the usual place...
......

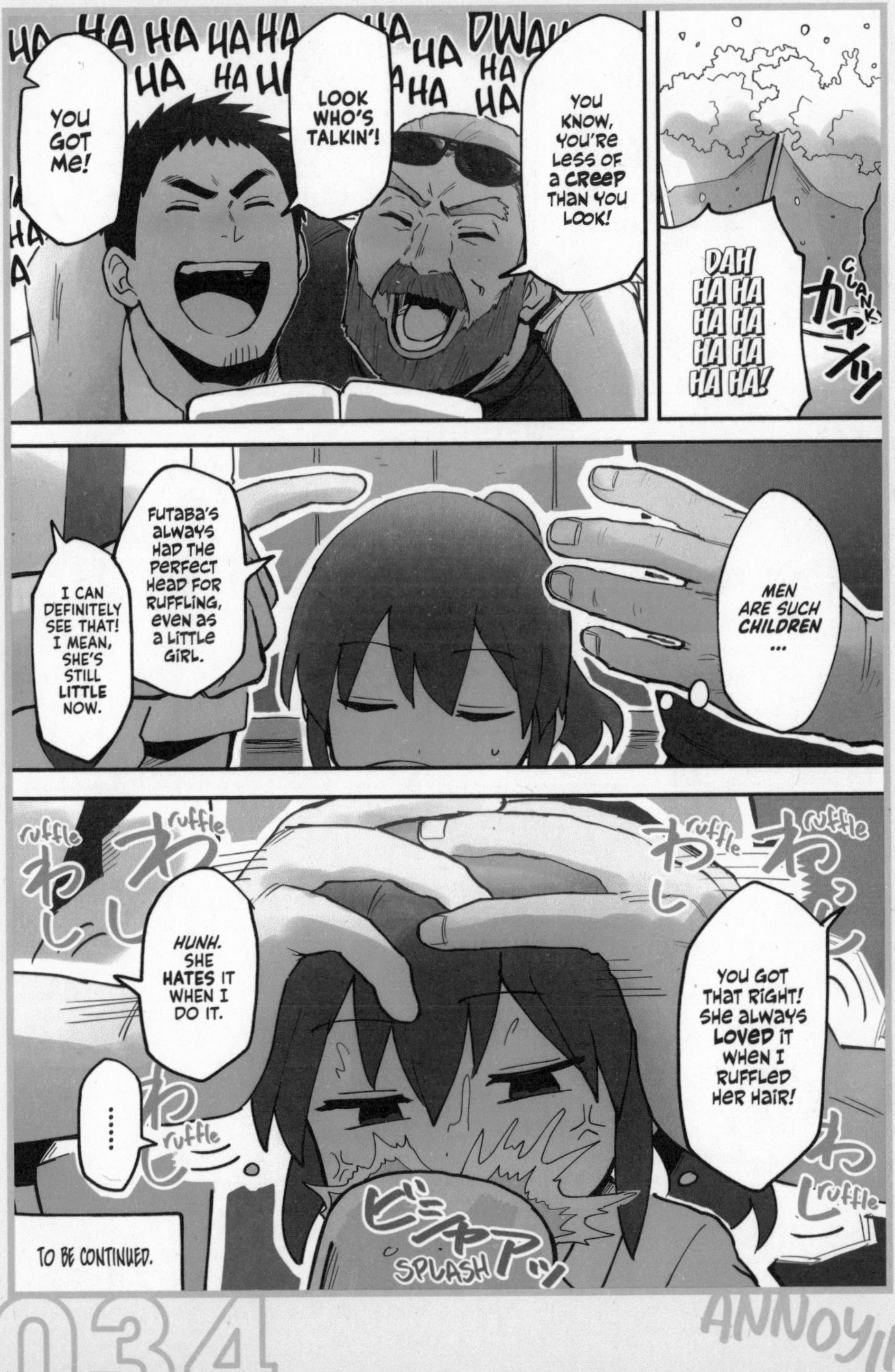
DAH HA HA HA HA HA HA HA HA!
CLANK
DWAH HA HA HA HA
YOU KNOW, YOU'RE LESS OF A CREEP THAN YOU LOOK!
LOOK WHO'S TALKIN'!
YOU GOT ME!
HA HA HA HA HA HA HA HA HA
MEN ARE SUCH CHILDREN...
FUTABA'S ALWAYS HAD THE PERFECT HEAD FOR RUFFLING, EVEN AS A LITTLE GIRL.
I CAN DEFINITELY SEE THAT! I MEAN, SHE'S STILL LITTLE NOW.
ruffle ruffle
YOU GOT THAT RIGHT! SHE ALWAYS LOVED IT WHEN I RUFFLED HER HAIR!
HUNH. SHE HATES IT WHEN I DO IT.
......
ruffle ruffle
SPLASH
TO BE CONTINUED.

034

ANNOYIN

Chapter 27

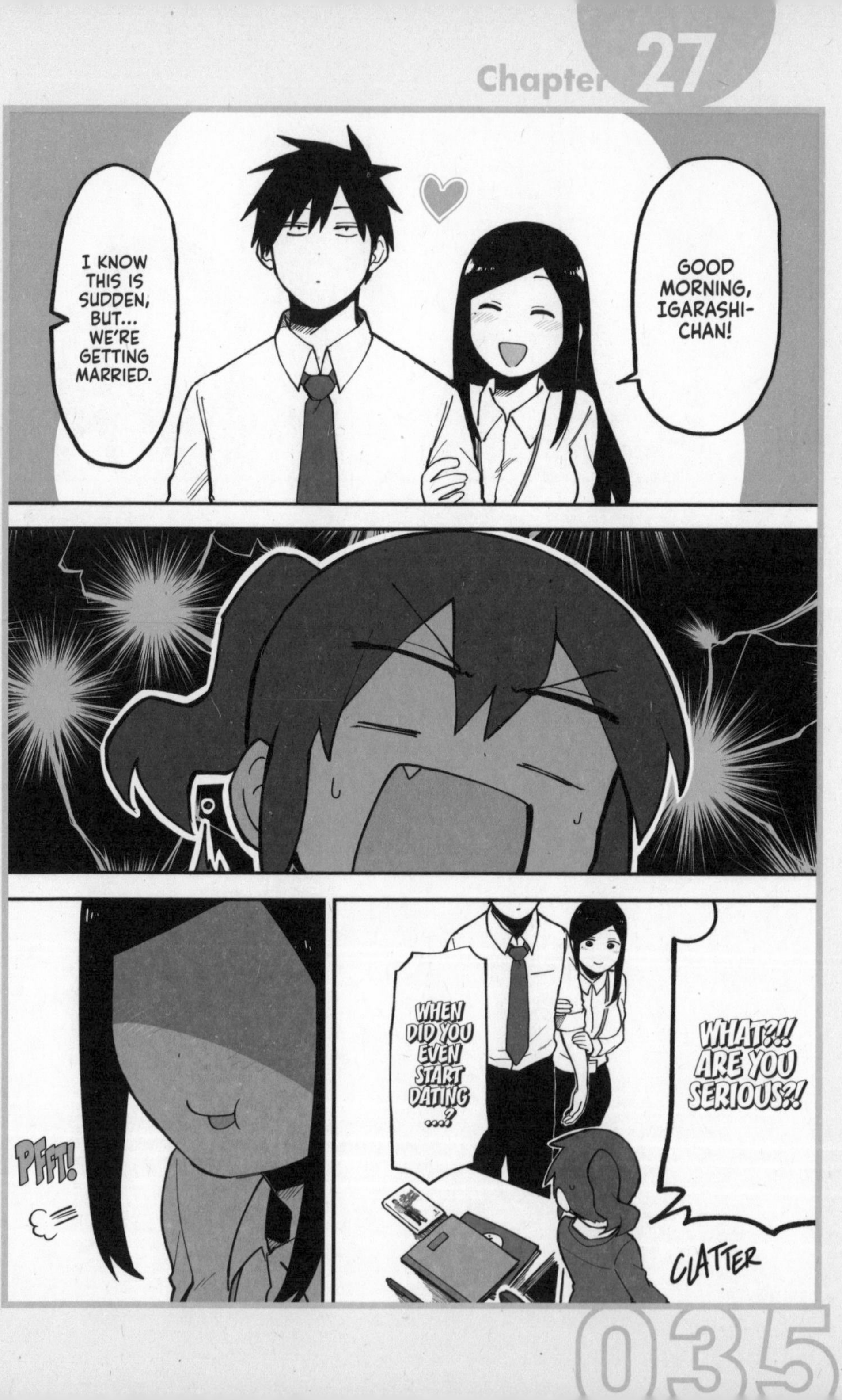
GOOD MORNING, IGARASHI-CHAN!
I KNOW THIS IS SUDDEN, BUT... WE'RE GETTING MARRIED.
WHAT?!! ARE YOU SERIOUS?!
WHEN DID YOU EVEN START DATING ...?
CLATTER
PFFT!

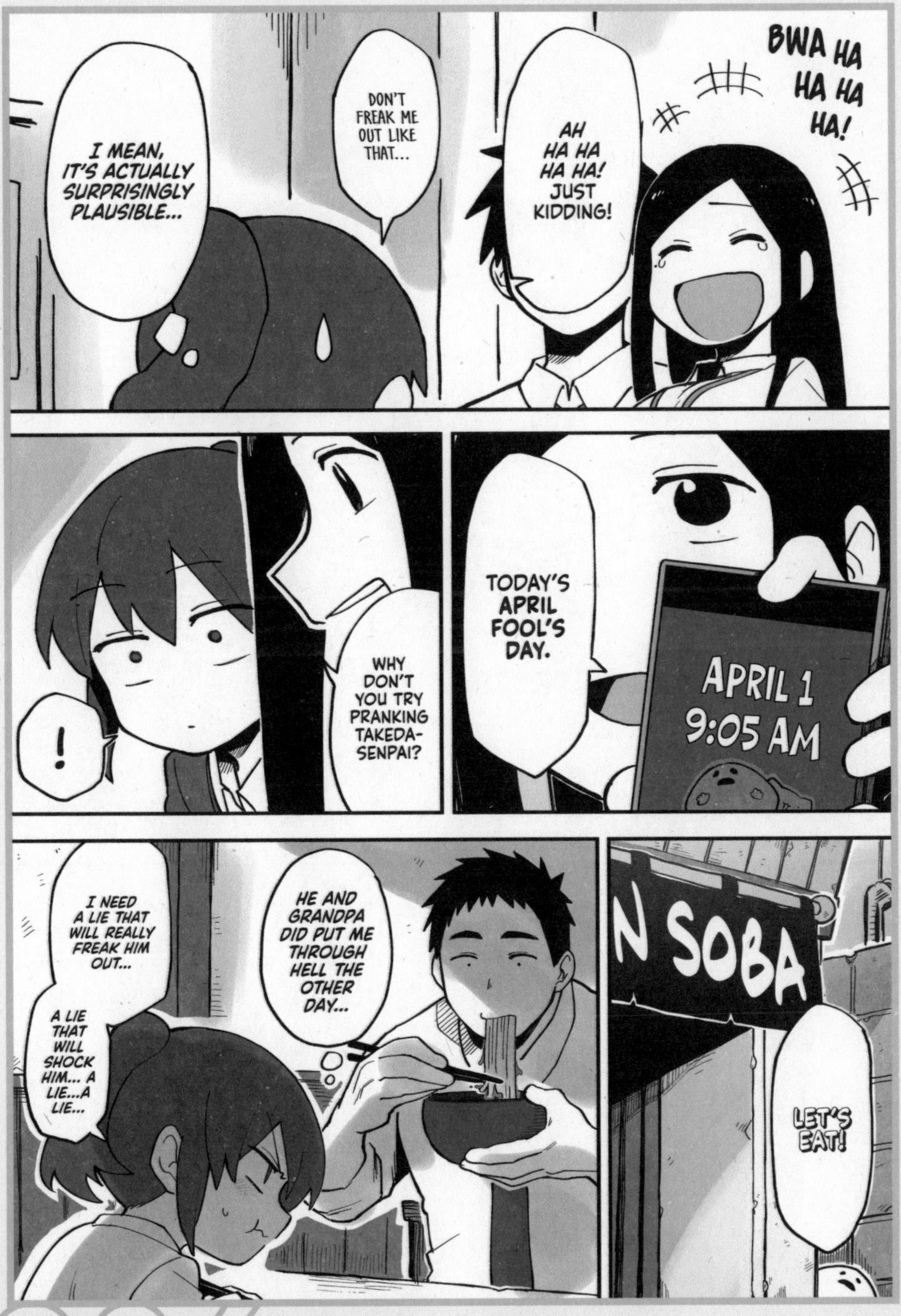
BWA HA HA HA HA!
AH HA HA HA HA! JUST KIDDING!
DON'T FREAK ME OUT LIKE THAT...
I MEAN, IT'S ACTUALLY SURPRISINGLY PLAUSIBLE...
TODAY'S APRIL FOOL'S DAY.
APRIL 1 9:05 AM
WHY DON'T YOU TRY PRANKING TAKEDA-SENPAI?
!
N SOBA
LET'S EAT!
HE AND GRANDPA DID PUT ME THROUGH HELL THE OTHER DAY...
I NEED A LIE THAT WILL REALLY FREAK HIM OUT...
A LIE THAT WILL SHOCK HIM... A LIE...A LIE...

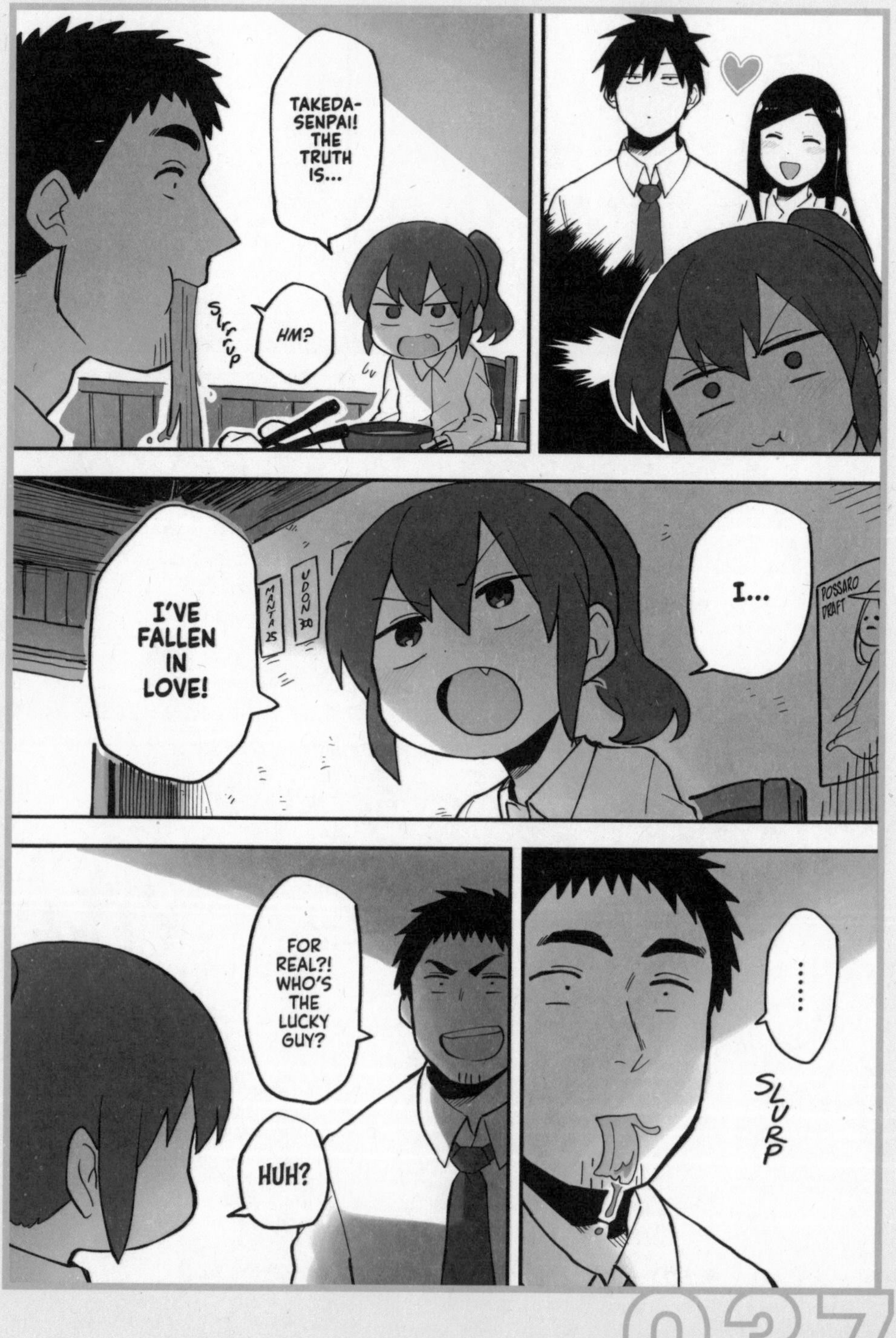
TAKEDA-SENPAI! THE TRUTH IS...
HM?
SLRRRUP
I...
I'VE FALLEN IN LOVE!
MANTA 25
UDON 300
POSSARO DRAFT
......
SLURP
FOR REAL?! WHO'S THE LUCKY GUY?
HUH?

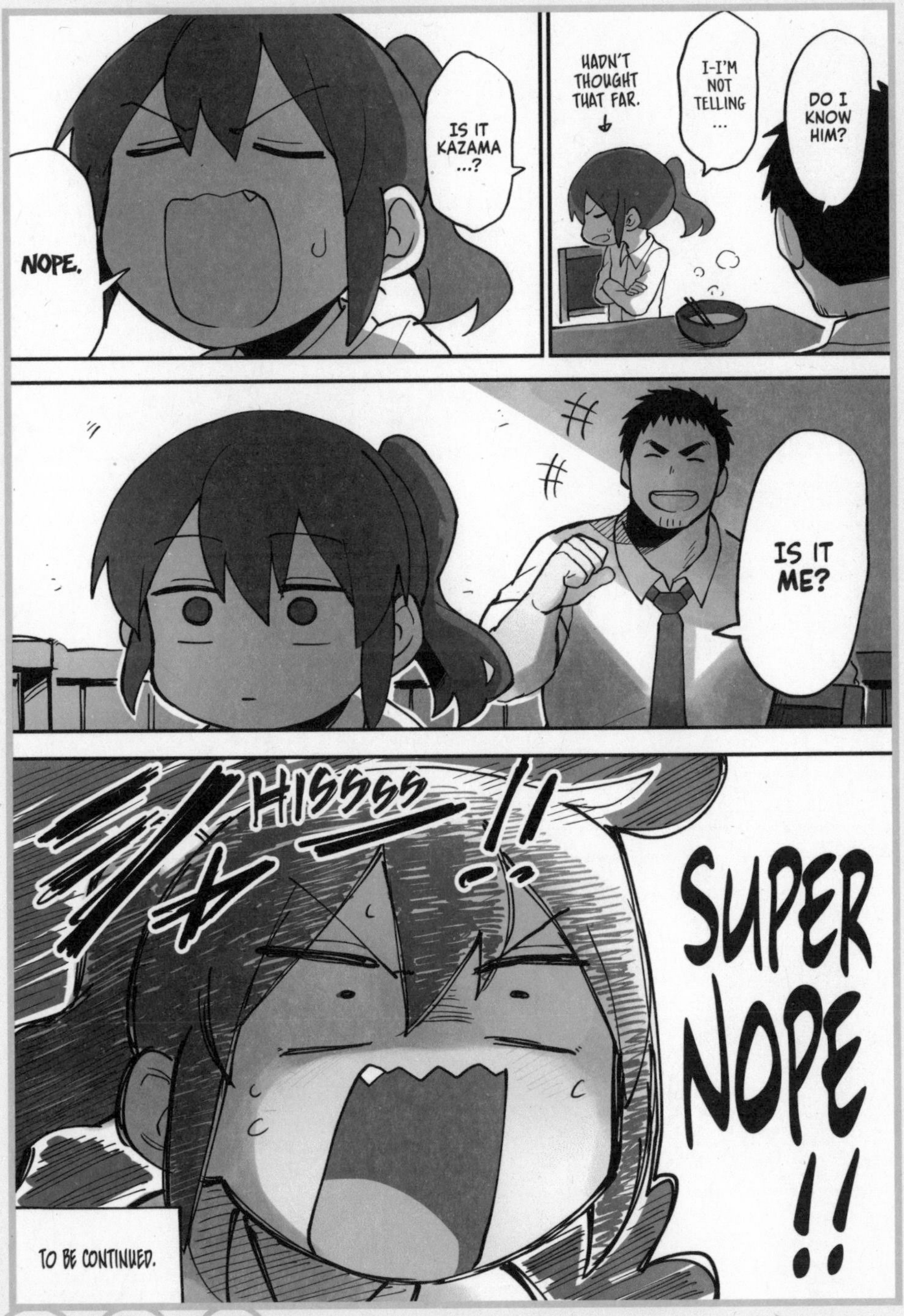
DO I KNOW HIM?
I-I'M NOT TELLING...
HADN'T THOUGHT THAT FAR.
IS IT KAZAMA...?
NOPE.
IS IT ME?
HISSSS
SUPER NOPE!!
TO BE CONTINUED.

Chapter 28

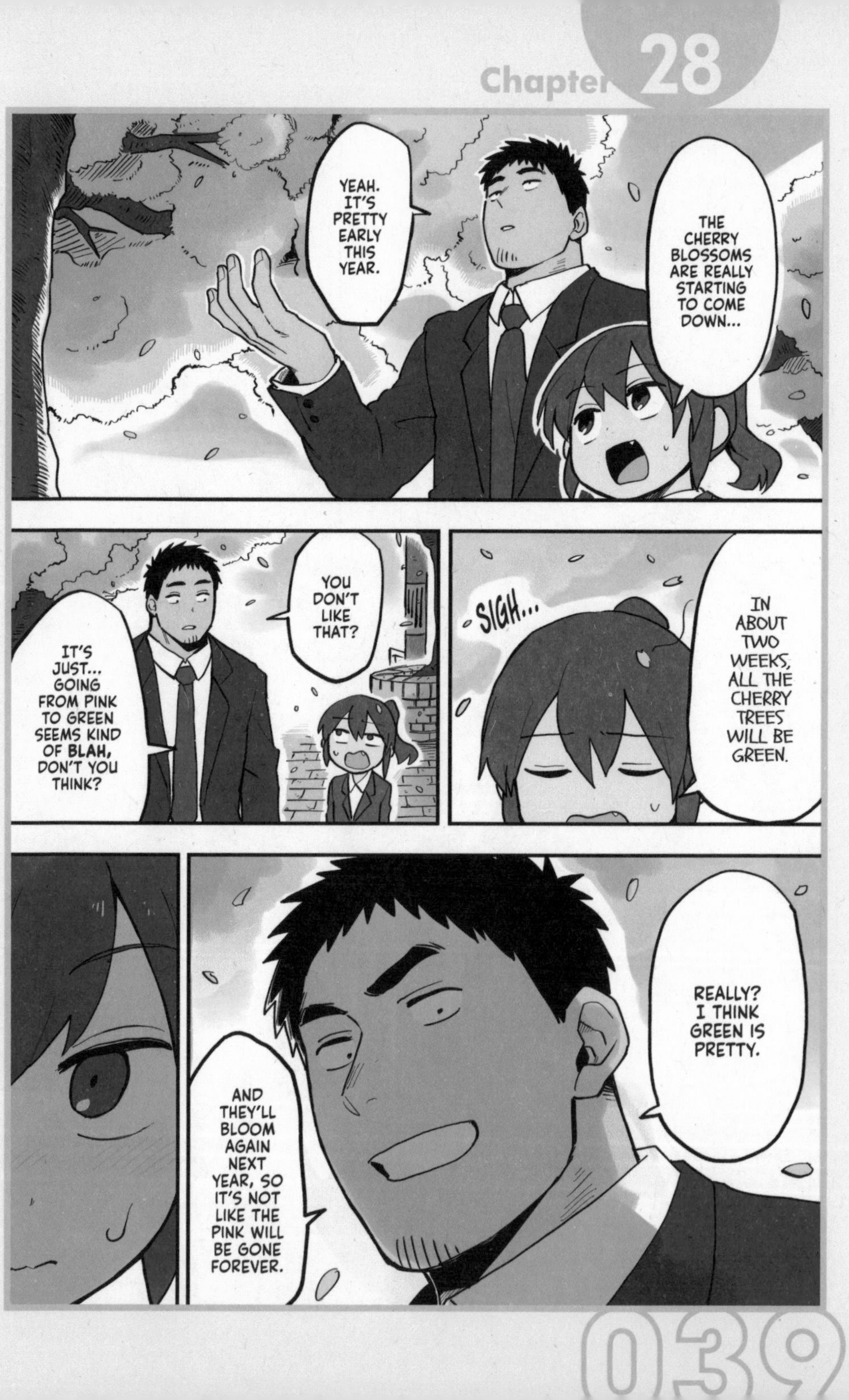
THE CHERRY BLOSSOMS ARE REALLY STARTING TO COME DOWN...
YEAH. IT'S PRETTY EARLY THIS YEAR.
IN ABOUT TWO WEEKS, ALL THE CHERRY TREES WILL BE GREEN.
SIGH...
YOU DON'T LIKE THAT?
IT'S JUST... GOING FROM PINK TO GREEN SEEMS KIND OF **BLAH**, DON'T YOU THINK?
REALLY? I THINK GREEN IS PRETTY.
AND THEY'LL BLOOM AGAIN NEXT YEAR, SO IT'S NOT LIKE THE PINK WILL BE GONE FOREVER.

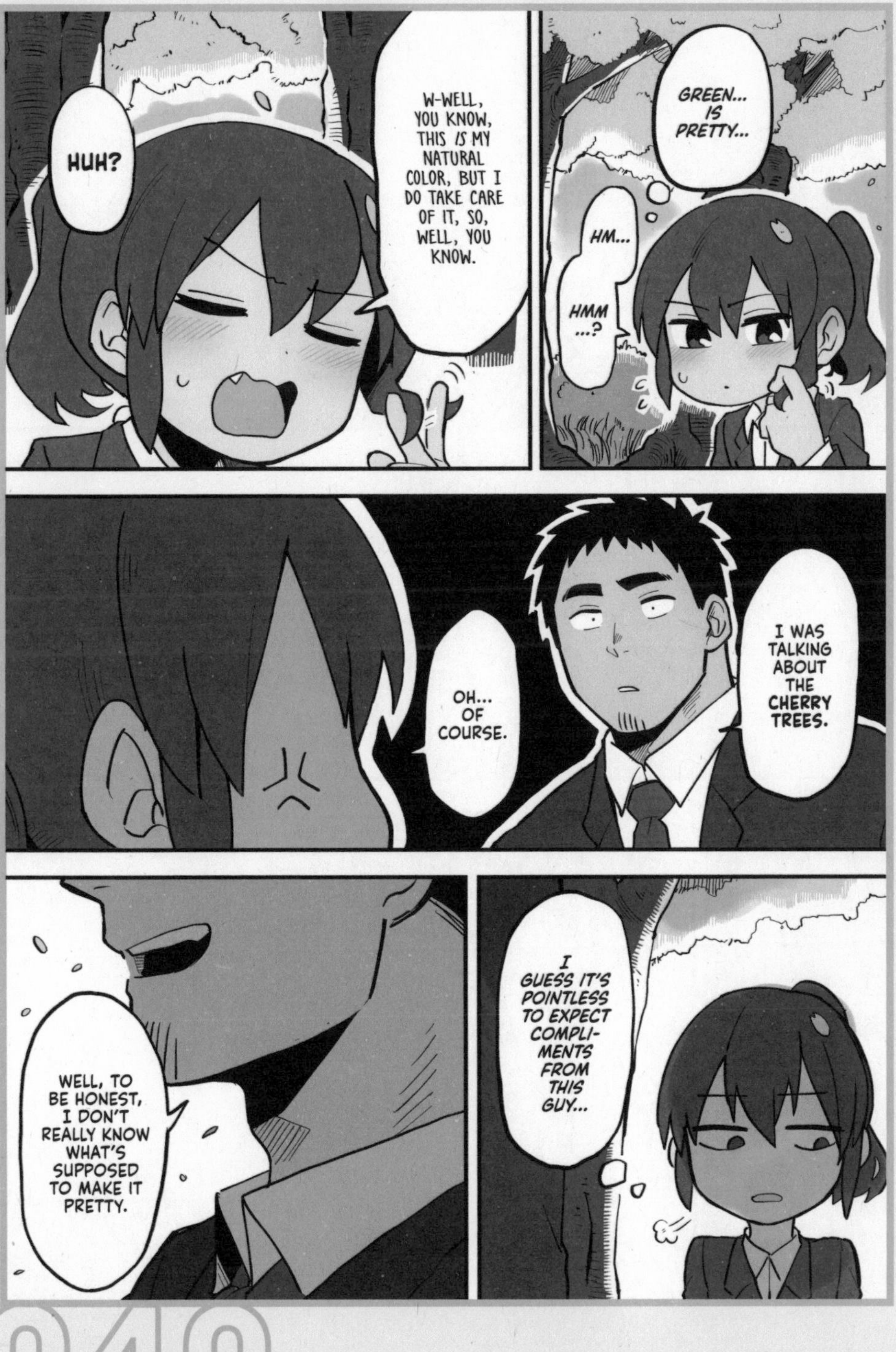
GREEN... IS PRETTY...
HM...
HMM ...?
W-WELL, YOU KNOW, THIS *IS* MY NATURAL COLOR, BUT I DO TAKE CARE OF IT, SO, WELL, YOU KNOW.
HUH?
I WAS TALKING ABOUT THE **CHERRY TREES.**
OH... OF COURSE.
I GUESS IT'S POINTLESS TO EXPECT COMPLI-MENTS FROM THIS GUY...
WELL, TO BE HONEST, I DON'T REALLY KNOW WHAT'S SUPPOSED TO MAKE IT PRETTY.

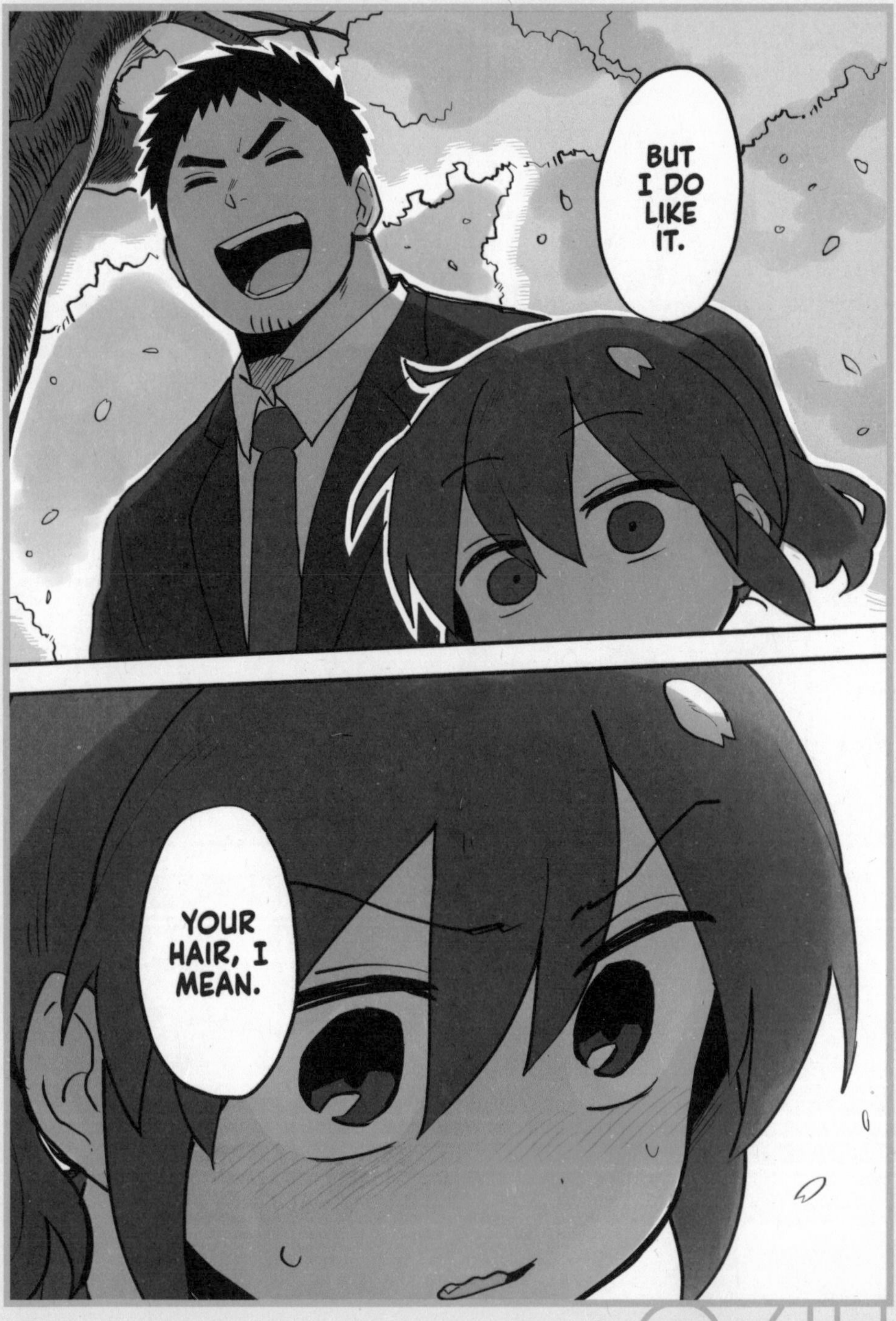
BUT I DO LIKE IT.
YOUR HAIR, I MEAN.

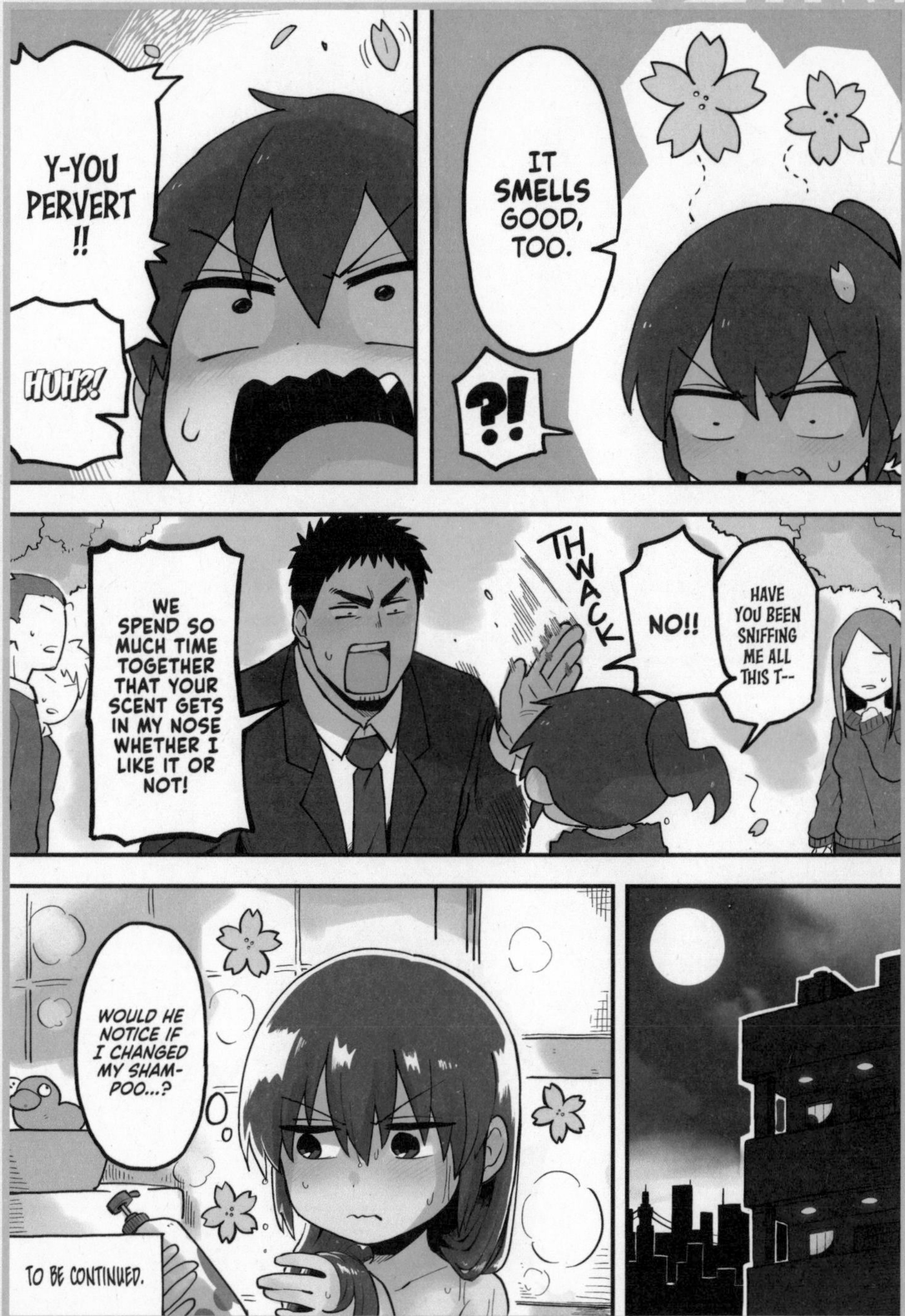
IT SMELLS GOOD, TOO.
?!
Y-YOU PERVERT !!
HUH?!
HAVE YOU BEEN SNIFFING ME ALL THIS T--
NO!!
THWACK
WE SPEND SO MUCH TIME TOGETHER THAT YOUR SCENT GETS IN MY NOSE WHETHER I LIKE IT OR NOT!
WOULD HE NOTICE IF I CHANGED MY SHAM-POO...?
TO BE CONTINUED.

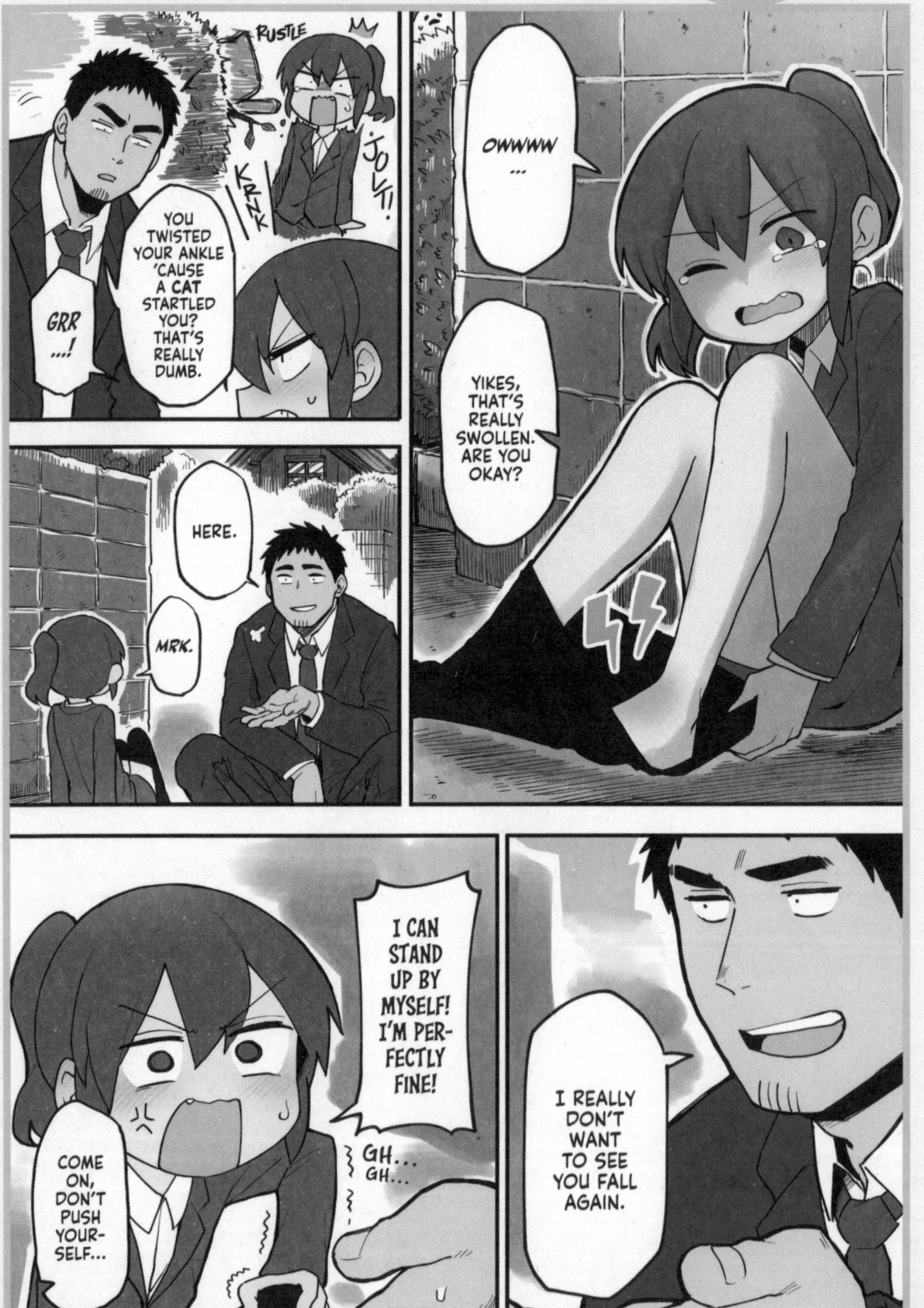
OWWWW...
YIKES, THAT'S REALLY SWOLLEN. ARE YOU OKAY?
RUSTLE
JOLT!
KRINK
YOU TWISTED YOUR ANKLE 'CAUSE A CAT STARTLED YOU? THAT'S REALLY DUMB.
GRR...!
HERE.
MRK.
I REALLY DON'T WANT TO SEE YOU FALL AGAIN.
I CAN STAND UP BY MYSELF! I'M PERFECTLY FINE!
GH... GH...
COME ON, DON'T PUSH YOURSELF...

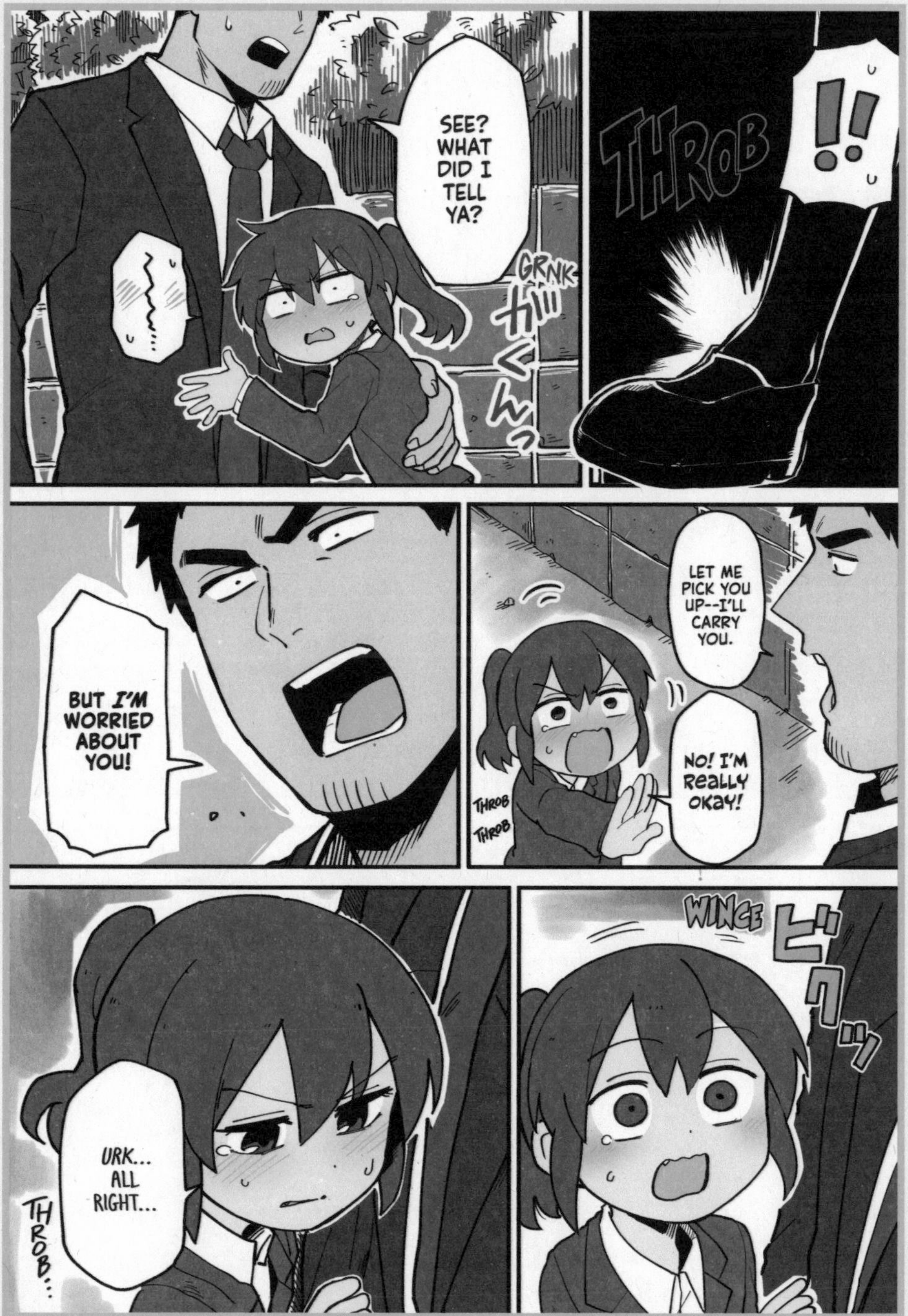
THROB
!!
SEE? WHAT DID I TELL YA?
~~~...
GRNK
がくんっ
LET ME PICK YOU UP--I'LL CARRY YOU.
NO! I'M REALLY OKAY!
THROB
THROB
BUT *I'M* WORRIED ABOUT YOU!
WINCE
ビクッ
URK... ALL RIGHT...
THROB...
~~~

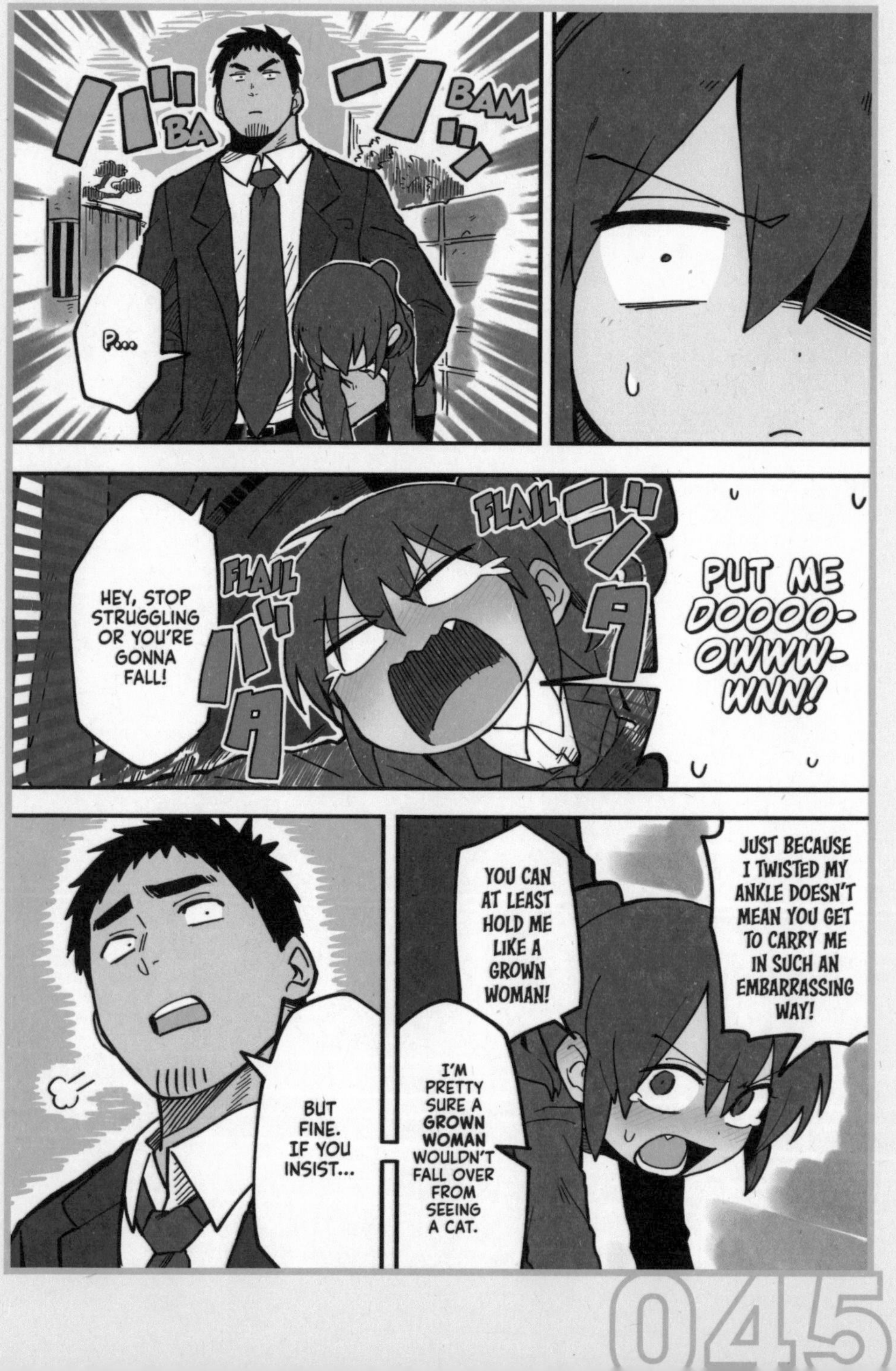
BAM
BA
P...
PUT ME DOOOO-OWWW-WNN!
FLAIL
FLAIL
HEY, STOP STRUGGLING OR YOU'RE GONNA FALL!
JUST BECAUSE I TWISTED MY ANKLE DOESN'T MEAN YOU GET TO CARRY ME IN SUCH AN EMBARRASSING WAY!
YOU CAN AT LEAST HOLD ME LIKE A GROWN WOMAN!
I'M PRETTY SURE A GROWN WOMAN WOULDN'T FALL OVER FROM SEEING A CAT.
BUT FINE. IF YOU INSIST...

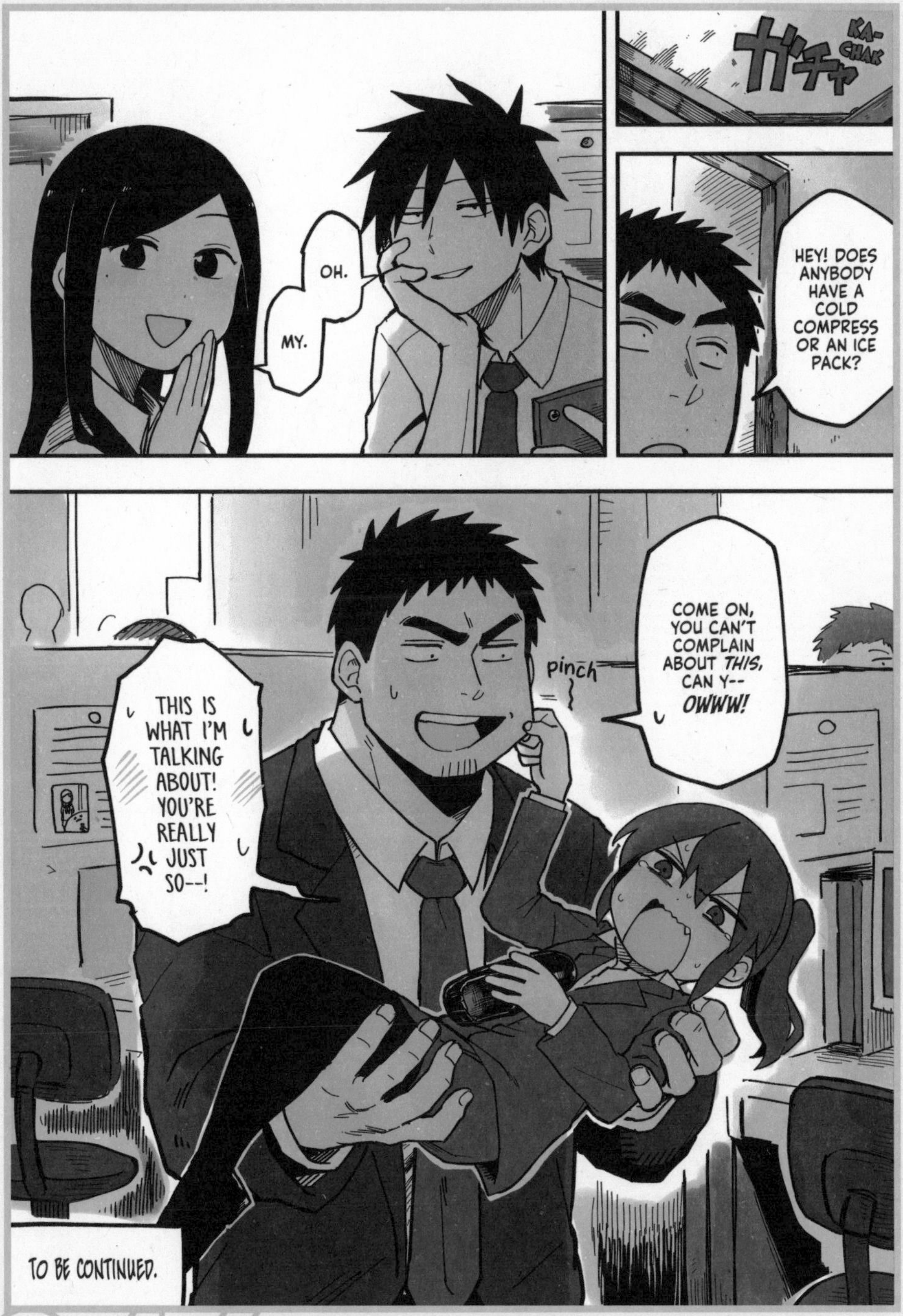
ガチャ KA-CHAK
HEY! DOES ANYBODY HAVE A COLD COMPRESS OR AN ICE PACK?
OH.
MY.
COME ON, YOU CAN'T COMPLAIN ABOUT *THIS*, CAN Y-- ***OWWW!***
pinch
THIS IS WHAT I'M TALKING ABOUT! YOU'RE REALLY JUST SO--!
TO BE CONTINUED.

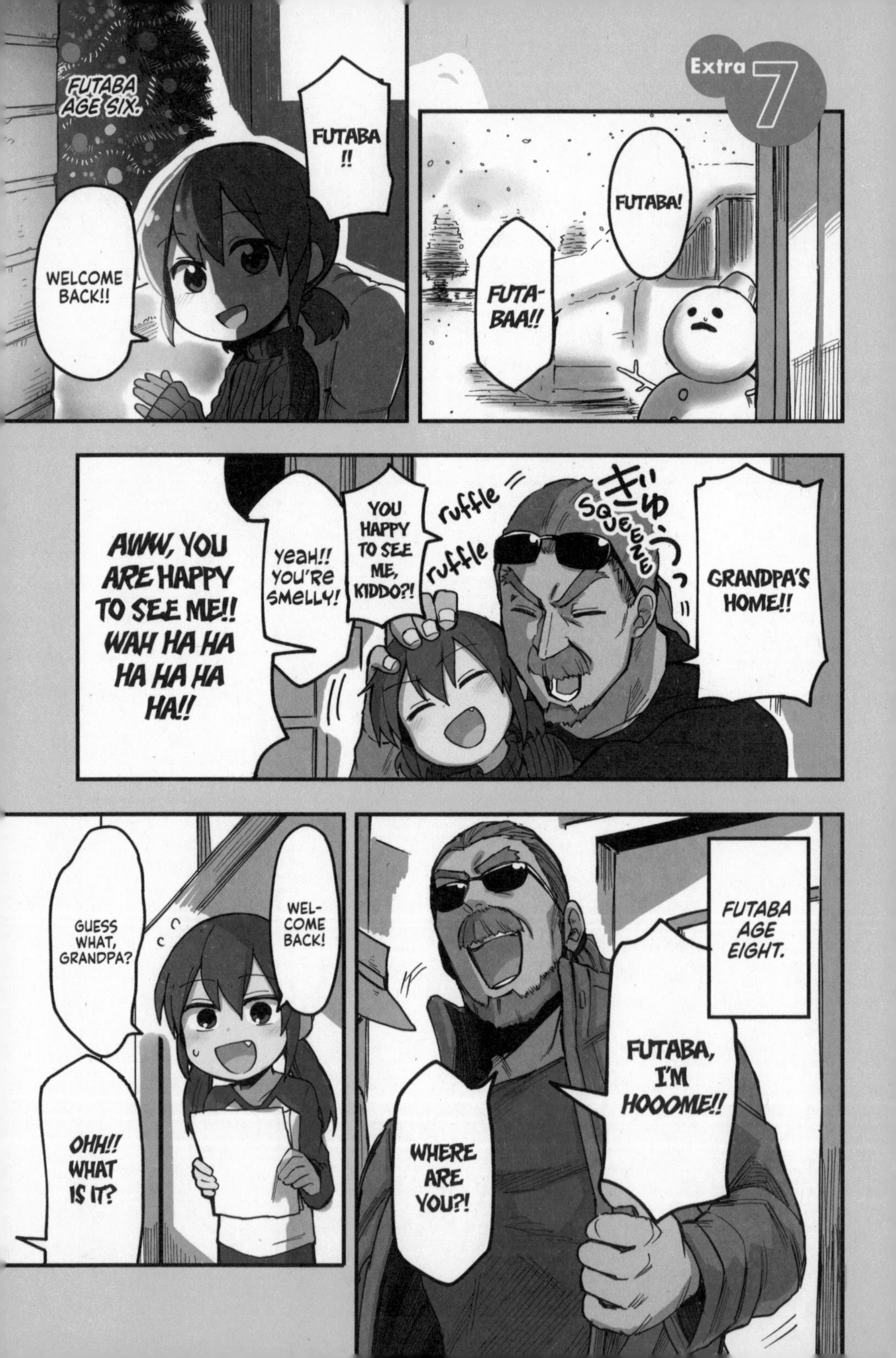
Extra 7
FUTABA!
FUTA-BAA!!
FUTABA!!
FUTABA AGE SIX.
WELCOME BACK!!
GRANDPA'S HOME!!
ぎゅっ
SQUEEZE
ruffle
ruffle
YOU HAPPY TO SEE ME, KIDDO?!
Yeah!! You're smelly!
AWW, YOU ARE HAPPY TO SEE ME!! WAH HA HA HA HA HA HA!!
FUTABA AGE EIGHT.
FUTABA, I'M HOOOME!!
WHERE ARE YOU?!
WEL-COME BACK!
GUESS WHAT, GRANDPA?
OHH!! WHAT IS IT?

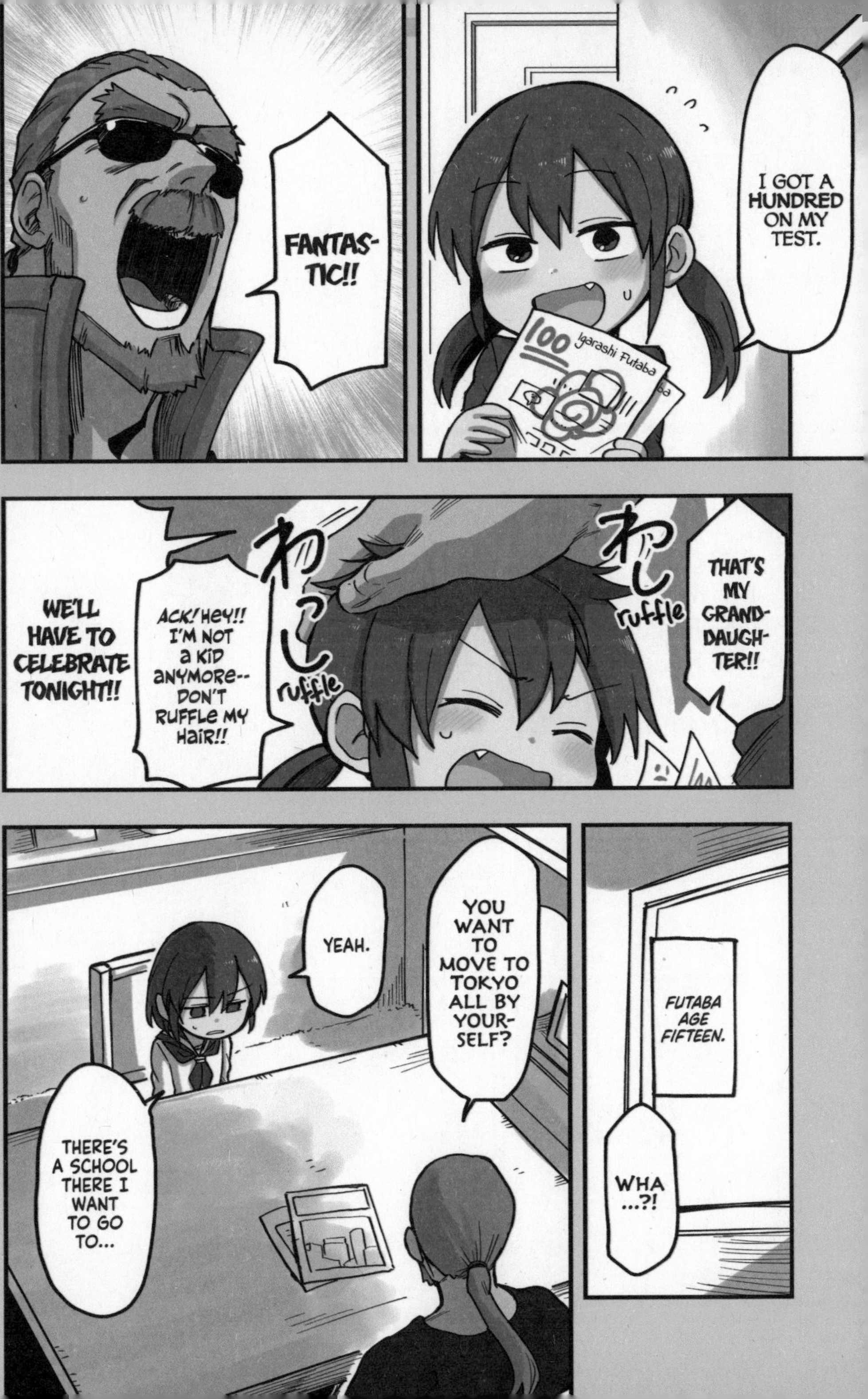
I GOT A HUNDRED ON MY TEST.
100 Igarashi Futaba
FANTAS-TIC!!
THAT'S MY GRAND-DAUGH-TER!!
わし ruffle
わし ruffle
ACK! HEY!! I'M NOT a KID anymore-- DON'T RUFFLE MY HaIR!!
WE'LL HAVE TO CELEBRATE TONIGHT!!
FUTABA AGE FIFTEEN.
WHA ...?!
YOU WANT TO MOVE TO TOKYO ALL BY YOUR-SELF?
YEAH.
THERE'S A SCHOOL THERE I WANT TO GO TO...

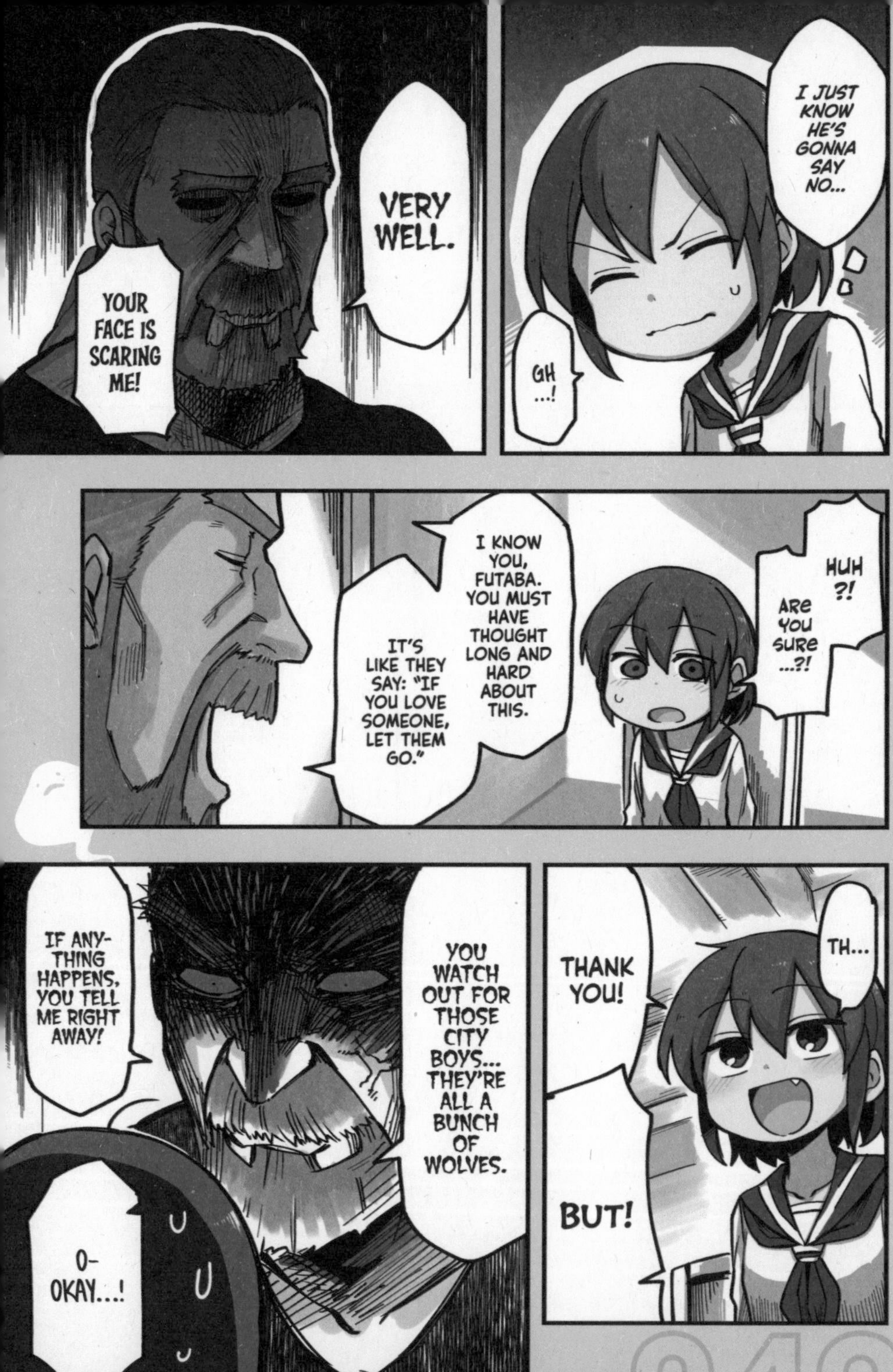
I JUST KNOW HE'S GONNA SAY NO...
GH ...!
VERY WELL.
YOUR FACE IS SCARING ME!
HUH ?!
Are you sure ...?!
I KNOW YOU, FUTABA. YOU MUST HAVE THOUGHT LONG AND HARD ABOUT THIS.
IT'S LIKE THEY SAY: "IF YOU LOVE SOMEONE, LET THEM GO."
TH...
THANK YOU!
BUT!
YOU WATCH OUT FOR THOSE CITY BOYS... THEY'RE ALL A BUNCH OF WOLVES.
IF ANYTHING HAPPENS, YOU TELL ME RIGHT AWAY!
O-OKAY...!

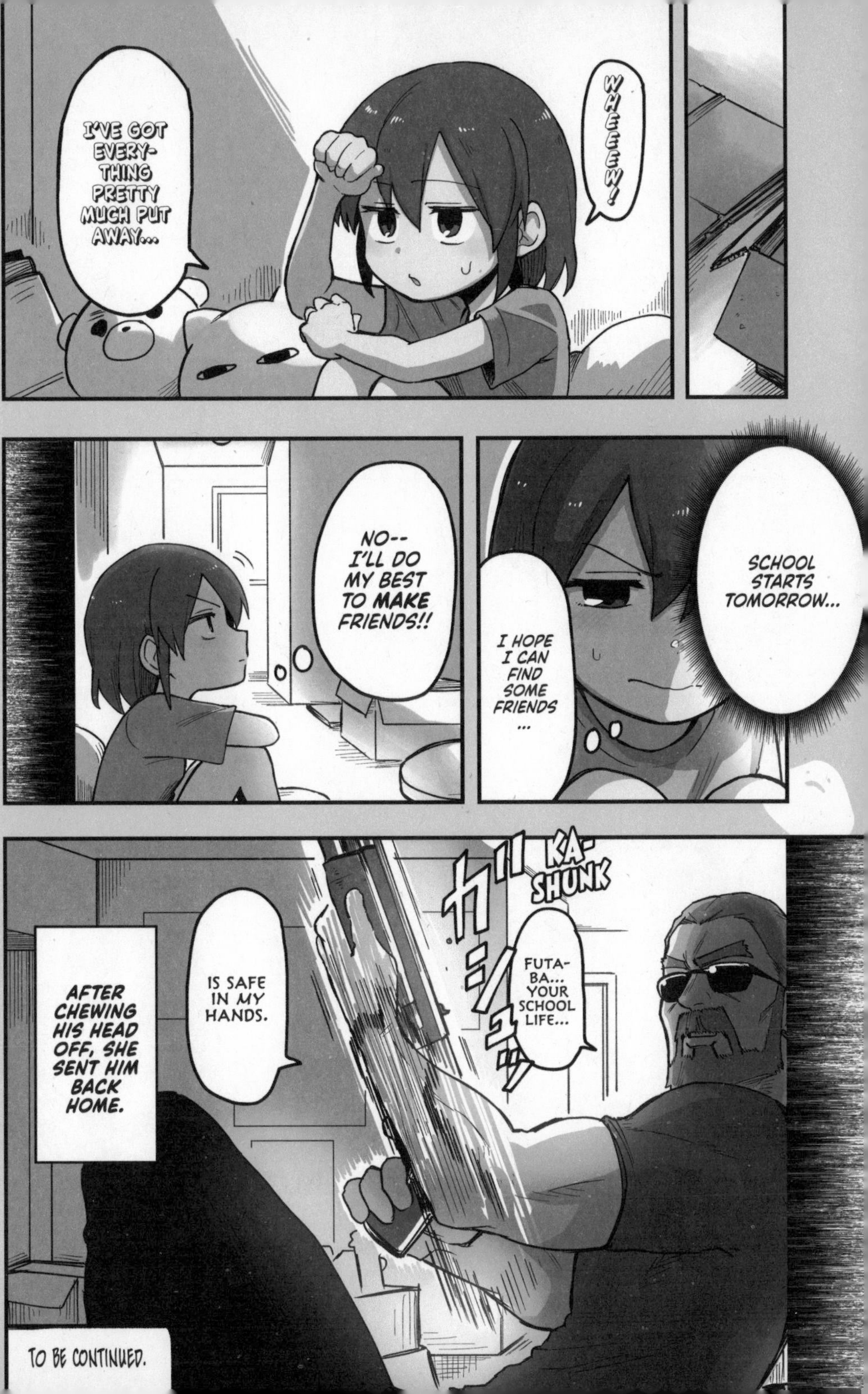
WHEEEEW!
I'VE GOT EVERY-THING PRETTY MUCH PUT AWAY...
SCHOOL STARTS TOMORROW...
I HOPE I CAN FIND SOME FRIENDS ...
NO-- I'LL DO MY BEST TO MAKE FRIENDS!!
KA-SHUNK
FUTA-BA... YOUR SCHOOL LIFE...
IS SAFE IN MY HANDS.
AFTER CHEWING HIS HEAD OFF, SHE SENT HIM BACK HOME.
TO BE CONTINUED.

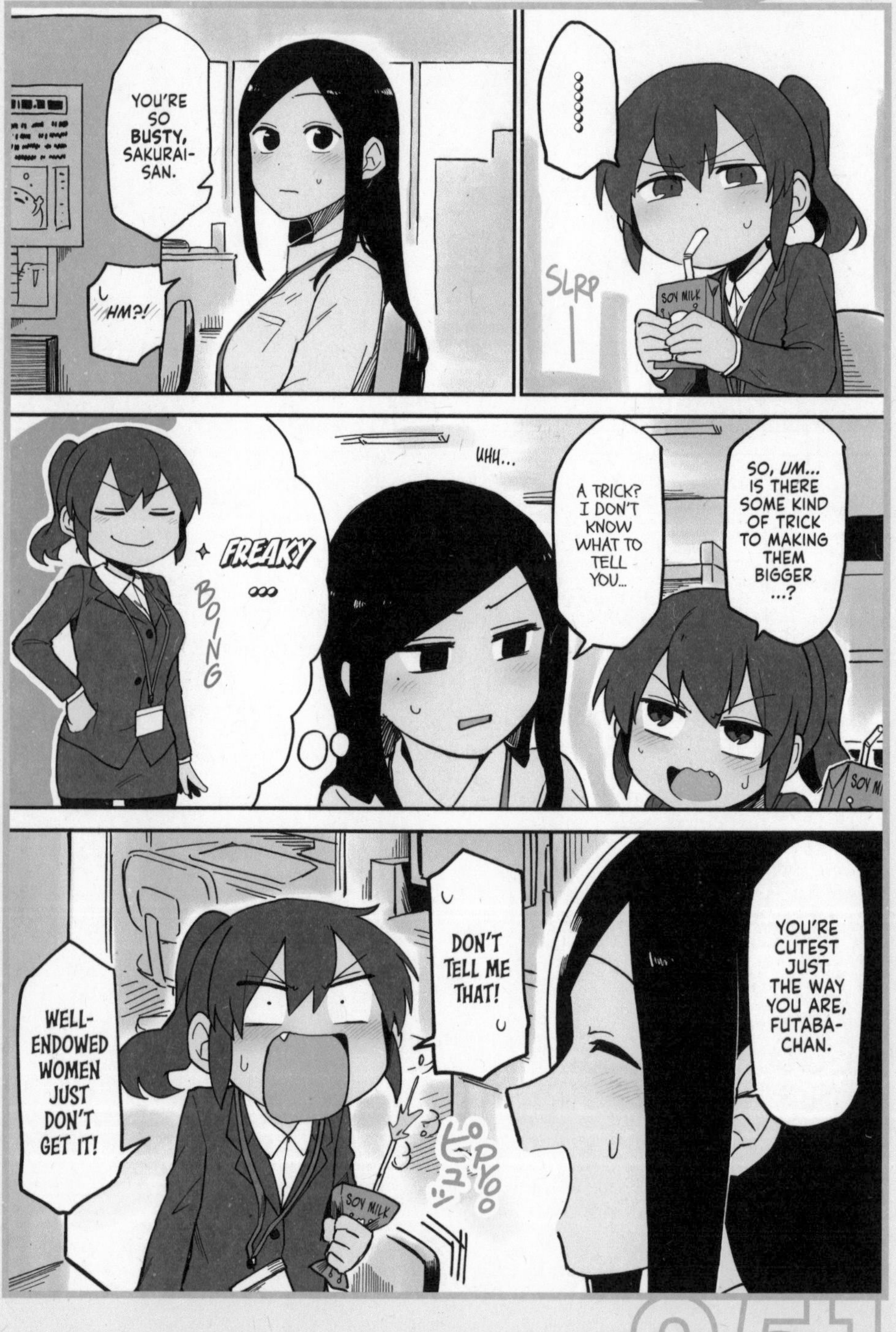
......
SLRP
SOY MILK
YOU'RE SO BUSTY, SAKURAI-SAN.
HM?!
SO, UM... IS THERE SOME KIND OF TRICK TO MAKING THEM BIGGER ...?
A TRICK? I DON'T KNOW WHAT TO TELL YOU...
UHH...
FREAKY
BOING
...
YOU'RE CUTEST JUST THE WAY YOU ARE, FUTABA-CHAN.
DON'T TELL ME THAT!
WELL-ENDOWED WOMEN JUST DON'T GET IT!
ピュッ
PYOO
SOY MILK

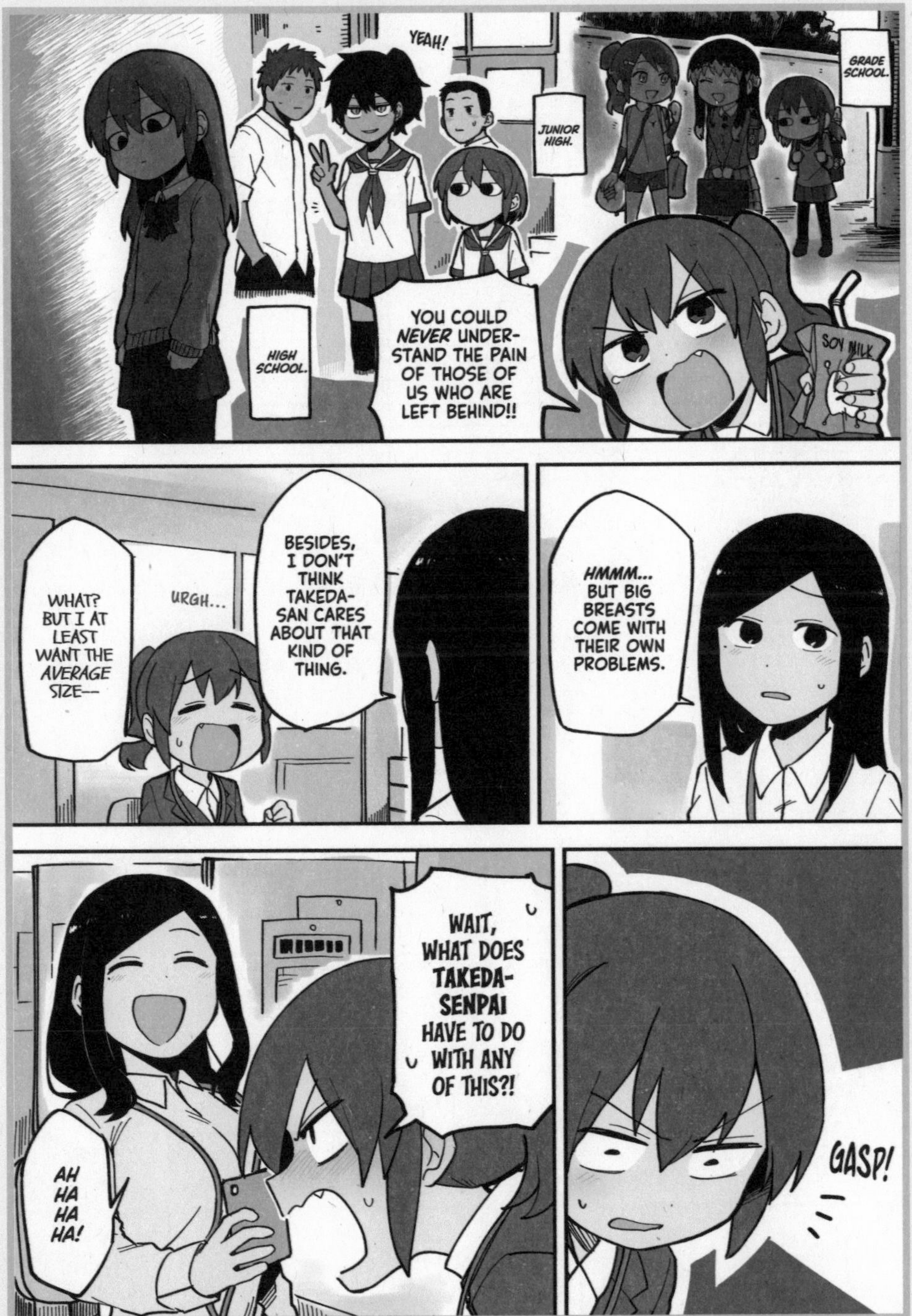
GRADE SCHOOL.
JUNIOR HIGH.
YEAH!
YOU COULD *NEVER* UNDERSTAND THE PAIN OF THOSE OF US WHO ARE LEFT BEHIND!!
SOY MILK
HIGH SCHOOL.
HMMM... BUT BIG BREASTS COME WITH THEIR OWN PROBLEMS.
BESIDES, I DON'T THINK TAKEDA-SAN CARES ABOUT THAT KIND OF THING.
URGH...
WHAT? BUT I AT LEAST WANT THE *AVERAGE* SIZE--
GASP!
WAIT, WHAT DOES TAKEDA-SENPAI HAVE TO DO WITH ANY OF THIS?!
AH HA HA HA!

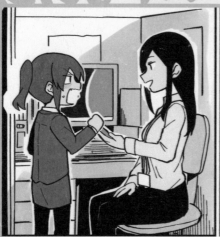

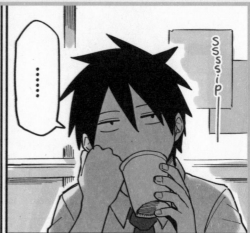

…….

SSSsip

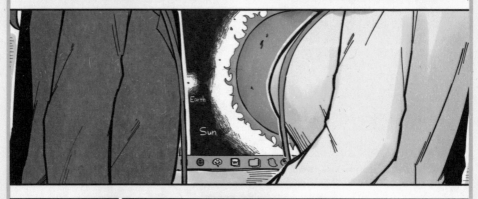

Earth

Sun

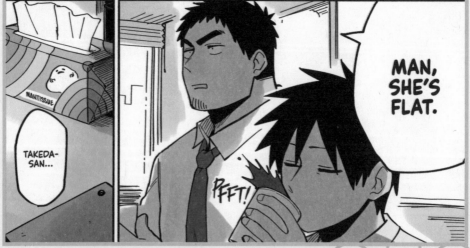

MANTISSUE

TAKEDA-
SAN…

PFFT!

MAN,
SHE'S
FLAT.

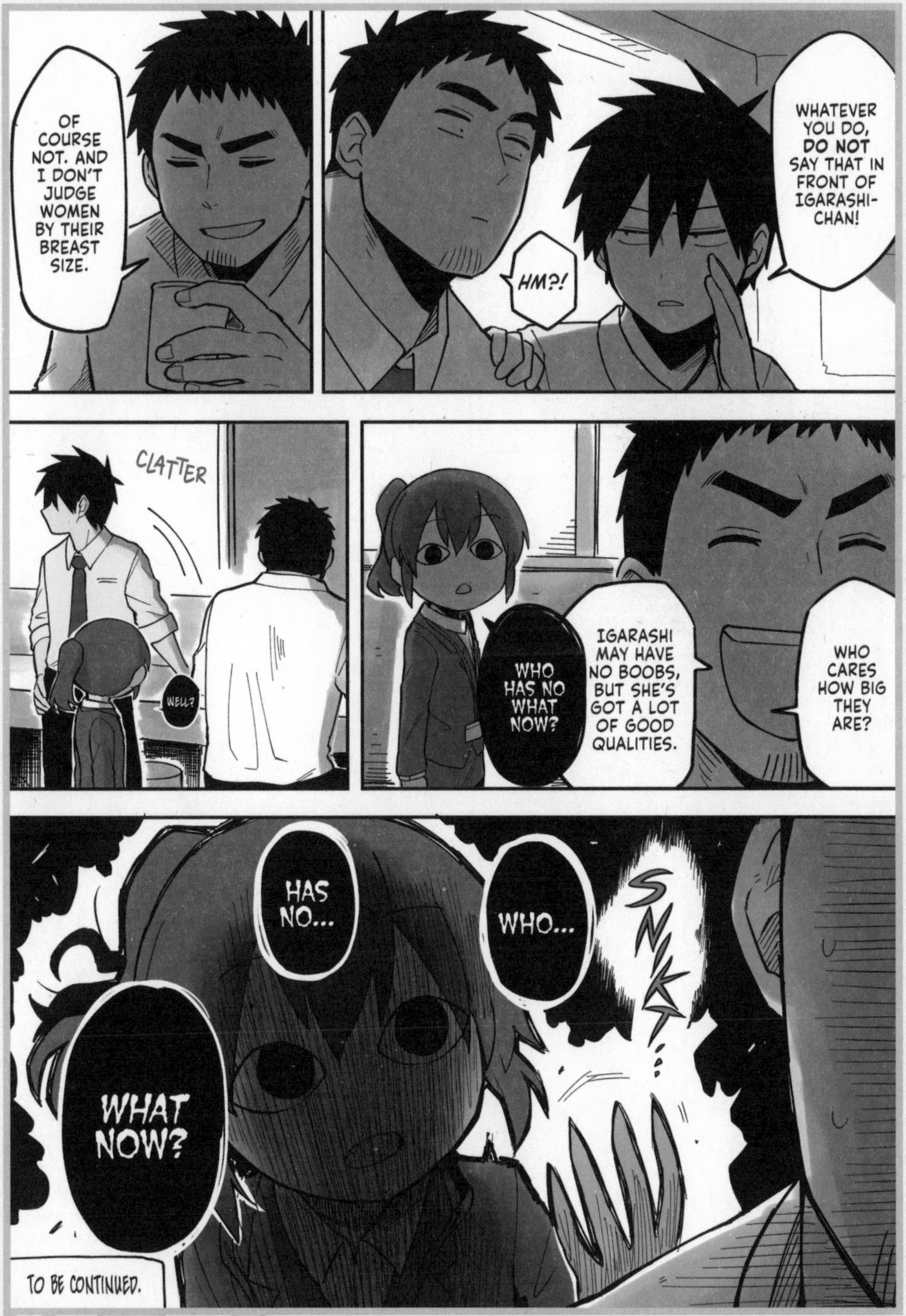
WHATEVER YOU DO, **DO NOT** SAY THAT IN FRONT OF IGARASHI-CHAN!
HM?!
OF COURSE NOT. AND I DON'T JUDGE WOMEN BY THEIR BREAST SIZE.
WHO CARES HOW BIG THEY ARE?
IGARASHI MAY HAVE NO BOOBS, BUT SHE'S GOT A LOT OF GOOD QUALITIES.
WHO HAS NO WHAT NOW?
CLATTER
WELL?
SNIKT
WHO...
HAS NO...
WHAT NOW?
TO BE CONTINUED.

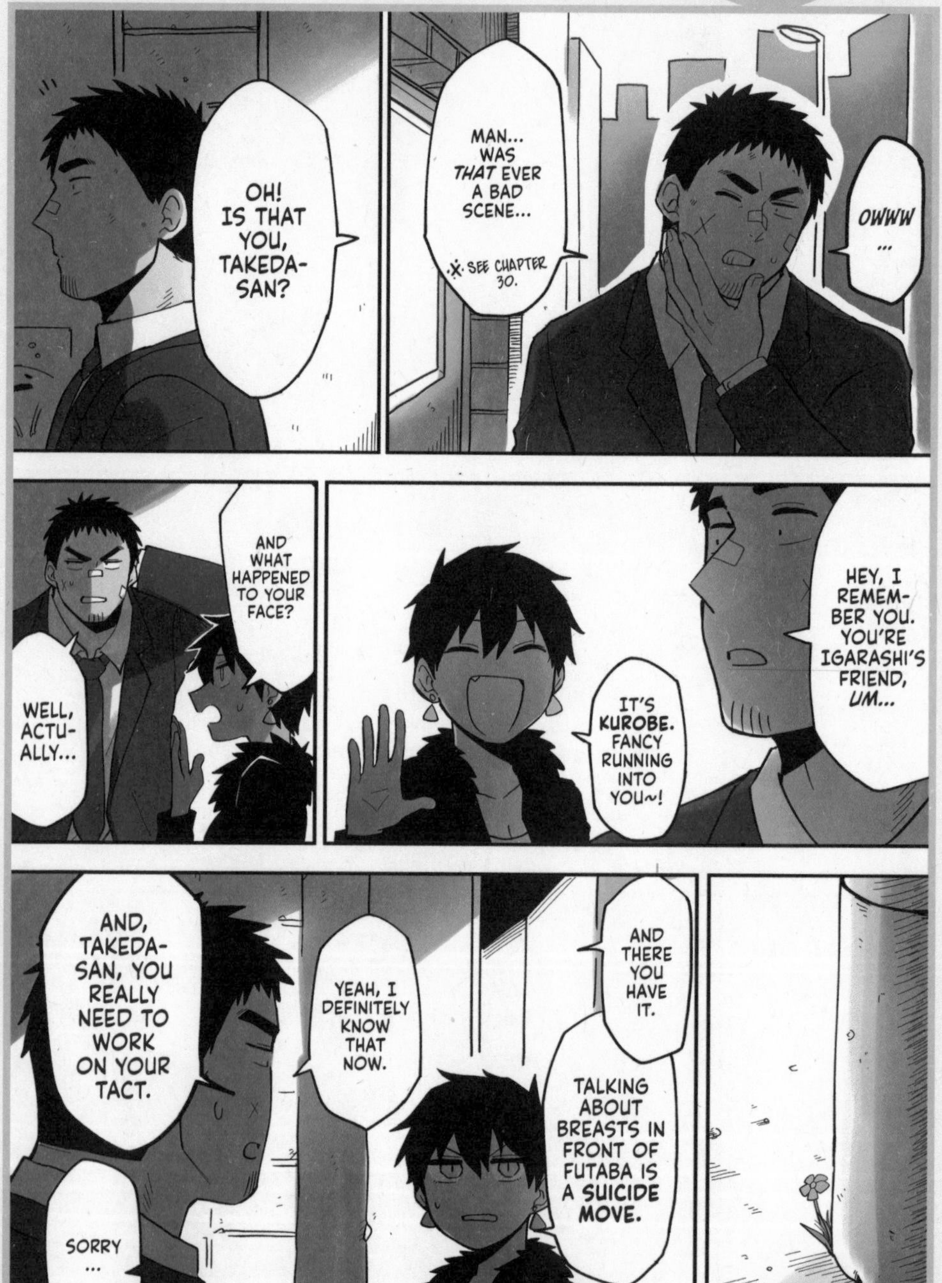
OWWW ...
MAN... WAS *THAT* EVER A BAD SCENE...
※ SEE CHAPTER 30.
OH! IS THAT YOU, TAKEDA-SAN?
HEY, I REMEMBER YOU. YOU'RE IGARASHI'S FRIEND, *UM*...
IT'S **KUROBE.** FANCY RUNNING INTO YOU~!
AND WHAT HAPPENED TO YOUR FACE?
WELL, ACTUALLY...
AND THERE YOU HAVE IT.
TALKING ABOUT BREASTS IN FRONT OF FUTABA IS A **SUICIDE MOVE.**
YEAH, I DEFINITELY KNOW THAT NOW.
AND, TAKEDA-SAN, YOU REALLY NEED TO WORK ON YOUR TACT.
SORRY ...

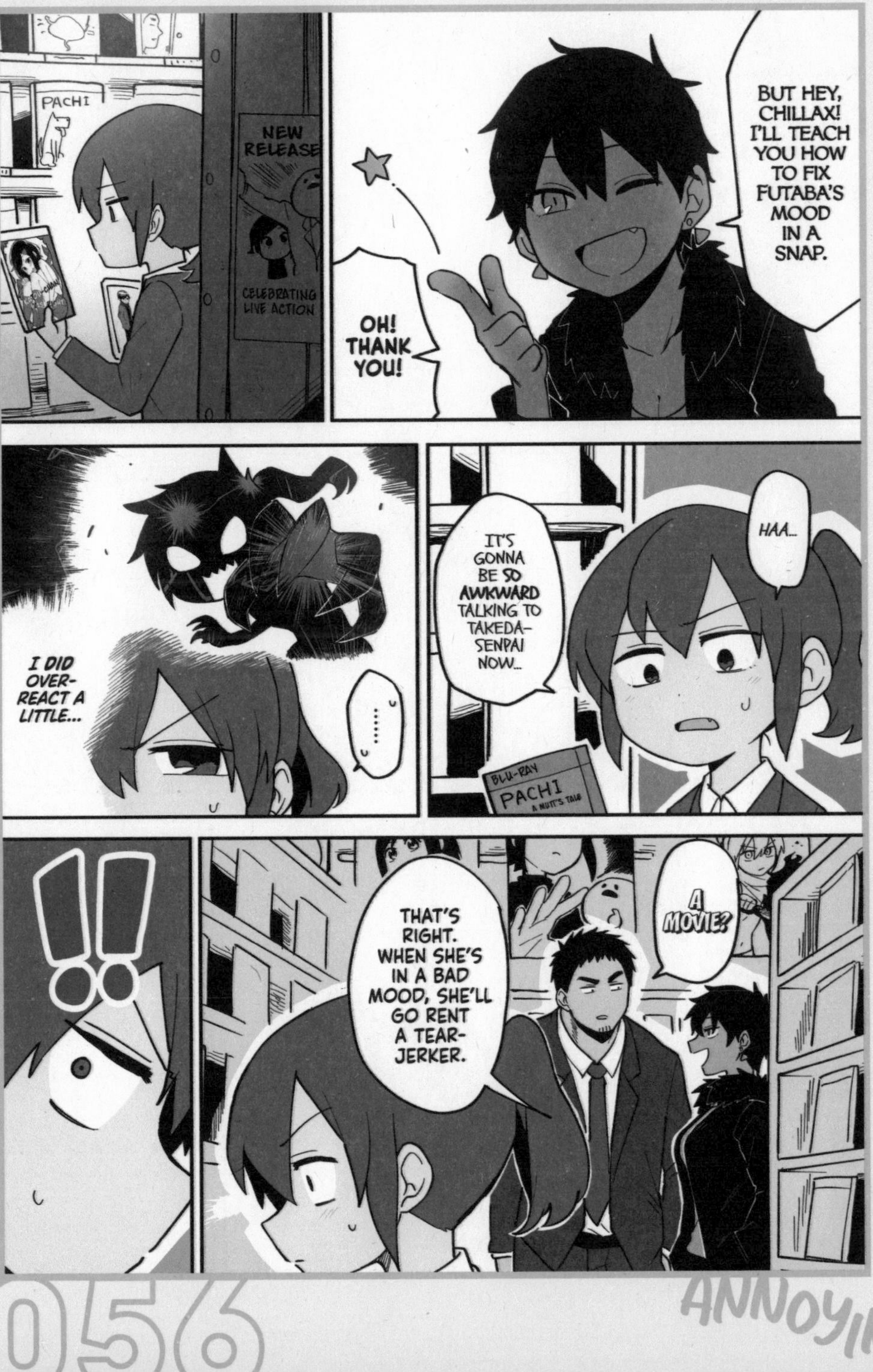
BUT HEY, CHILLAX! I'LL TEACH YOU HOW TO FIX FUTABA'S MOOD IN A SNAP.
OH! THANK YOU!
PACHI
NEW RELEASE
CELEBRATING LIVE ACTION
HAA...
IT'S GONNA BE SO AWKWARD TALKING TO TAKEDA-SENPAI NOW...
BLU-RAY
PACHI
I DID OVER-REACT A LITTLE...
......
A MOVIE?
THAT'S RIGHT. WHEN SHE'S IN A BAD MOOD, SHE'LL GO RENT A TEAR-JERKER.
!!

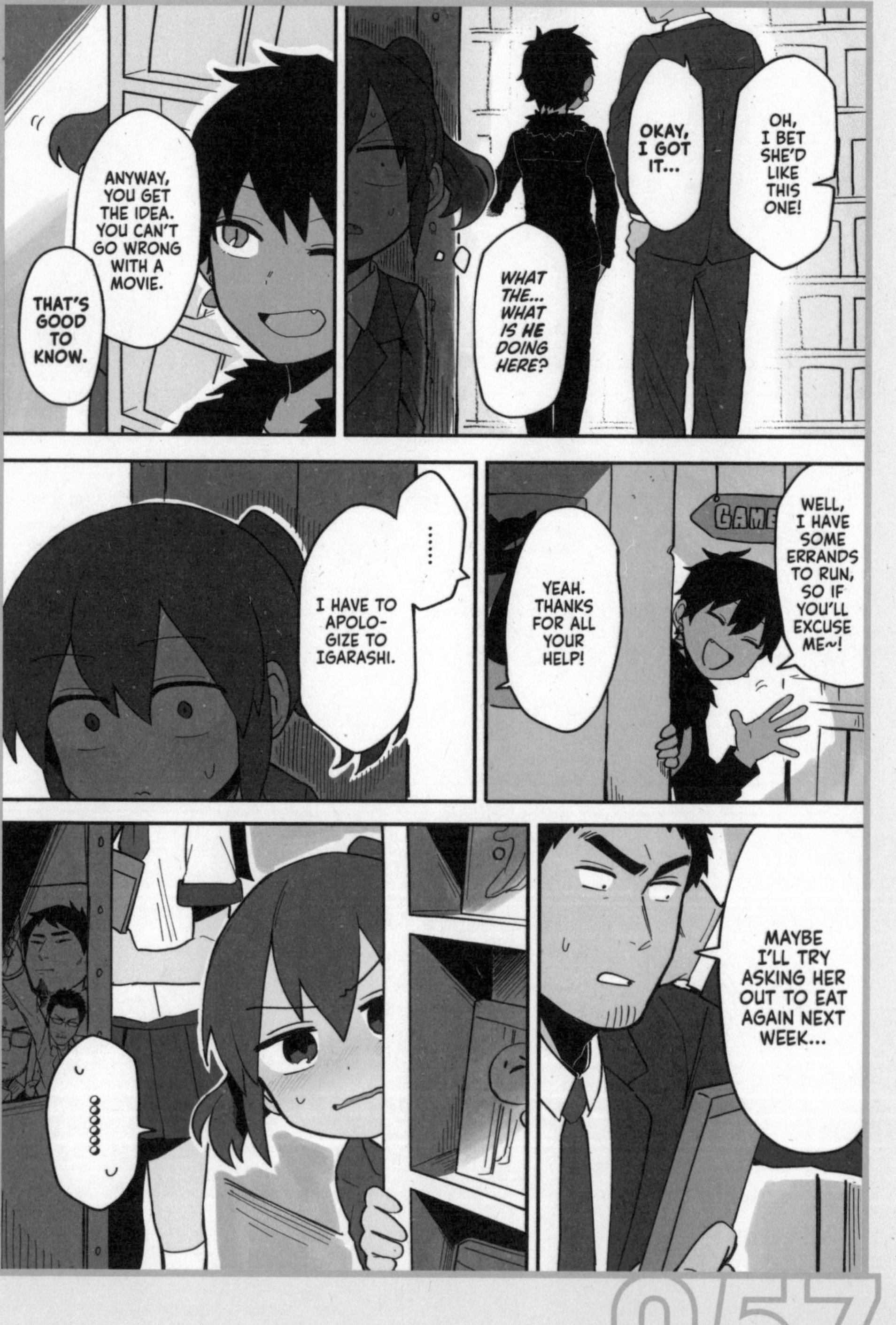
OH, I BET SHE'D LIKE THIS ONE!
OKAY, I GOT IT...
WHAT THE... WHAT IS HE DOING HERE?
ANYWAY, YOU GET THE IDEA. YOU CAN'T GO WRONG WITH A MOVIE.
THAT'S GOOD TO KNOW.
WELL, I HAVE SOME ERRANDS TO RUN, SO IF YOU'LL EXCUSE ME~!
GAME
YEAH. THANKS FOR ALL YOUR HELP!
......
I HAVE TO APOLO-GIZE TO IGARASHI.
MAYBE I'LL TRY ASKING HER OUT TO EAT AGAIN NEXT WEEK...
......

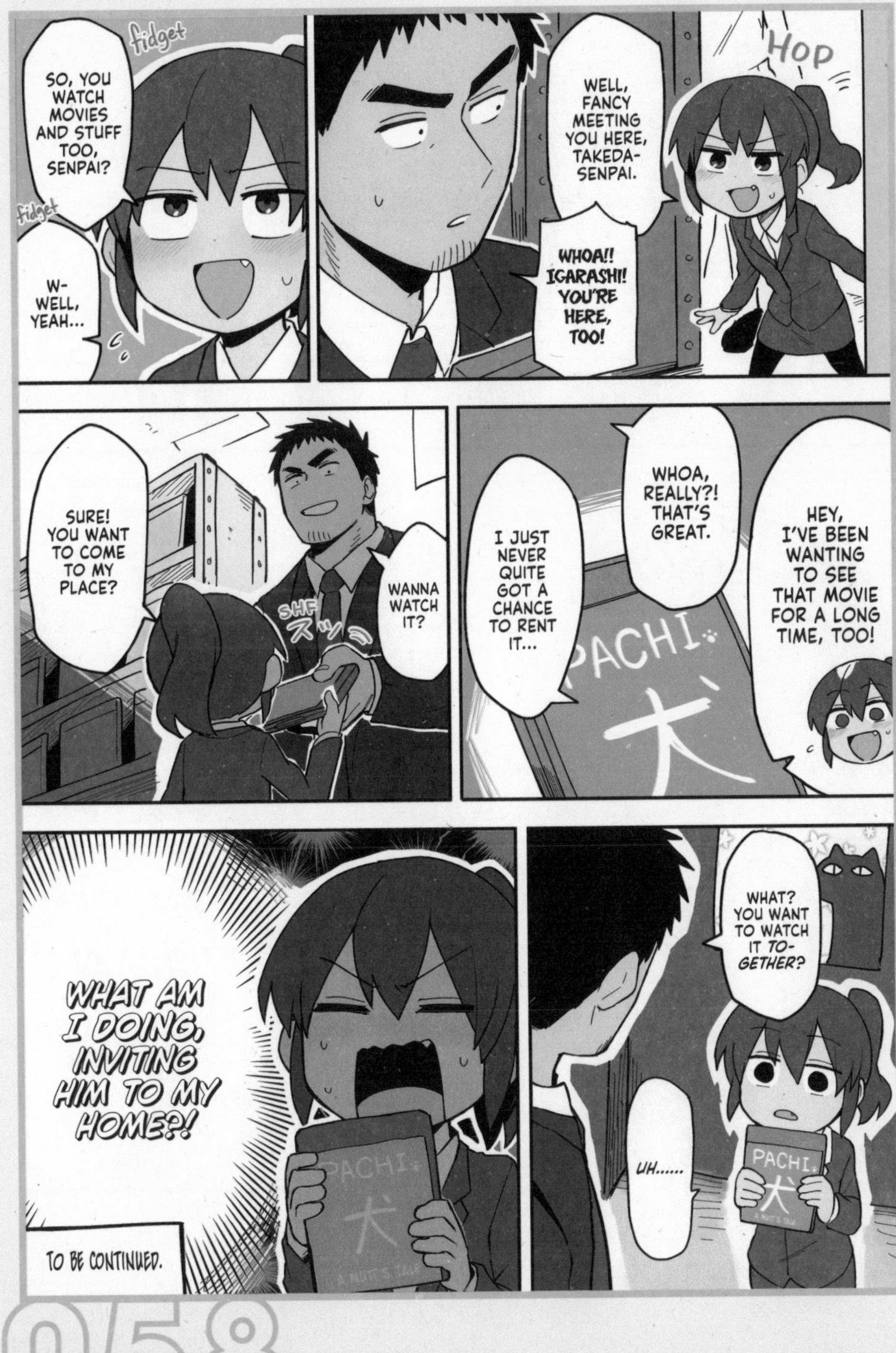
HOP
WELL, FANCY MEETING YOU HERE, TAKEDA-SENPAI.
WHOA!! IGARASHI! YOU'RE HERE, TOO!
fidget
SO, YOU WATCH MOVIES AND STUFF TOO, SENPAI?
fidget
W-WELL, YEAH...
HEY, I'VE BEEN WANTING TO SEE THAT MOVIE FOR A LONG TIME, TOO!
WHOA, REALLY?! THAT'S GREAT.
I JUST NEVER QUITE GOT A CHANCE TO RENT IT...
PACHI
犬
WANNA WATCH IT?
SHF
スッ
SURE! YOU WANT TO COME TO MY PLACE?
WHAT? YOU WANT TO WATCH IT TO-GETHER?
PACHI
犬
A MUTT'S TALE
UH......
WHAT AM I DOING, INVITING HIM TO MY HOME?!
TO BE CONTINUED.

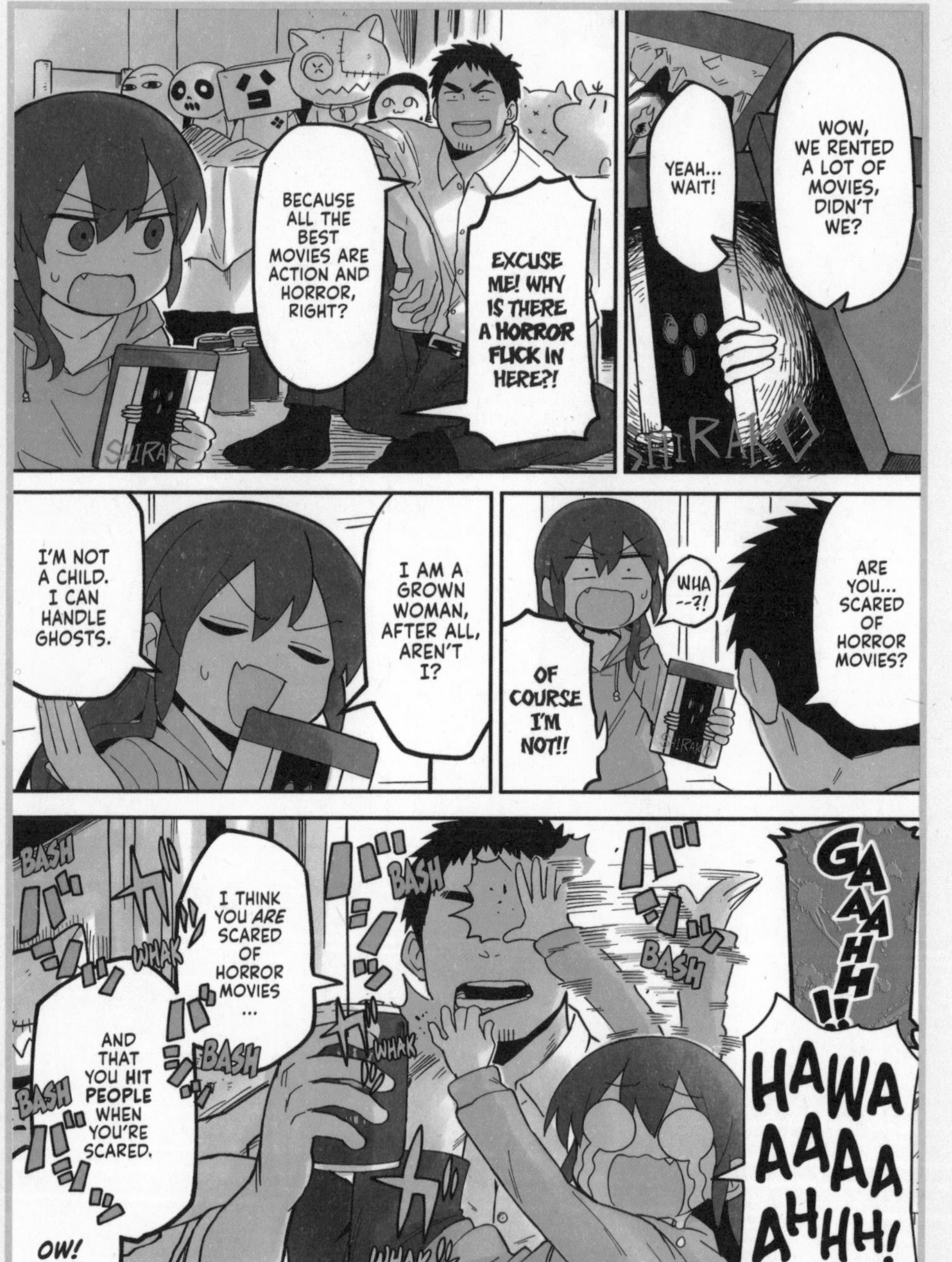
WOW, WE RENTED A LOT OF MOVIES, DIDN'T WE?
YEAH... WAIT!
SHIRAKO
EXCUSE ME! WHY IS THERE A HORROR FLICK IN HERE?!
BECAUSE ALL THE BEST MOVIES ARE ACTION AND HORROR, RIGHT?
ARE YOU... SCARED OF HORROR MOVIES?
WHA--?!
OF COURSE I'M NOT!!
SHIRAKO
I AM A GROWN WOMAN, AFTER ALL, AREN'T I?
I'M NOT A CHILD. I CAN HANDLE GHOSTS.
GAAAHH!!
HAWAAAAAAHHH!
BASH
BASH
WHAK
WHAK
I THINK YOU *ARE* SCARED OF HORROR MOVIES ...
AND THAT YOU HIT PEOPLE WHEN YOU'RE SCARED.
BASH
WHAK
BASH
BASH
OW! OW!

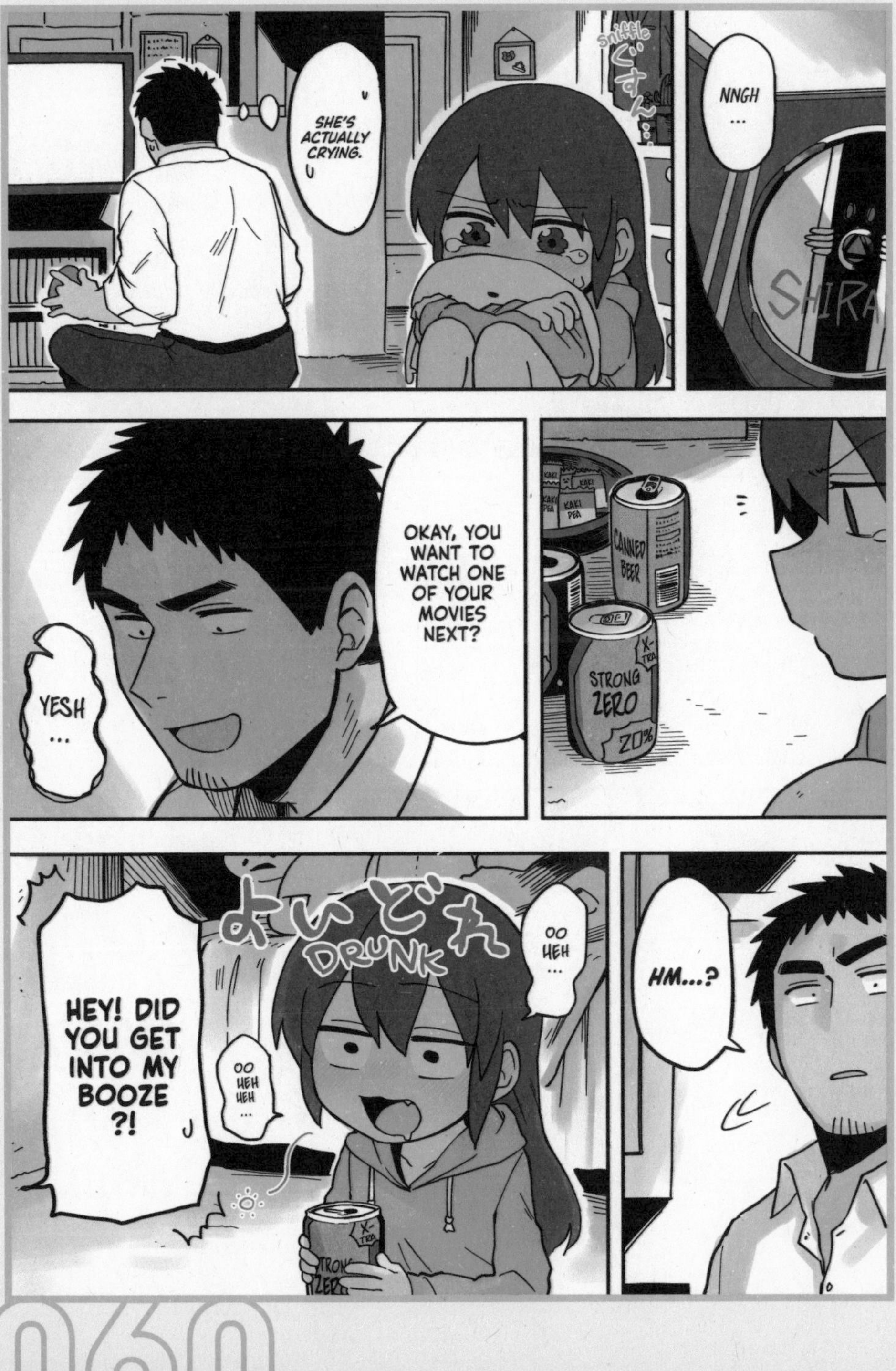
NNGH ...
sniffle ぐすん...
SHE'S ACTUALLY CRYING.
KAKI PEA
CANNED BEER
X-TRA
STRONG ZERO
20%
OKAY, YOU WANT TO WATCH ONE OF YOUR MOVIES NEXT?
YESH ...
HM...?
OO HEH ...
よいどれ DRUNK
HEY! DID YOU GET INTO MY BOOZE ?!
OO HEH HEH ...

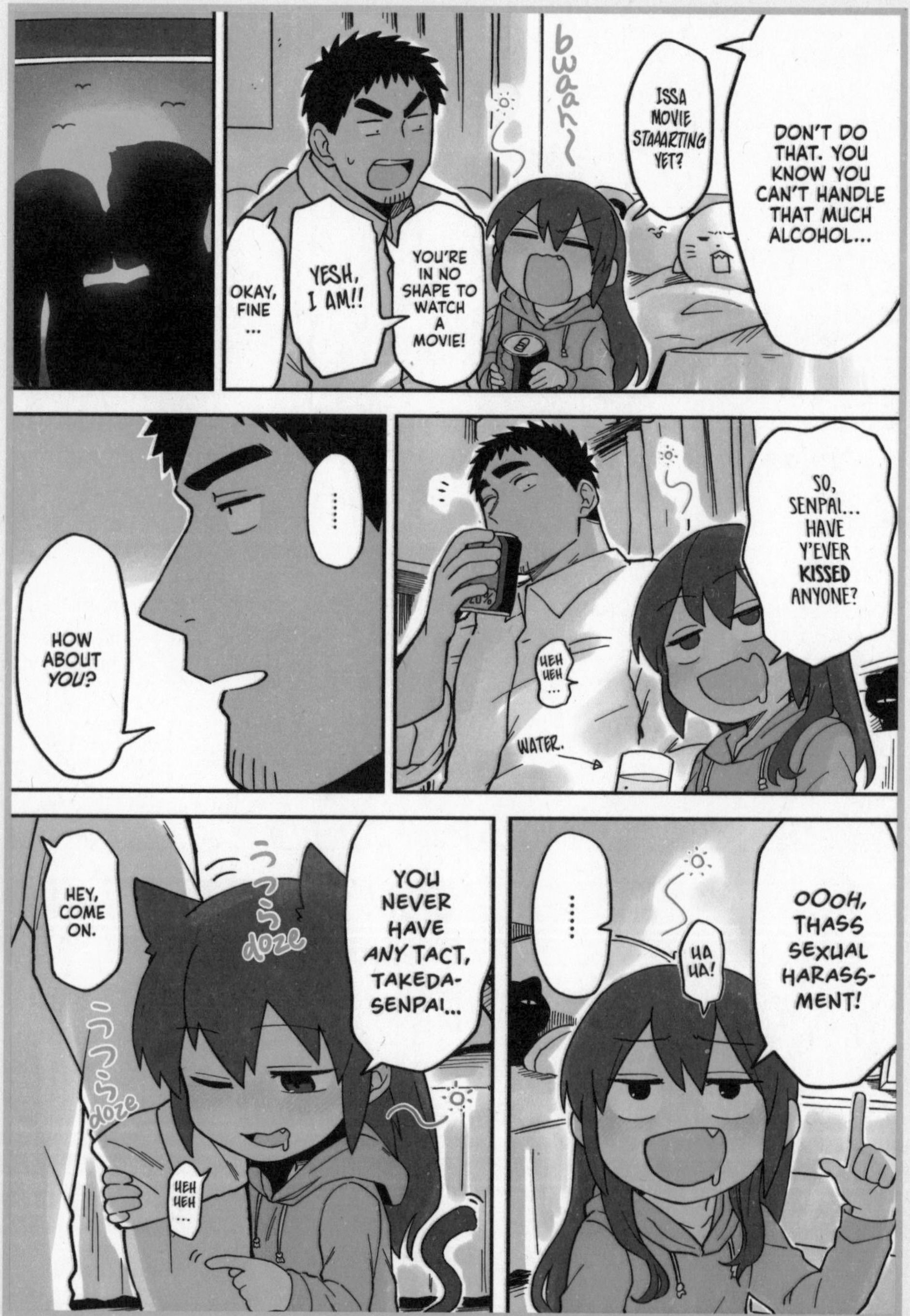
DON'T DO THAT. YOU KNOW YOU CAN'T HANDLE THAT MUCH ALCOHOL...
ISSA MOVIE STAAARTING YET?
bwaah~
YOU'RE IN NO SHAPE TO WATCH A MOVIE!
YESH, I AM!!
OKAY, FINE ...
SO, SENPAI... HAVE Y'EVER KISSED ANYONE?
HEH HEH ...
WATER.
......
HOW ABOUT YOU?
OOOH, THASS SEXUAL HARASS-MENT!
HA HA!
......
YOU NEVER HAVE ANY TACT, TAKEDA-SENPAI...
HEY, COME ON.
doze
doze
HEH HEH ...

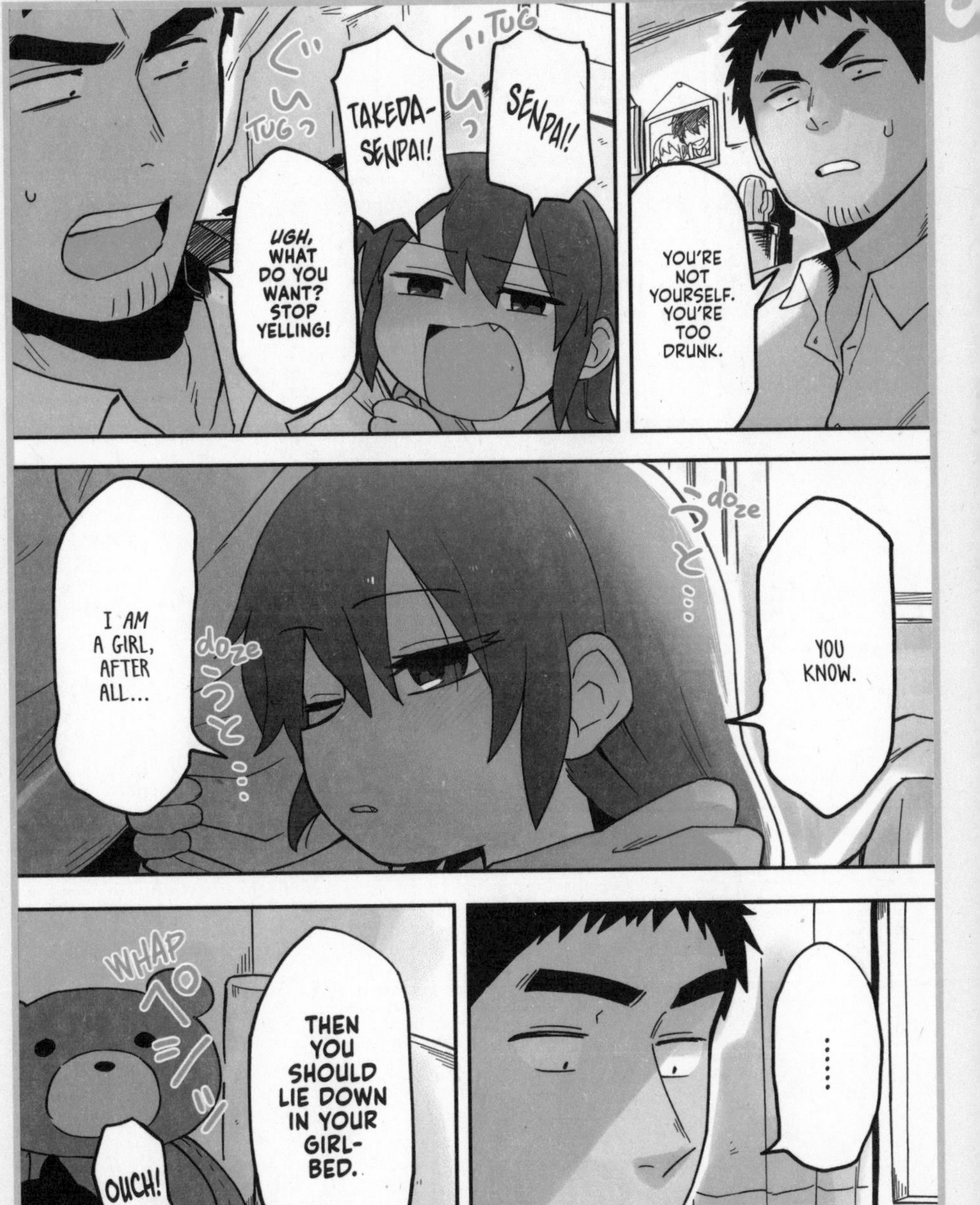
YOU'RE NOT YOURSELF. YOU'RE TOO DRUNK.
TUG
SENPAI!
TUG
TAKEDA-SENPAI!
UGH, WHAT DO YOU WANT? STOP YELLING!
doze
YOU KNOW.
I AM A GIRL, AFTER ALL...
doze
......
THEN YOU SHOULD LIE DOWN IN YOUR GIRL-BED.
WHAP
OUCH!
TO BE CONTINUED.

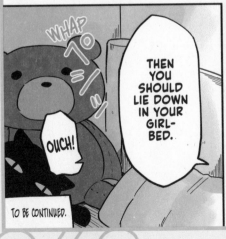

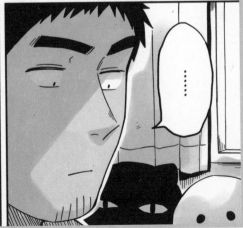

Chapter 33

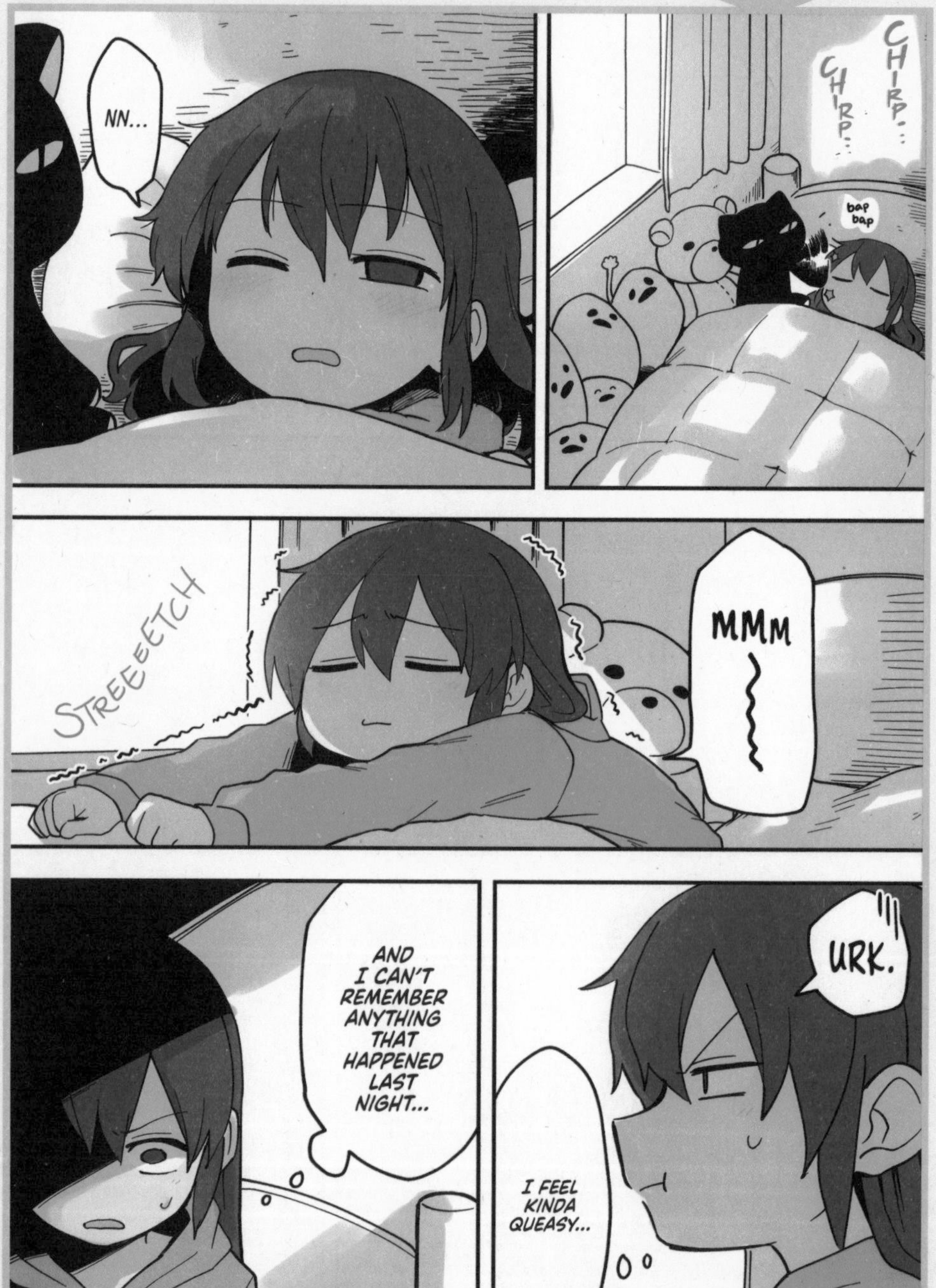
CHIRP...
CHIRP...
bap bap
NN...
MMM~
STREEEETCH
URK.
I FEEL KINDA QUEASY...
AND I CAN'T REMEMBER ANYTHING THAT HAPPENED LAST NIGHT...

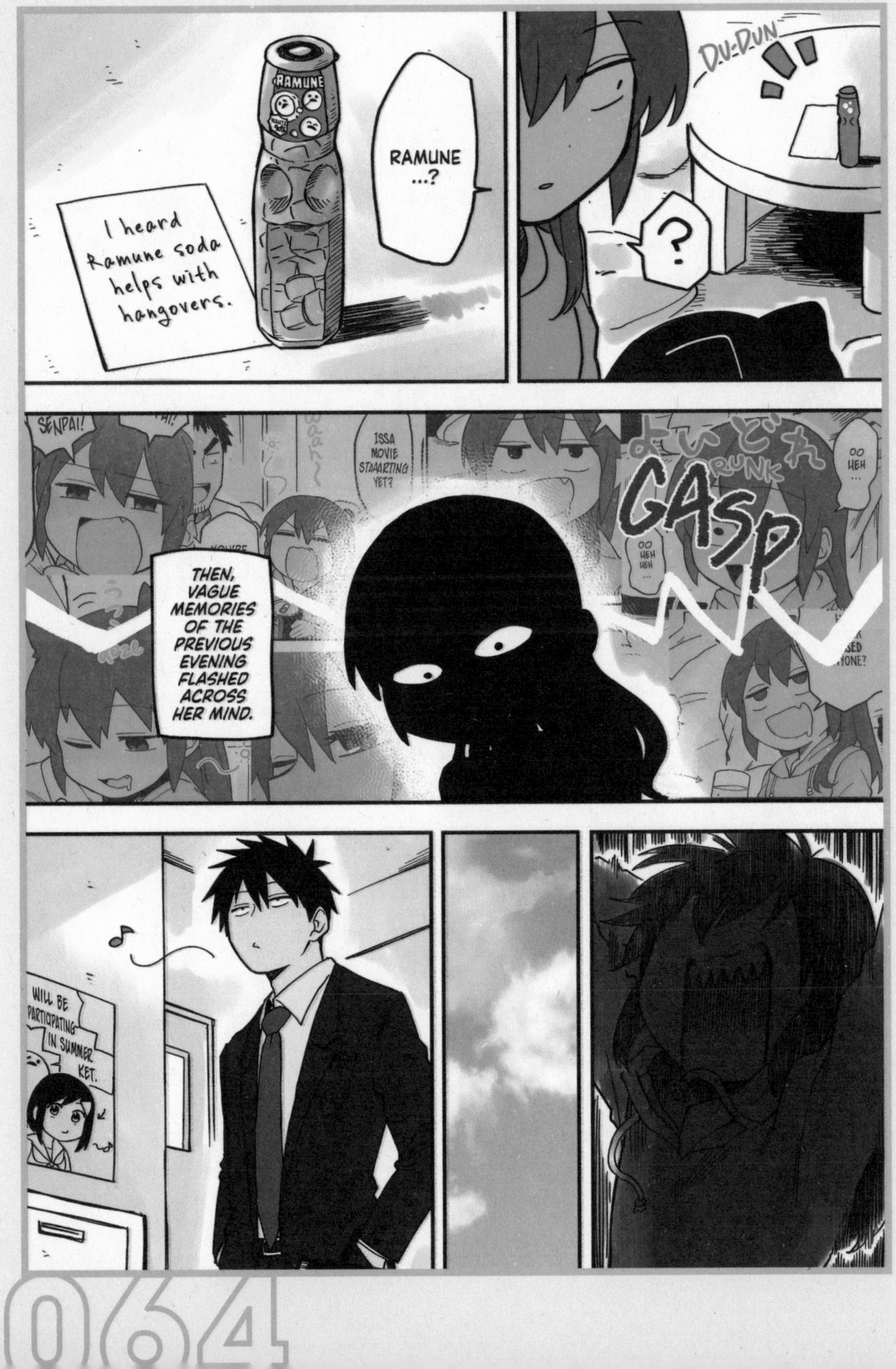
DU-DUN
?
I heard Ramune soda helps with hangovers.
RAMUNE
RAMUNE ...?
OO HEH ...
GASP
OO HEH HEH ...
ISSA MOVIE STAAARTING YET?
THEN, VAGUE MEMORIES OF THE PREVIOUS EVENING FLASHED ACROSS HER MIND.
SENPAI!
WILL BE PARTICIPATING IN SUMMER KET.

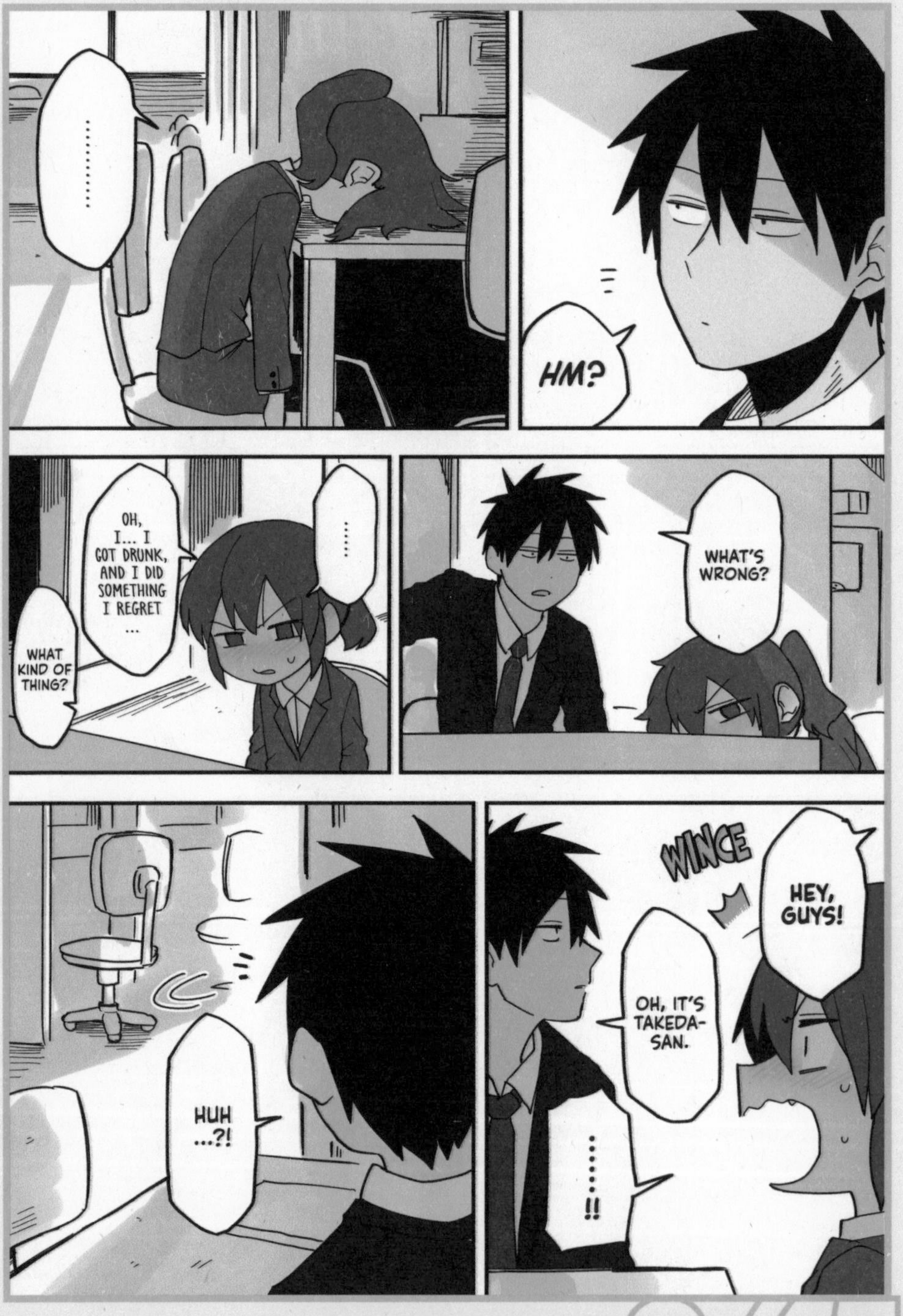
HM?
....
WHAT'S WRONG?
......
OH, I... I GOT DRUNK, AND I DID SOMETHING I REGRET ...
WHAT KIND OF THING?
HEY, GUYS!
WINCE
OH, IT'S TAKEDA-SAN.
......!!
HUH ...?!

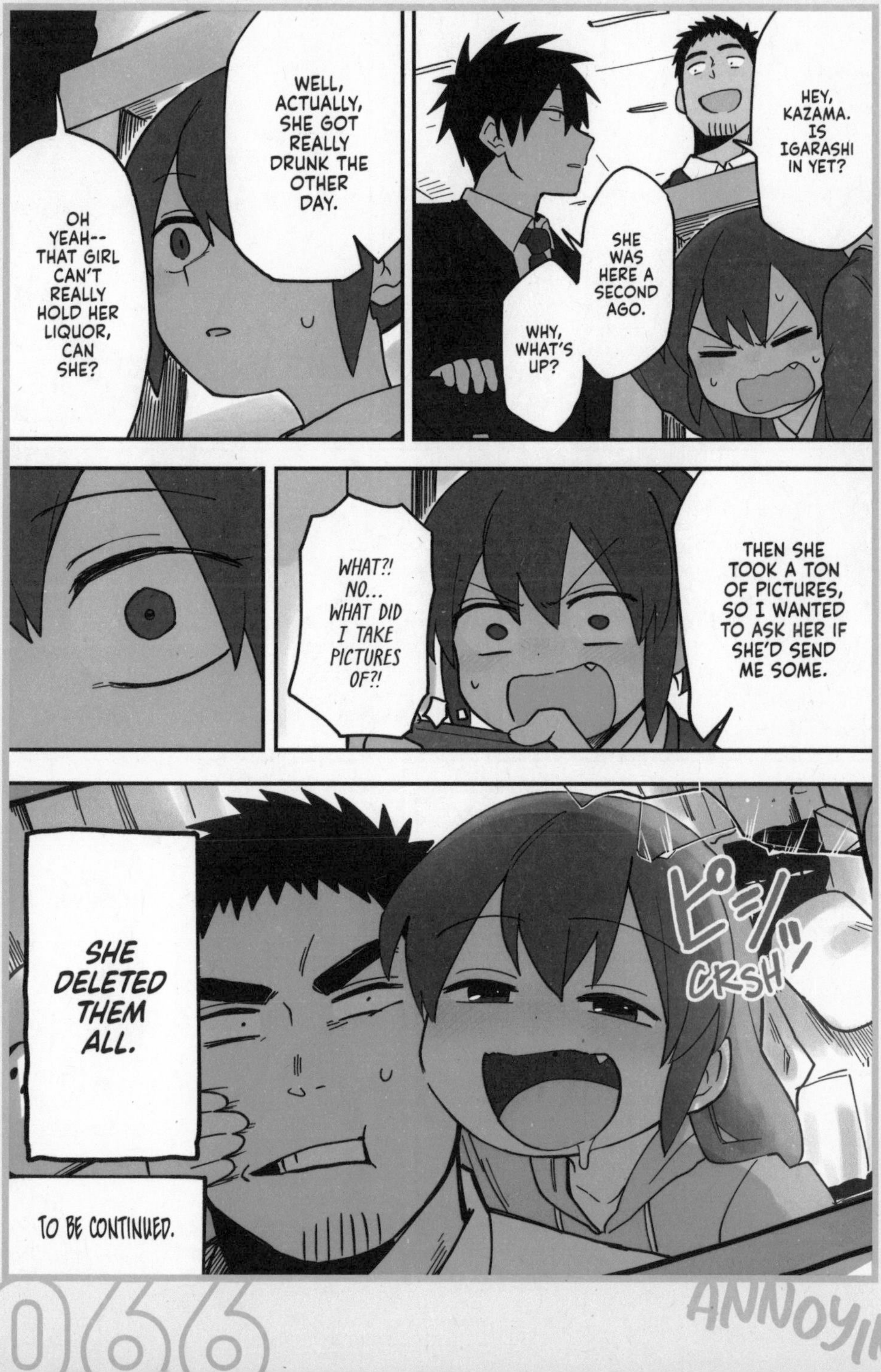
HEY, KAZAMA. IS IGARASHI IN YET?
SHE WAS HERE A SECOND AGO.
WHY, WHAT'S UP?
WELL, ACTUALLY, SHE GOT REALLY DRUNK THE OTHER DAY.
OH YEAH--THAT GIRL CAN'T REALLY HOLD HER LIQUOR, CAN SHE?
THEN SHE TOOK A TON OF PICTURES, SO I WANTED TO ASK HER IF SHE'D SEND ME SOME.
WHAT?! NO... WHAT DID I TAKE PICTURES OF?!
CRSH
SHE DELETED THEM ALL.
TO BE CONTINUED.

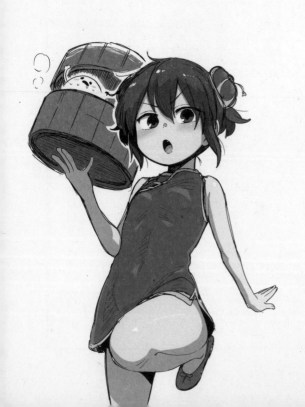

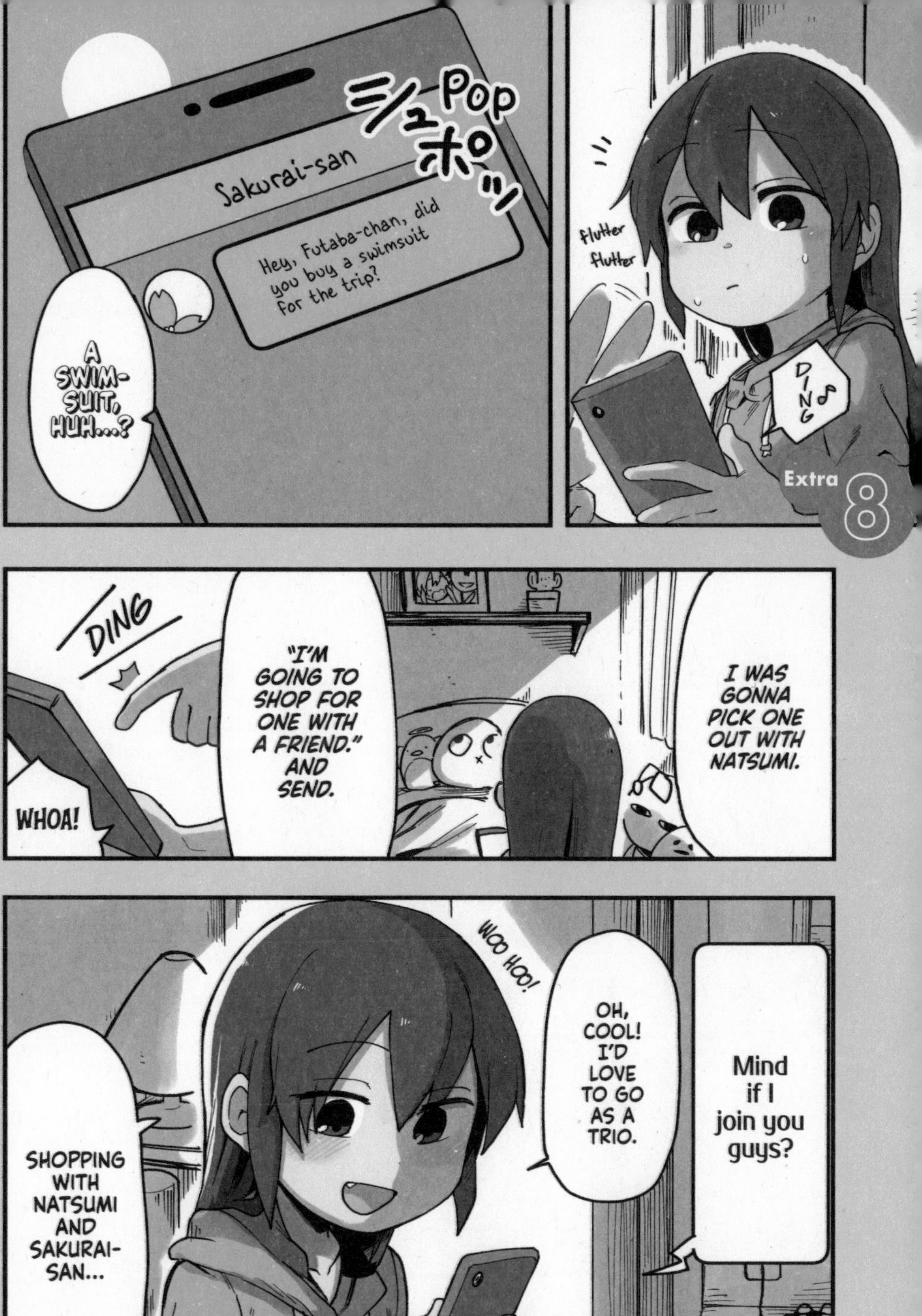
Extra 8
DING ♪
flutter flutter
シュポッ Pop
Sakurai-san
Hey, Futaba-chan, did you buy a swimsuit for the trip?
A SWIM-SUIT, HUH...?
I WAS GONNA PICK ONE OUT WITH NATSUMI.
"I'M GOING TO SHOP FOR ONE WITH A FRIEND." AND SEND.
DING
WHOA!
Mind if I join you guys?
OH, COOL! I'D LOVE TO GO AS A TRIO.
WOO HOO!
SHOPPING WITH NATSUMI AND SAKURAI-SAN...

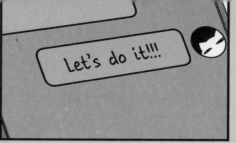

Let's do it!!!

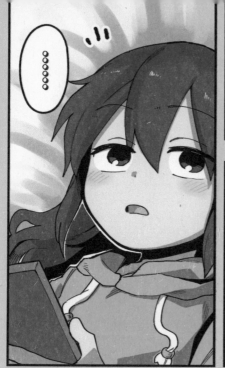

......

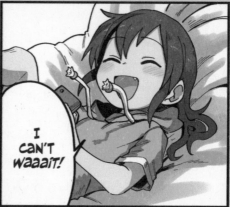

I can't waaait!

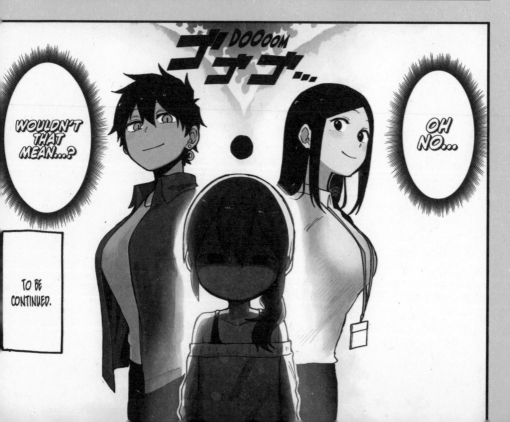

DOOOOM
ゴゴゴ...

WOULDN'T THAT MEAN...?

OH NO...

TO BE CONTINUED.

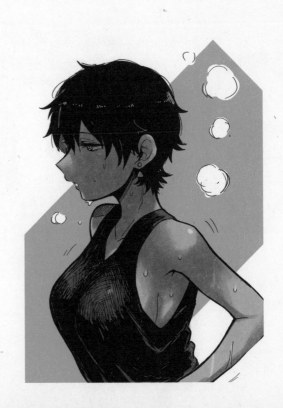

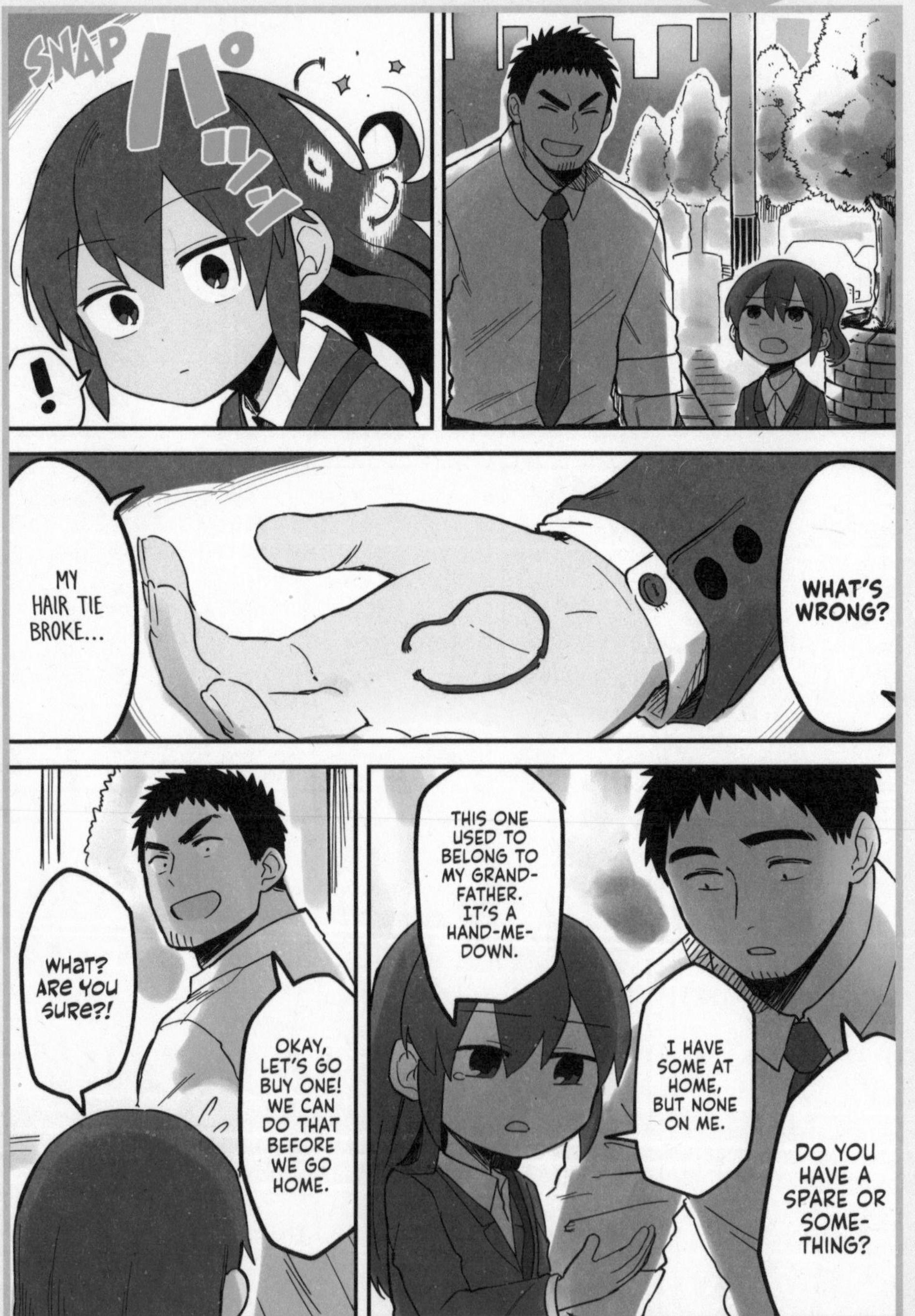
SNAP
!
WHAT'S WRONG?
MY HAIR TIE BROKE...
DO YOU HAVE A SPARE OR SOME-THING?
I HAVE SOME AT HOME, BUT NONE ON ME.
THIS ONE USED TO BELONG TO MY GRAND-FATHER. IT'S A HAND-ME-DOWN.
WHAT? ARE YOU SURE?!
OKAY, LET'S GO BUY ONE! WE CAN DO THAT BEFORE WE GO HOME.

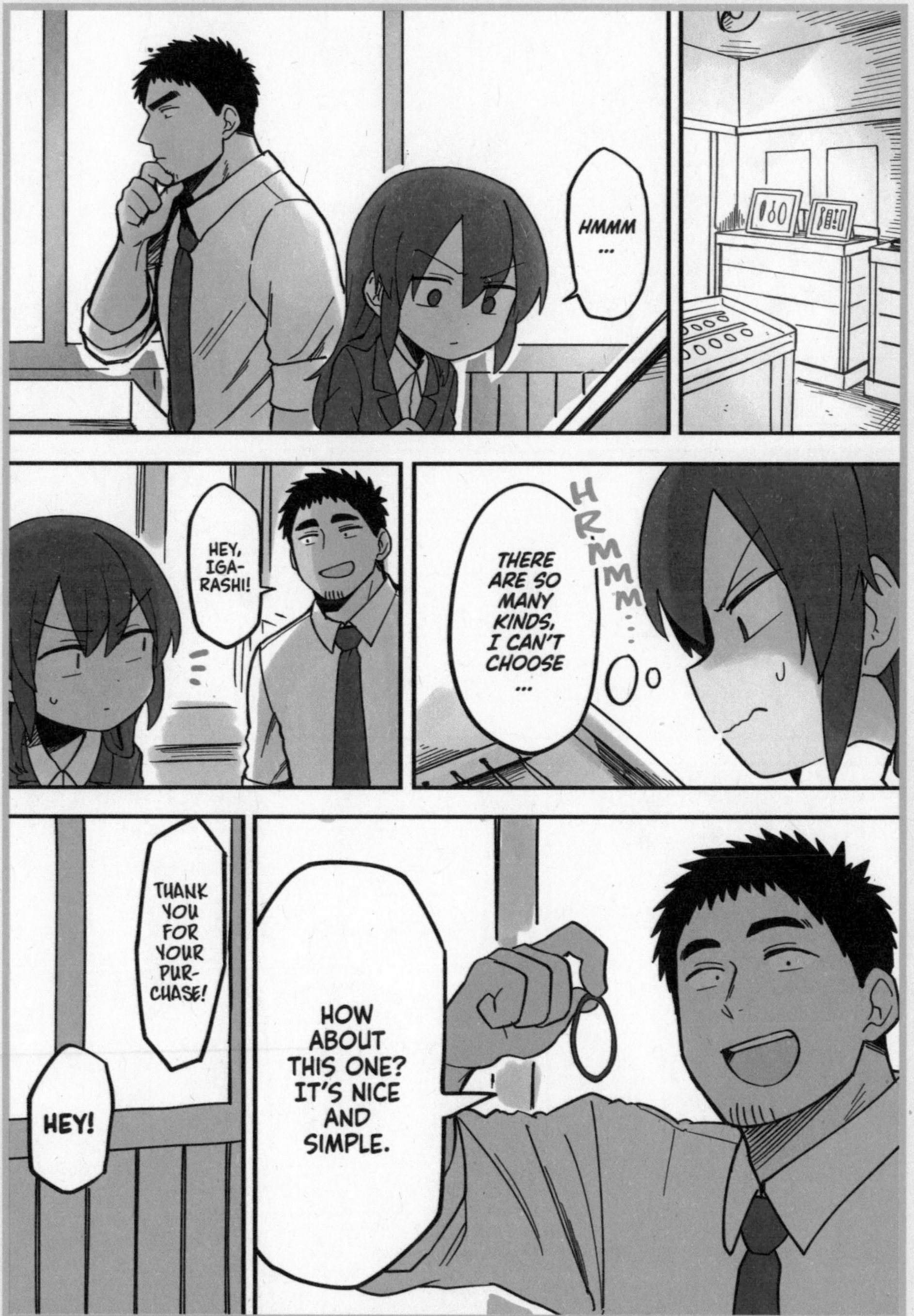
HMMM ...
HRMMM...
THERE ARE SO MANY KINDS, I CAN'T CHOOSE ...
HEY, IGA-RASHI!
HOW ABOUT THIS ONE? IT'S NICE AND SIMPLE.
THANK YOU FOR YOUR PUR-CHASE!
HEY!

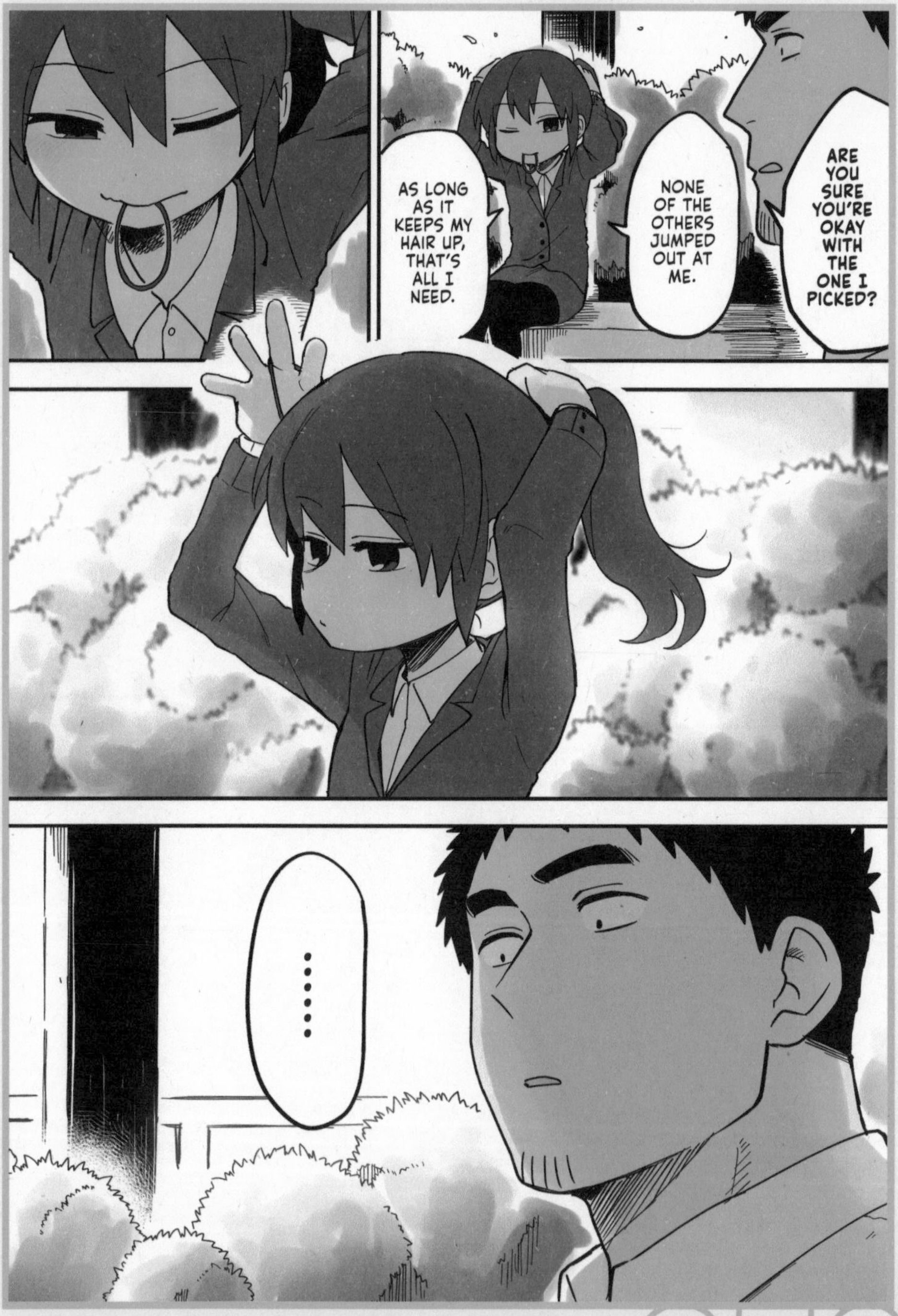
ARE YOU SURE YOU'RE OKAY WITH THE ONE I PICKED?
NONE OF THE OTHERS JUMPED OUT AT ME.
AS LONG AS IT KEEPS MY HAIR UP, THAT'S ALL I NEED.
......

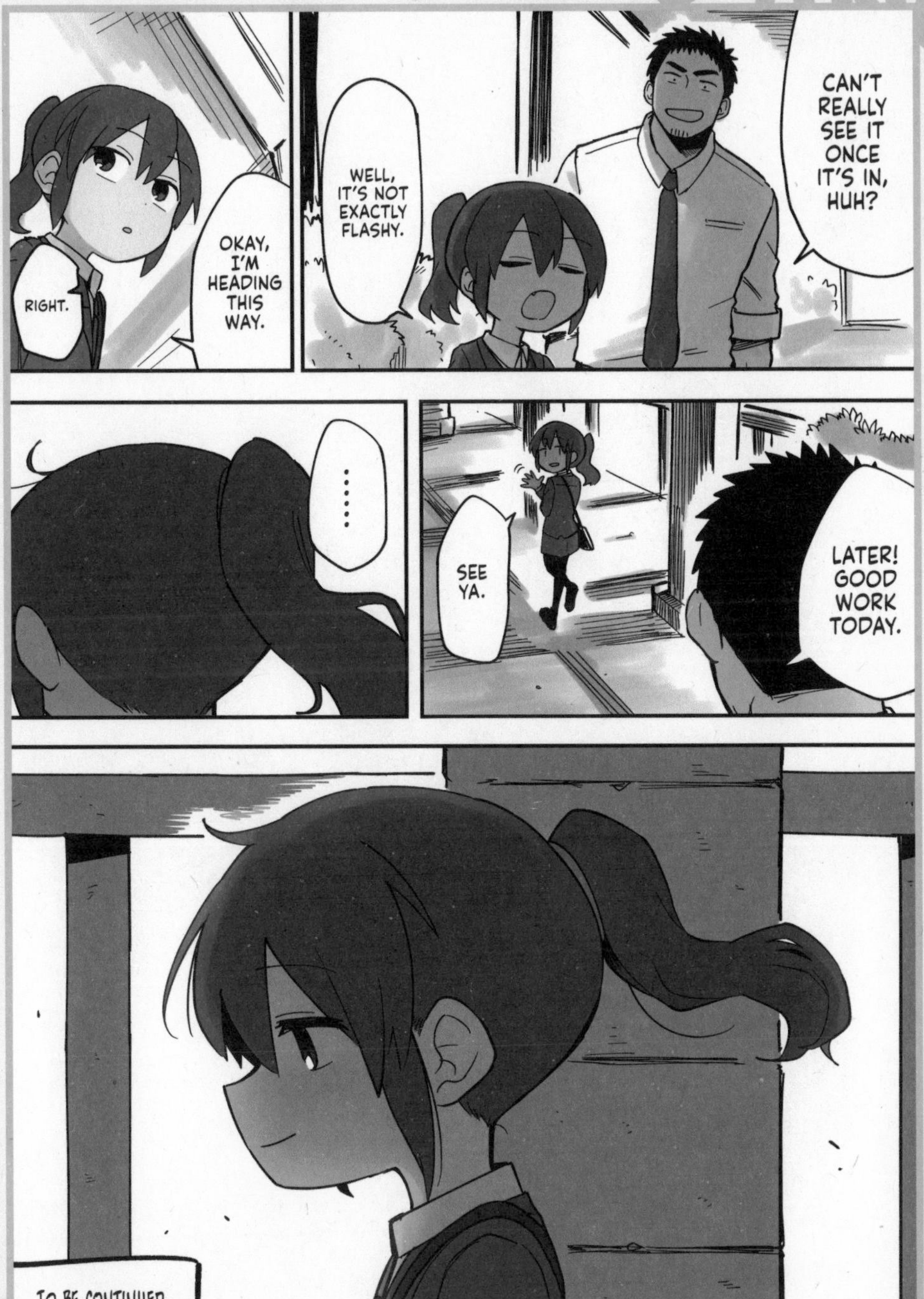
CAN'T REALLY SEE IT ONCE IT'S IN, HUH?
WELL, IT'S NOT EXACTLY FLASHY.
OKAY, I'M HEADING THIS WAY.
RIGHT.
LATER! GOOD WORK TODAY.
SEE YA.
......
TO BE CONTINUED.

Chapter 35

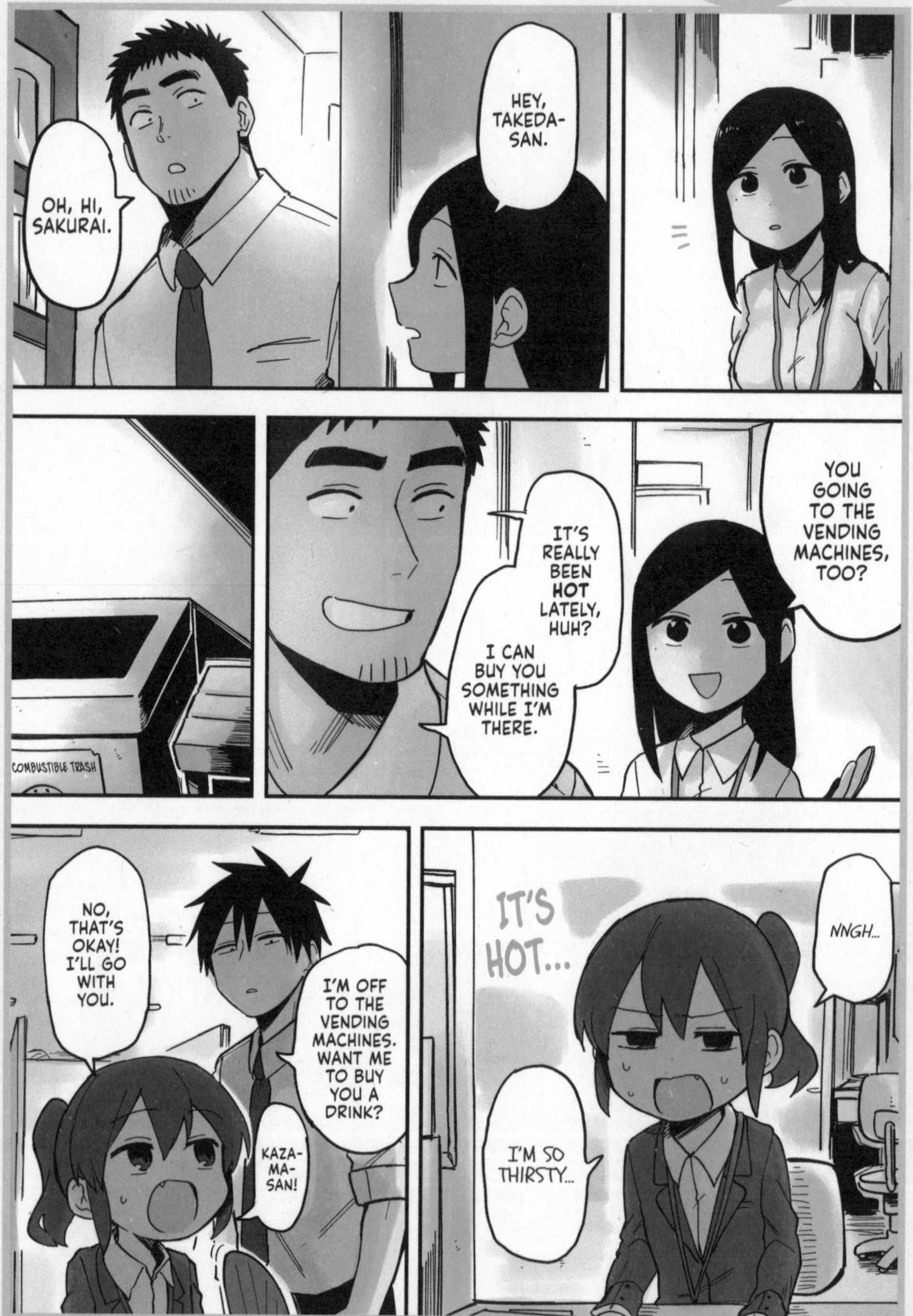

HEY, TAKEDA-SAN.
OH, HI, SAKURAI.
YOU GOING TO THE VENDING MACHINES, TOO?
IT'S REALLY BEEN HOT LATELY, HUH?
I CAN BUY YOU SOMETHING WHILE I'M THERE.
COMBUSTIBLE TRASH
NNGH...
IT'S HOT...
I'M SO THIRSTY...
KAZAMA-SAN!
I'M OFF TO THE VENDING MACHINES. WANT ME TO BUY YOU A DRINK?
NO, THAT'S OKAY! I'LL GO WITH YOU.

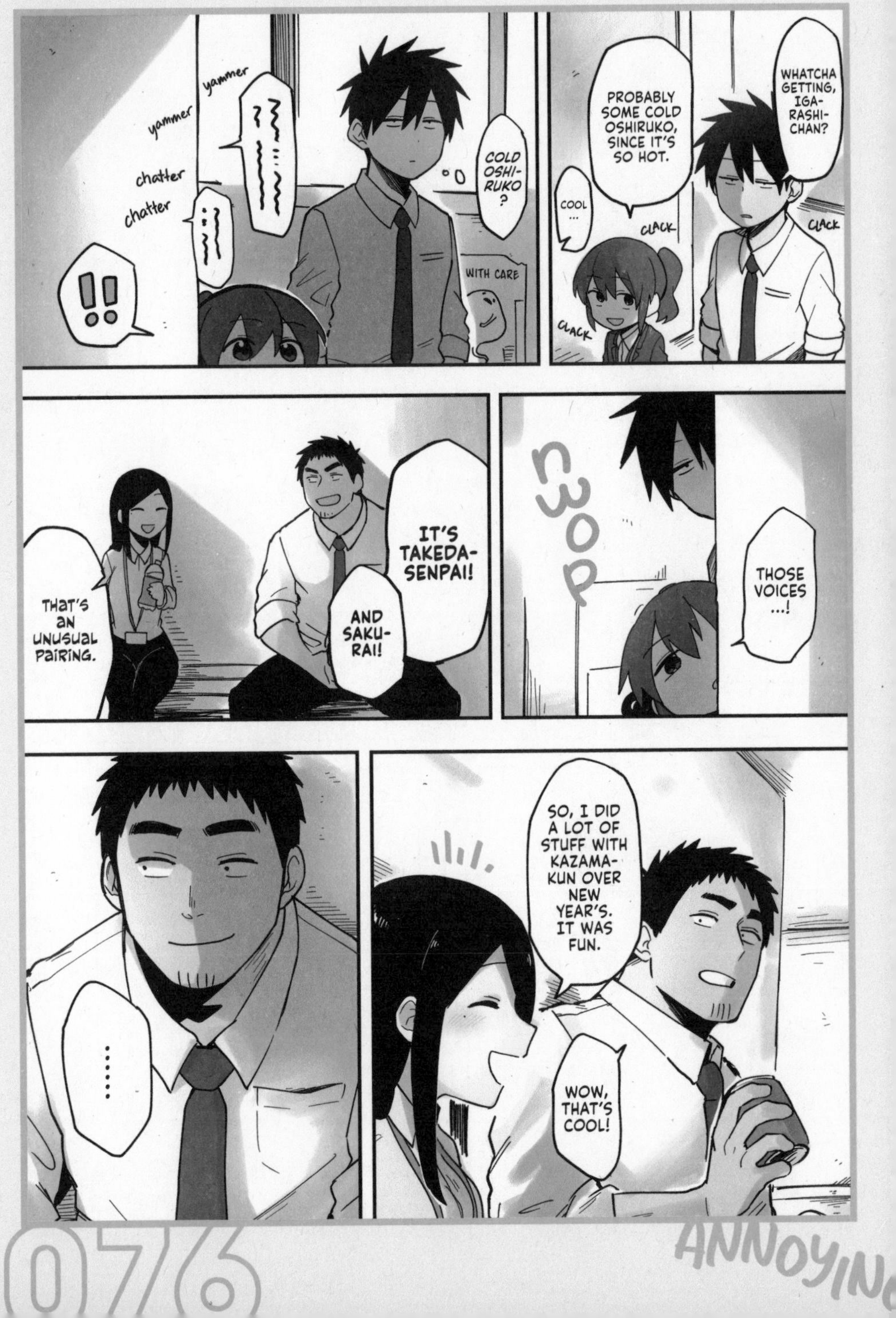
WHATCHA GETTING, IGA-RASHI-CHAN?
PROBABLY SOME COLD OSHIRUKO, SINCE IT'S SO HOT.
COOL...
CLACK
CLACK
CLACK
COLD OSHIRUKO?
WITH CARE
yammer yammer
chatter chatter
!!
THOSE VOICES ...!
IT'S TAKEDA-SENPAI!
AND SAKU-RAI!
THAT'S AN UNUSUAL PAIRING.
SO, I DID A LOT OF STUFF WITH KAZAMA-KUN OVER NEW YEAR'S. IT WAS FUN.
WOW, THAT'S COOL!
......

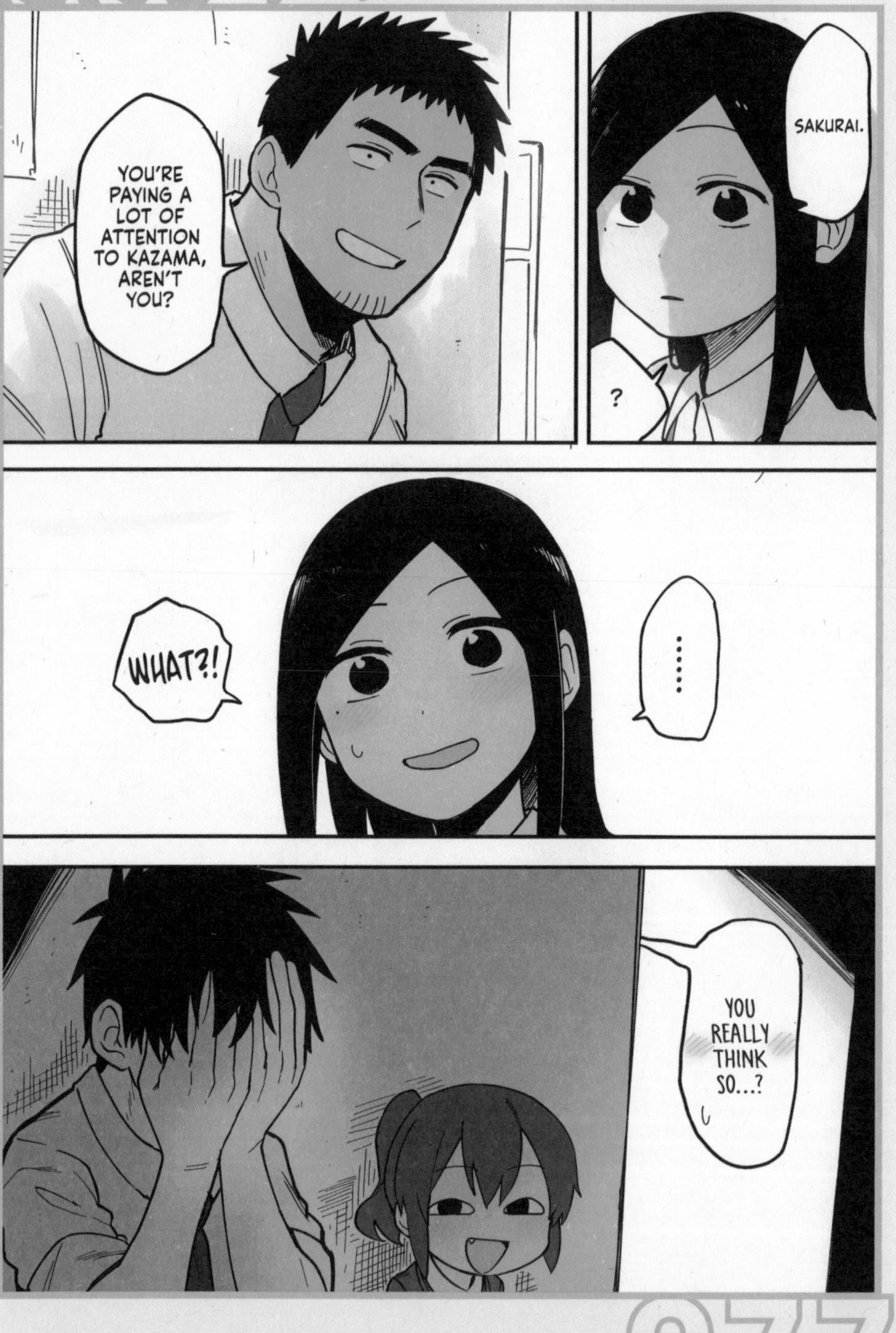
SAKURAI.
?
YOU'RE PAYING A LOT OF ATTENTION TO KAZAMA, AREN'T YOU?
......
WHAT?!
YOU REALLY THINK SO...?

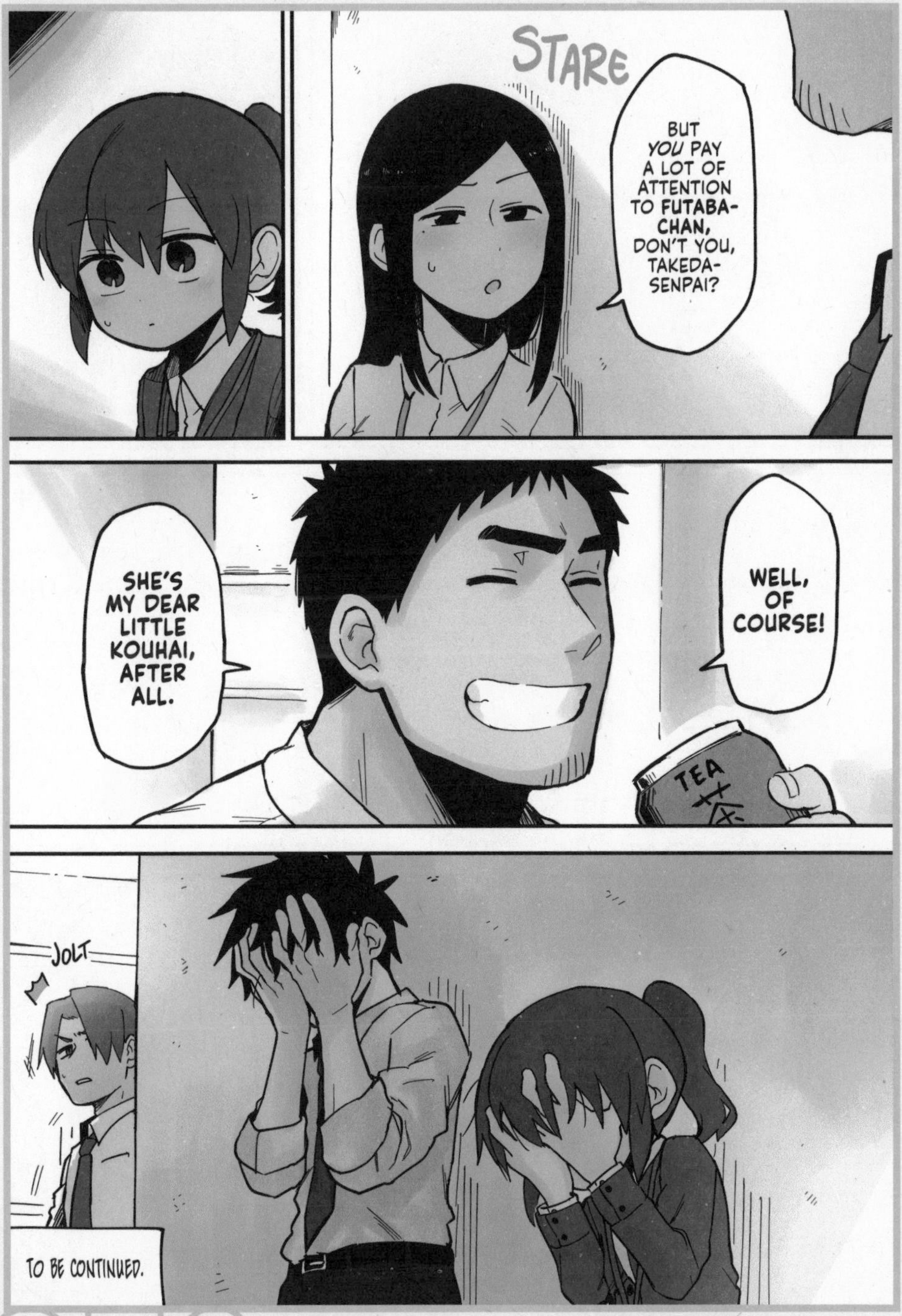
STARE
BUT *YOU* PAY A LOT OF ATTENTION TO FUTABA-CHAN, DON'T YOU, TAKEDA-SENPAI?
WELL, OF COURSE!
SHE'S MY DEAR LITTLE KOUHAI, AFTER ALL.
TEA
JOLT
TO BE CONTINUED.

Chapter 36

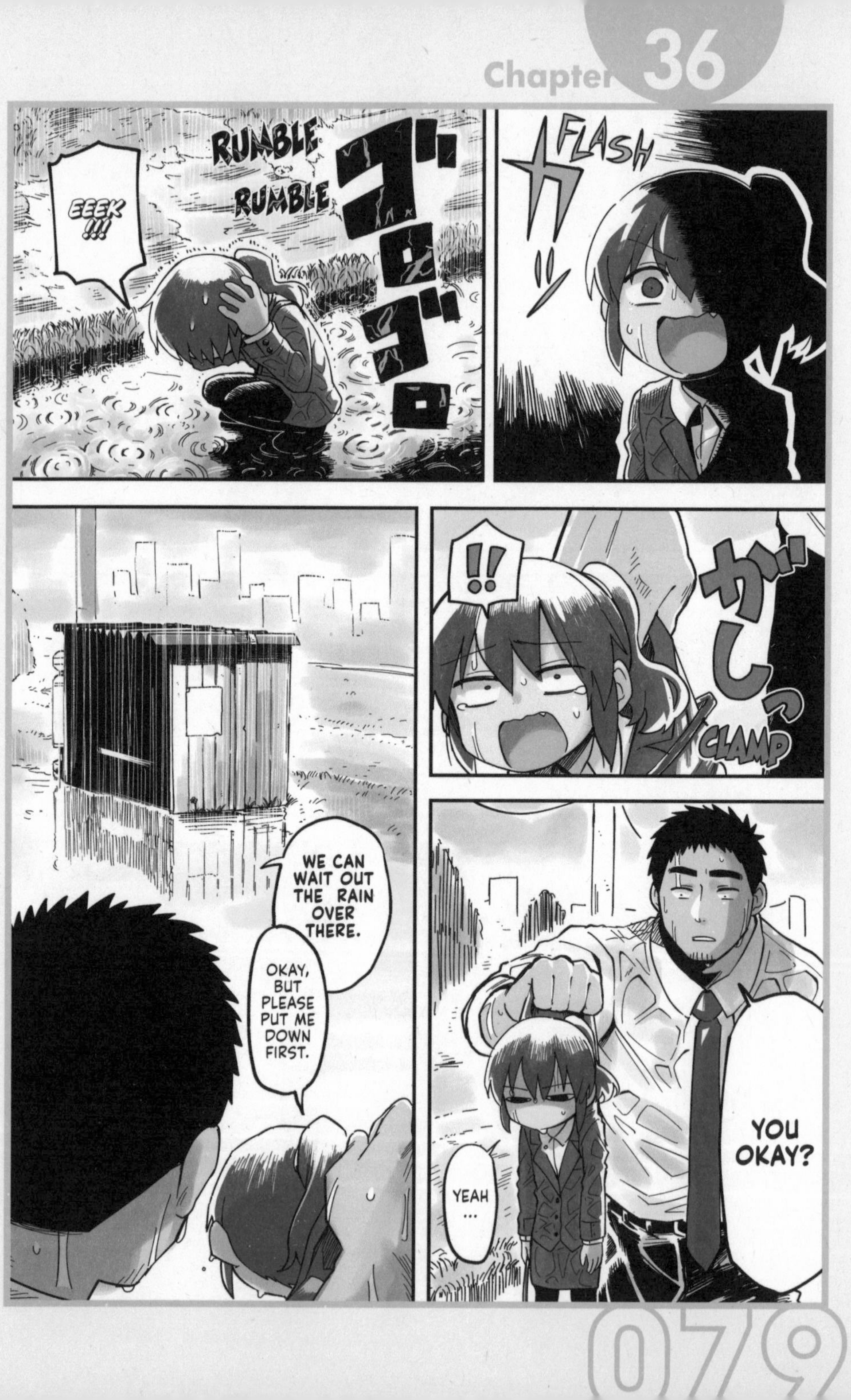

カッ
FLASH
!!
RUMBLE RUMBLE
ゴロゴロ
EEEK!!!
!!
がしっ
CLAMP
YOU OKAY?
YEAH...
WE CAN WAIT OUT THE RAIN OVER THERE.
OKAY, BUT PLEASE PUT ME DOWN FIRST.

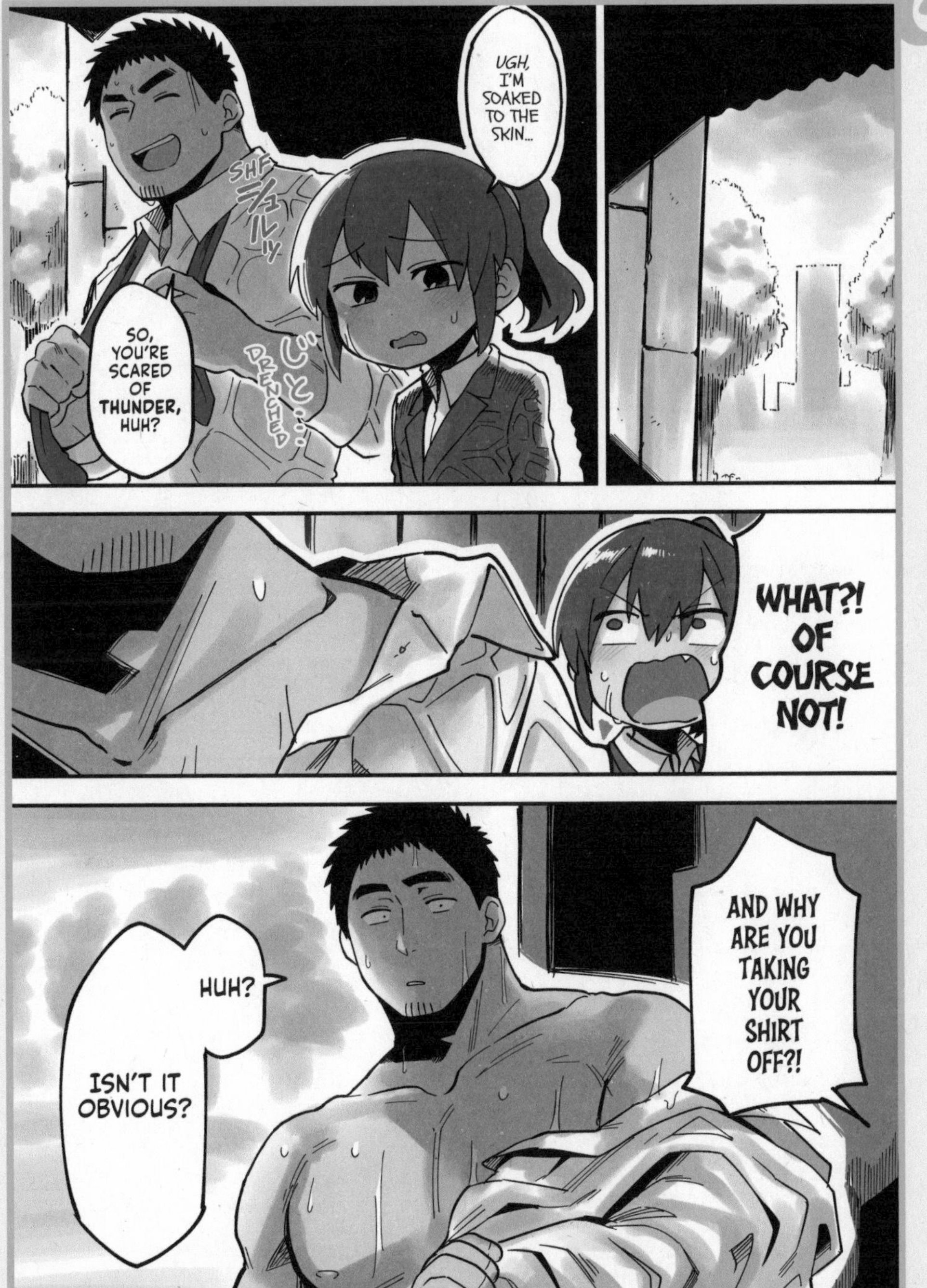
UGH, I'M SOAKED TO THE SKIN...
SHF
シュルッ
SO, YOU'RE SCARED OF THUNDER, HUH?
じと…
DRENCHED
WHAT?! OF COURSE NOT!
AND WHY ARE YOU TAKING YOUR SHIRT OFF?!
HUH?
ISN'T IT OBVIOUS?

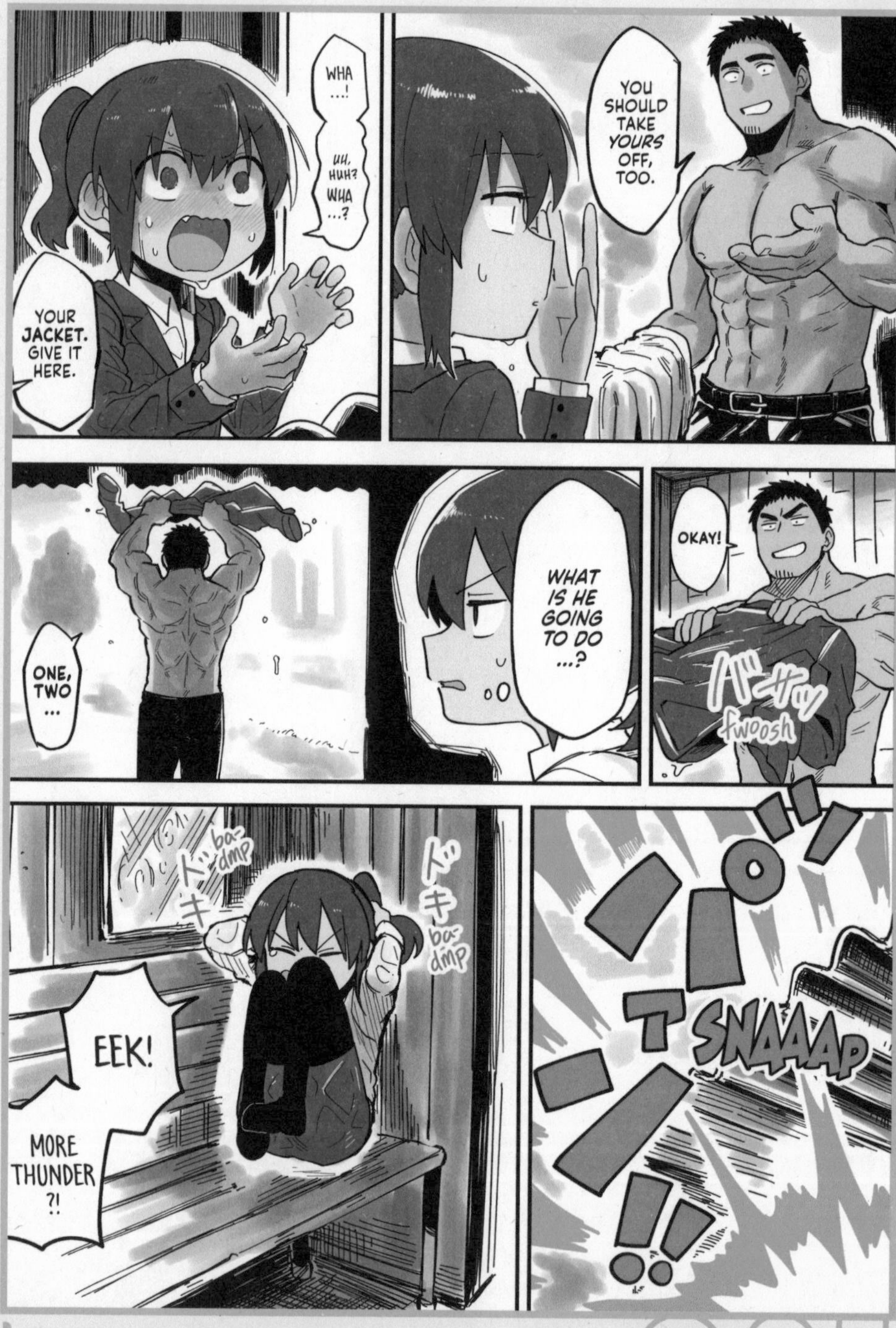
YOU SHOULD TAKE YOURS OFF, TOO.
WHA ...!
UH, HUH? WHA ...?
YOUR JACKET. GIVE IT HERE.
OKAY!
バサッ
fwoosh
WHAT IS HE GOING TO DO ...?
ONE, TWO ...
パァーン!!
SNAAAP
ドキ
ba-dmp
ドキ
ba-dmp
EEK!
MORE THUNDER ?!

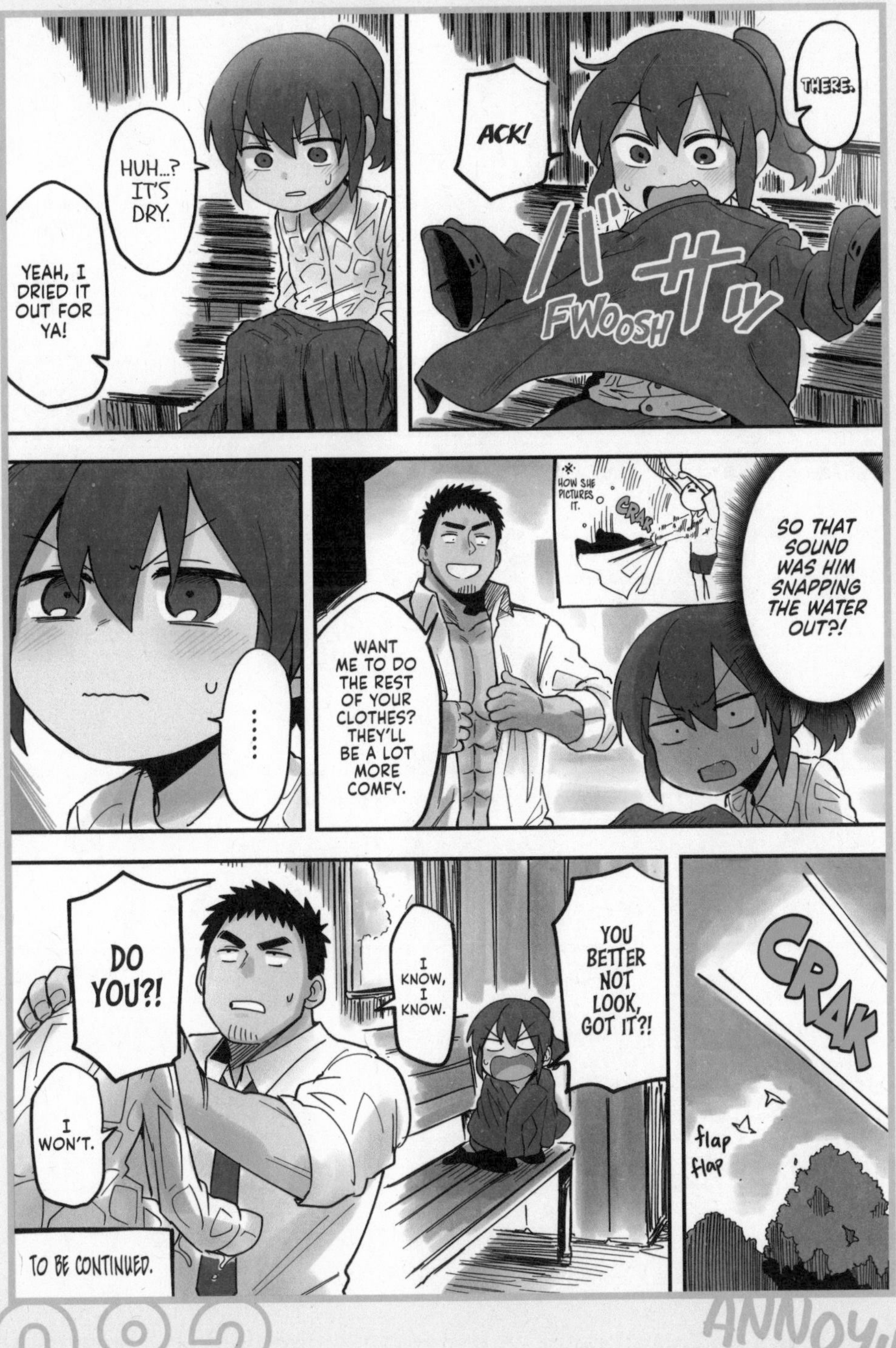
THERE.
ACK!
FWOOSH
HUH...? IT'S DRY.
YEAH, I DRIED IT OUT FOR YA!
※ HOW SHE PICTURES IT.
CRAK
SO THAT SOUND WAS HIM SNAPPING THE WATER OUT?!
WANT ME TO DO THE REST OF YOUR CLOTHES? THEY'LL BE A LOT MORE COMFY.
......
CRAK
flap flap
YOU BETTER NOT LOOK, GOT IT?!
I KNOW, I KNOW.
DO YOU?!
I WON'T.
TO BE CONTINUED.

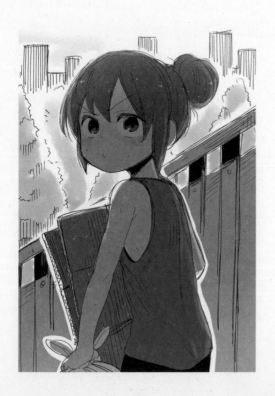

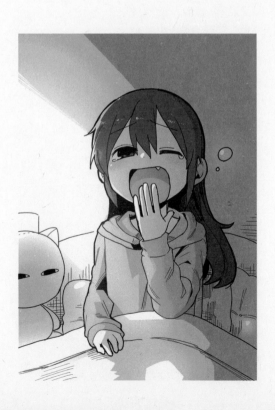

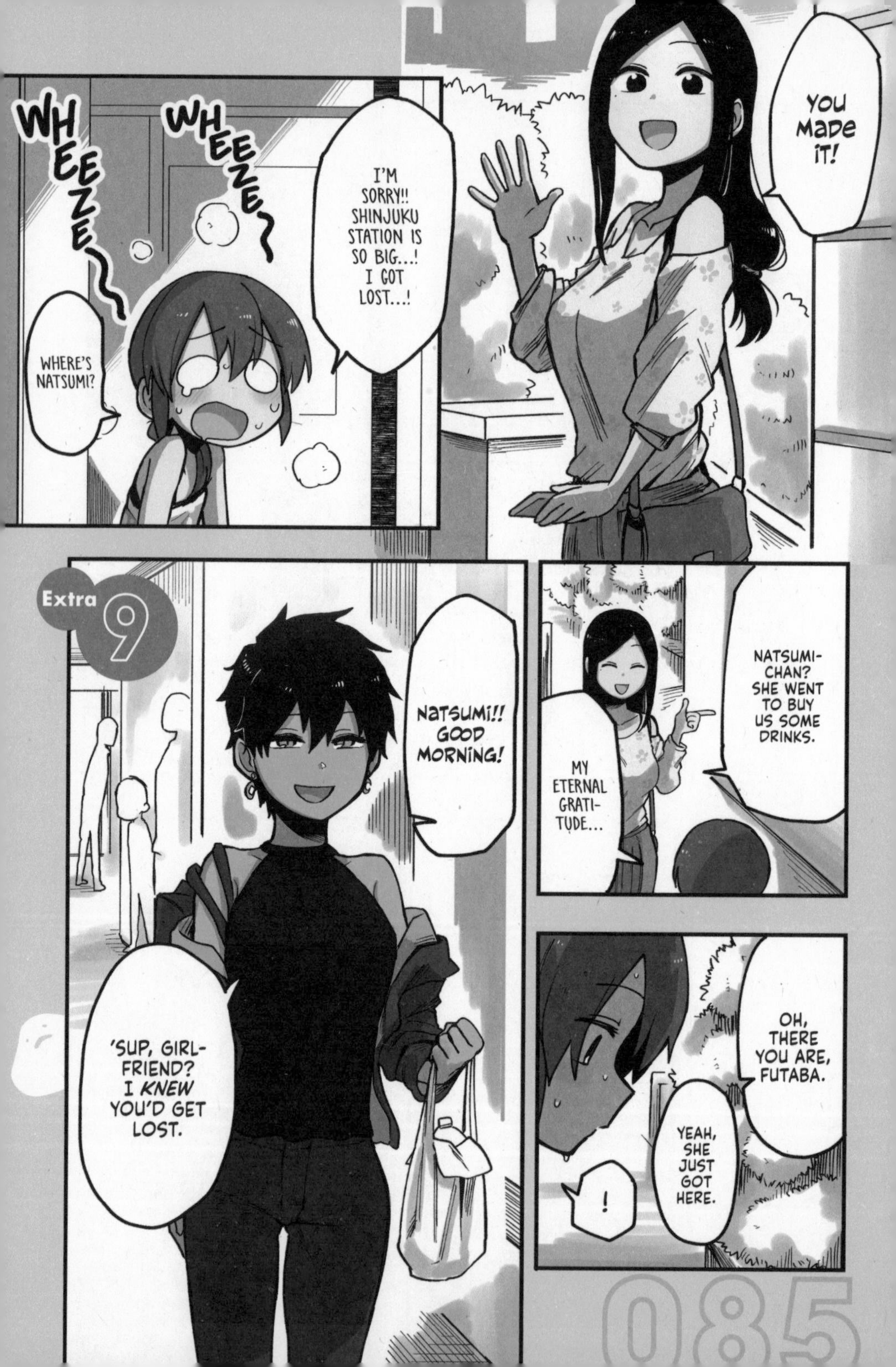
YOU MADE IT!
WHEEZE WHEEZE
I'M SORRY!! SHINJUKU STATION IS SO BIG...! I GOT LOST...!
WHERE'S NATSUMI?
NATSUMI-CHAN? SHE WENT TO BUY US SOME DRINKS.
MY ETERNAL GRATITUDE...
OH, THERE YOU ARE, FUTABA.
YEAH, SHE JUST GOT HERE.
!
Extra 9
NATSUMI!! GOOD MORNING!
'SUP, GIRL-FRIEND? I *KNEW* YOU'D GET LOST.

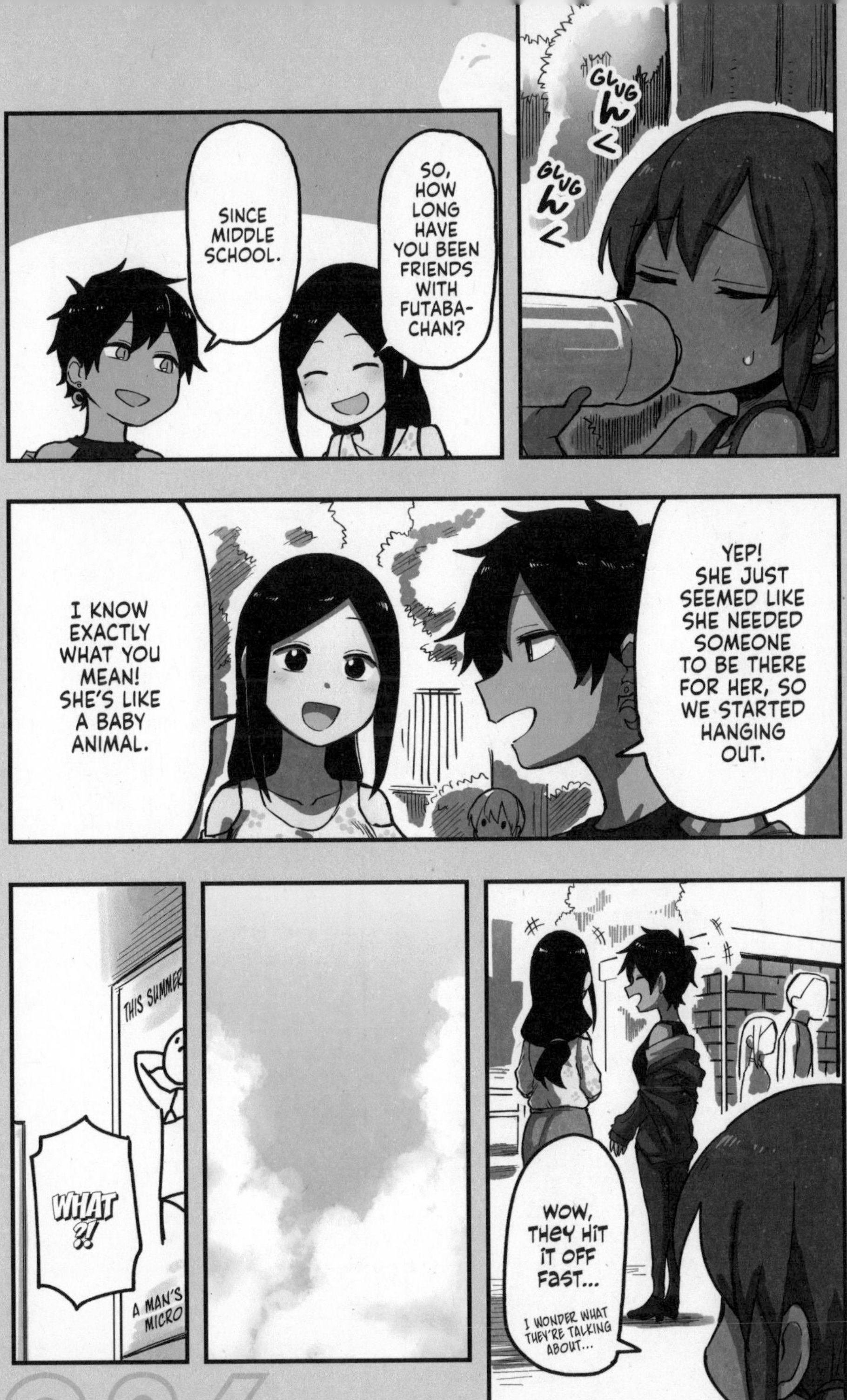
GLUG
GLUG
SO, HOW LONG HAVE YOU BEEN FRIENDS WITH FUTABA-CHAN?
SINCE MIDDLE SCHOOL.
YEP! SHE JUST SEEMED LIKE SHE NEEDED SOMEONE TO BE THERE FOR HER, SO WE STARTED HANGING OUT.
I KNOW EXACTLY WHAT YOU MEAN! SHE'S LIKE A BABY ANIMAL.
WOW, THEY HIT IT OFF FAST...
I WONDER WHAT THEY'RE TALKING ABOUT...
THIS SUMMER
WHAT ?!
A MAN'S MICRO

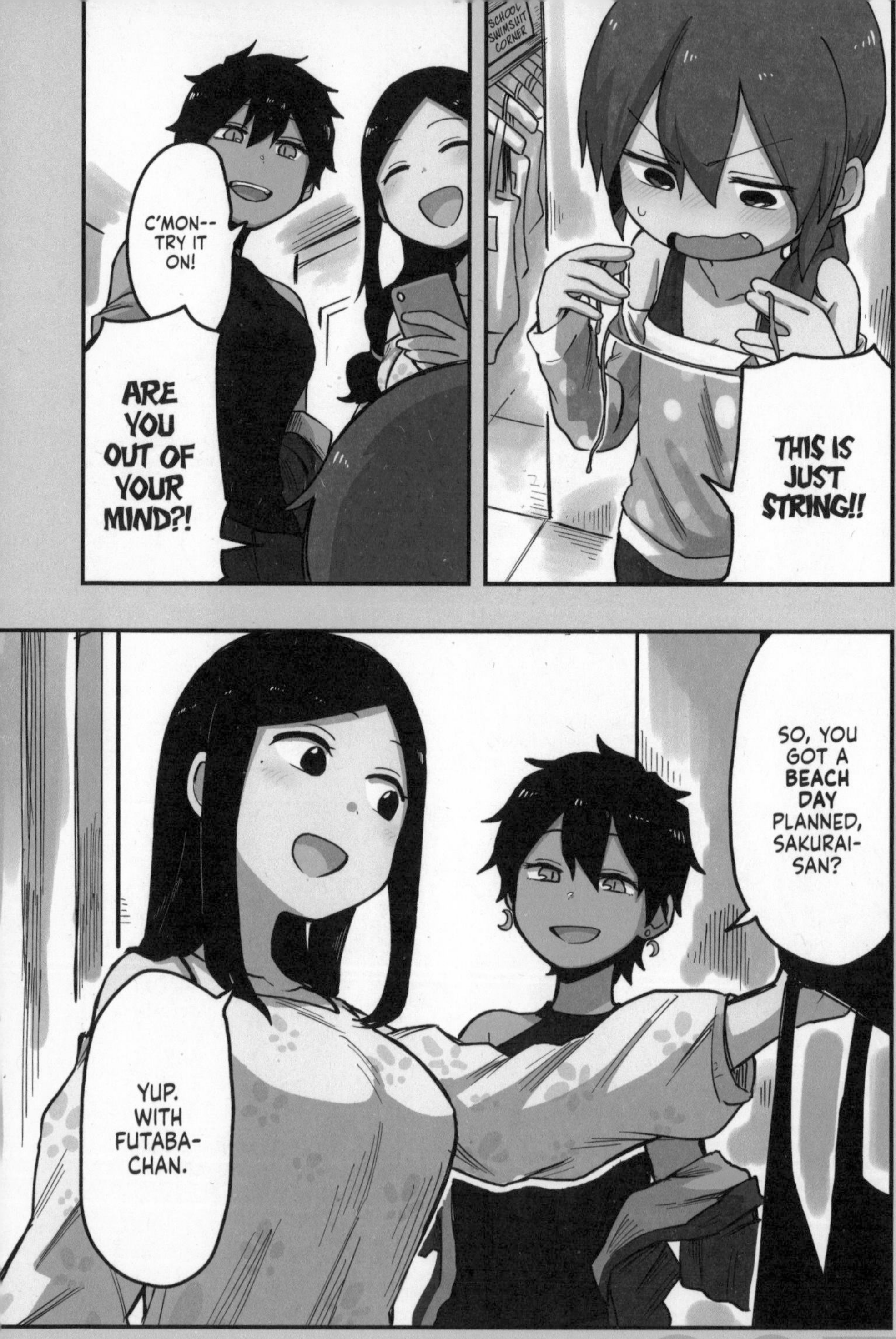
SCHOOL SWIMSUIT CORNER
THIS IS JUST STRING!!
C'MON-- TRY IT ON!
ARE YOU OUT OF YOUR MIND?!
SO, YOU GOT A BEACH DAY PLANNED, SAKURAI-SAN?
YUP. WITH FUTABA-CHAN.

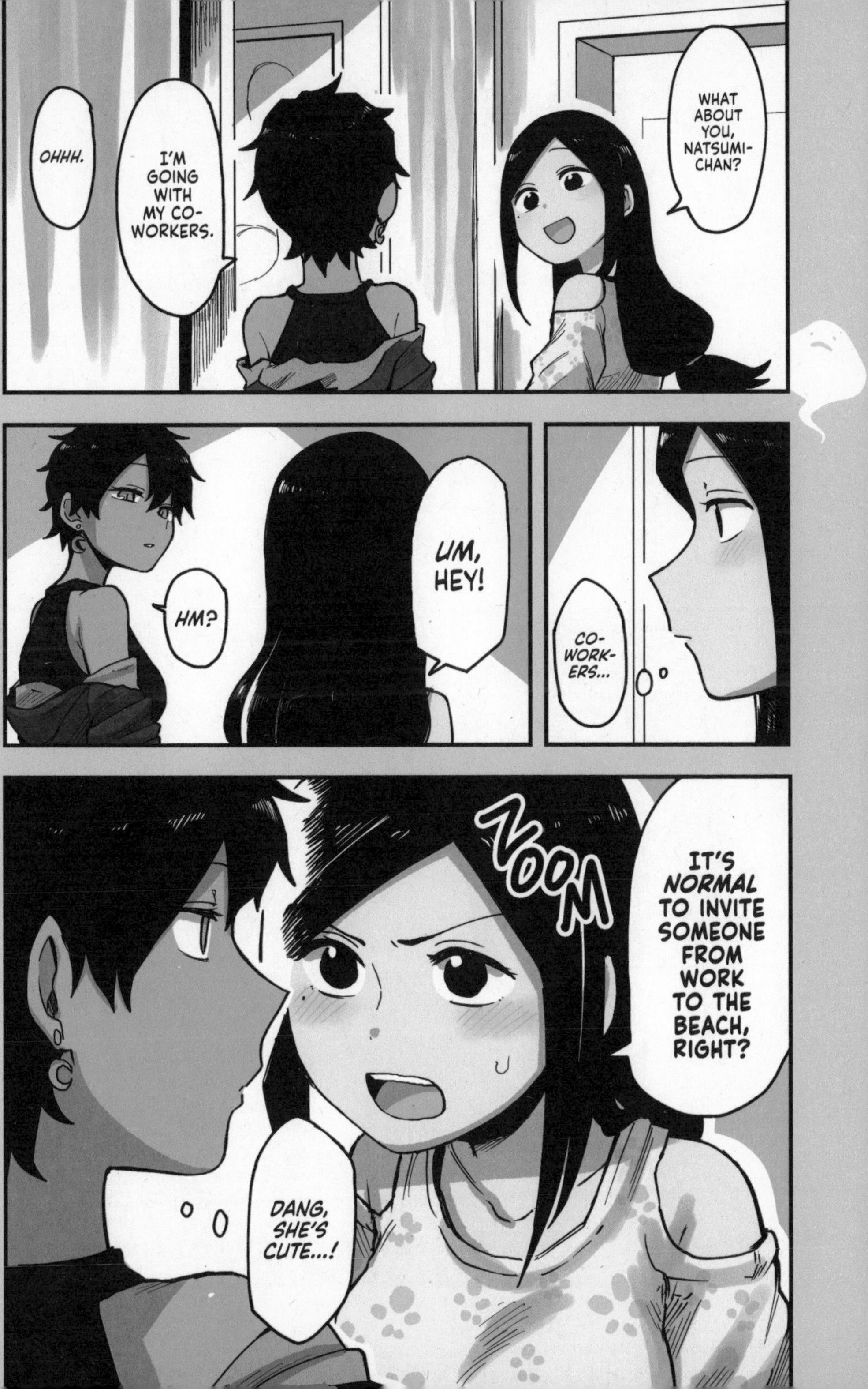
WHAT ABOUT YOU, NATSUMI-CHAN?
I'M GOING WITH MY CO-WORKERS.
OHHH.
CO-WORK-ERS...
UM, HEY!
HM?
NOOM
IT'S *NORMAL* TO INVITE SOMEONE FROM WORK TO THE BEACH, RIGHT?
DANG, SHE'S CUTE...!

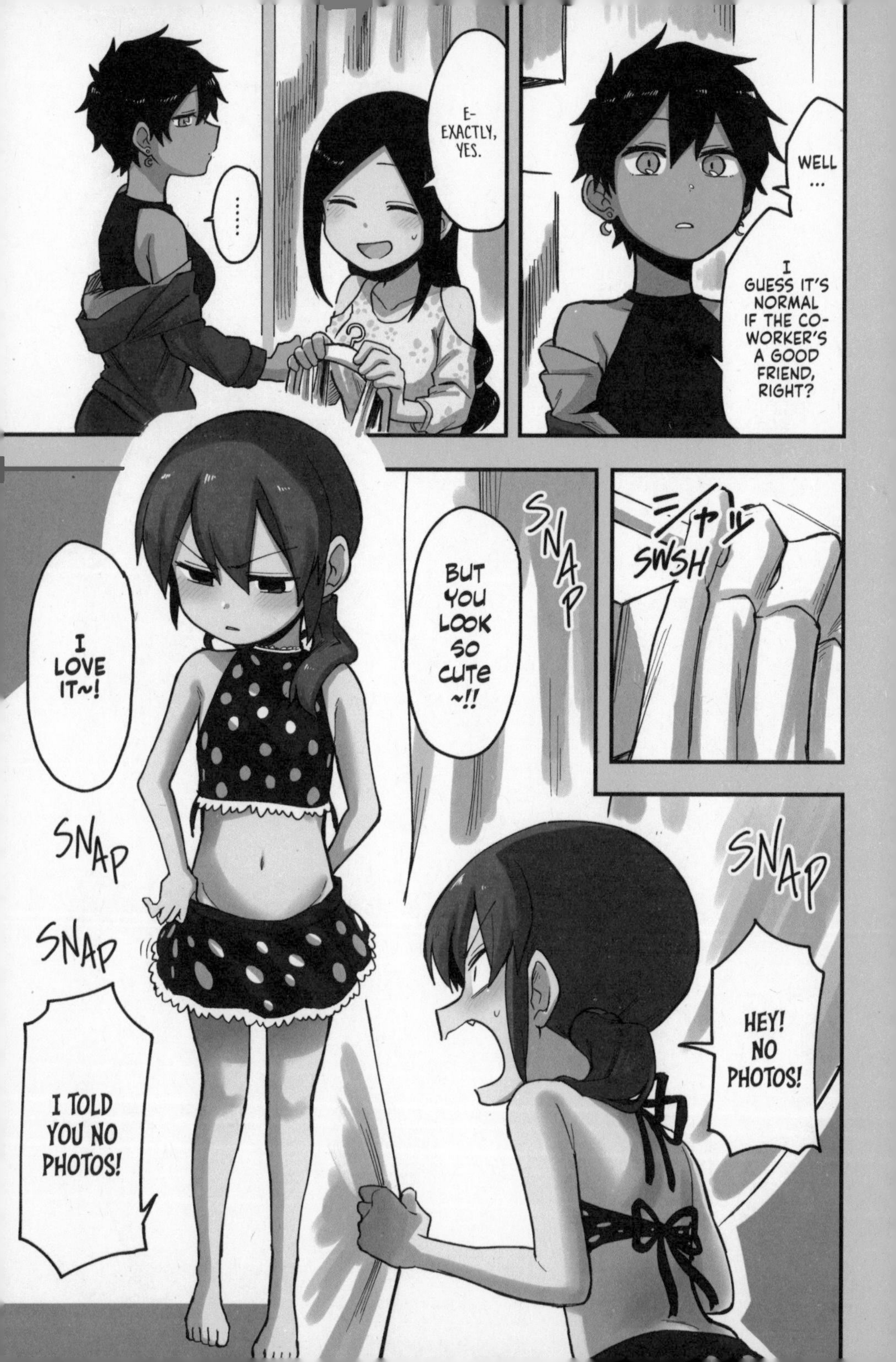
WELL ...
I GUESS IT'S NORMAL IF THE CO-WORKER'S A GOOD FRIEND, RIGHT?
E- EXACTLY, YES.
......
シャッ
SWSH
SNAP
BUT YOU LOOK SO CUTE ~!!
SNAP
HEY! NO PHOTOS!
I LOVE IT~!
SNAP
SNAP
I TOLD YOU NO PHOTOS!

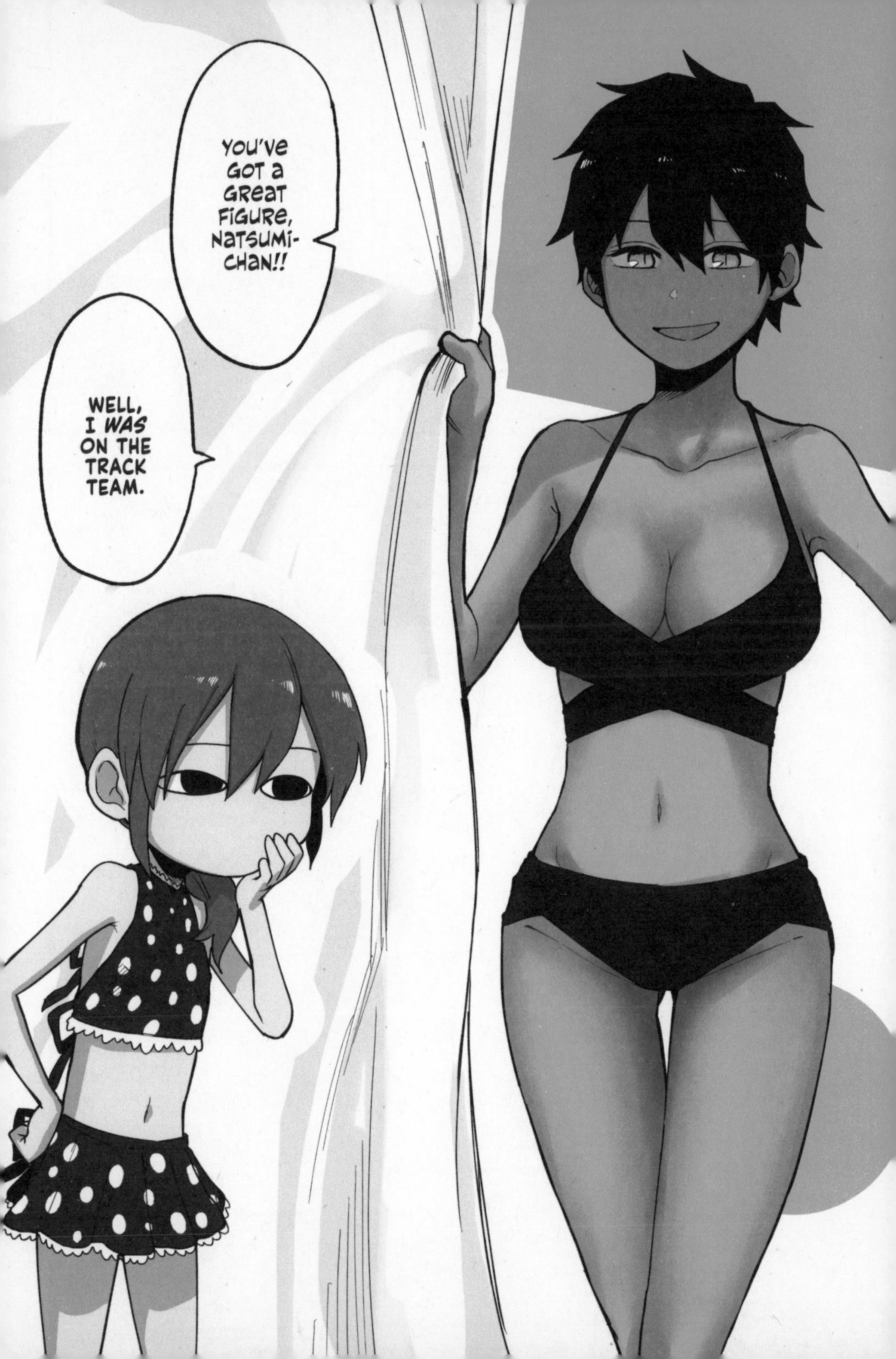
YOU'VE GOT A GREAT FIGURE, NATSUMI-CHAN!!
WELL, I *WAS* ON THE TRACK TEAM.

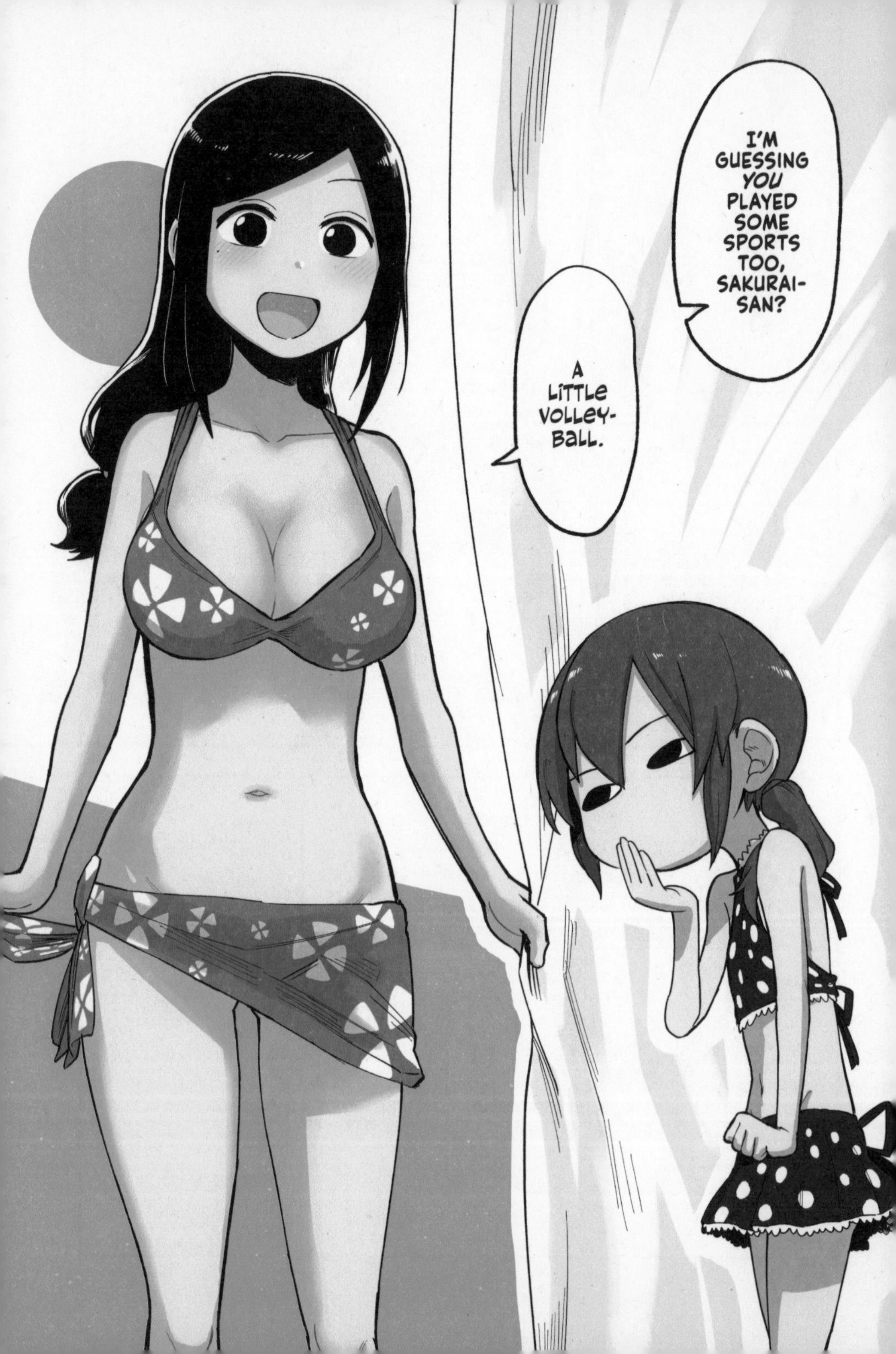
I'M GUESSING *YOU* PLAYED SOME SPORTS TOO, SAKURAI-SAN?
A LITTLE VOLLEY-BALL.

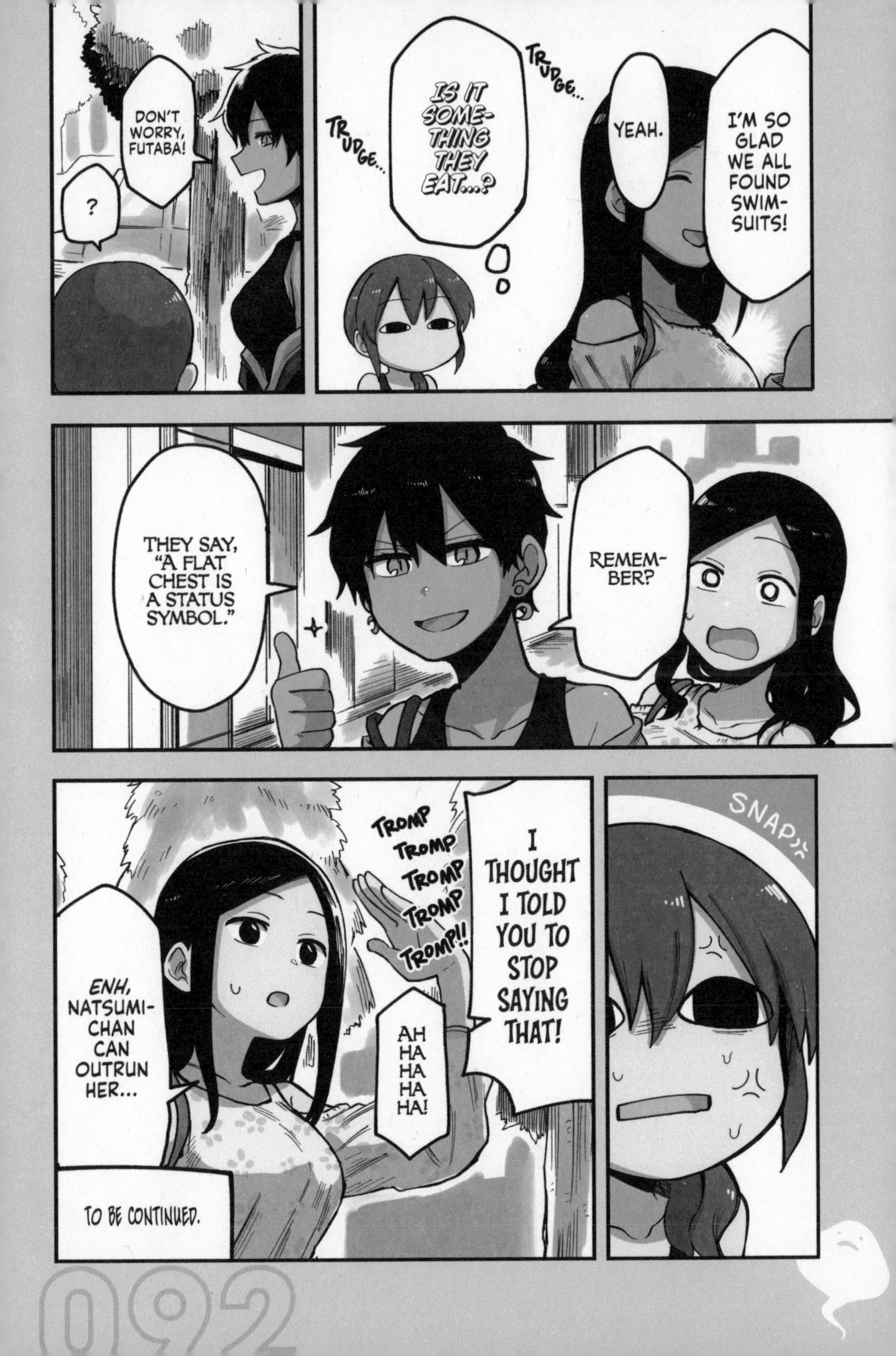
I'M SO GLAD WE ALL FOUND SWIM-SUITS!
YEAH.
TRUDGE...
IS IT SOME-THING THEY EAT...?
TRUDGE...
DON'T WORRY, FUTABA!
?
REMEM-BER?
THEY SAY, "A FLAT CHEST IS A STATUS SYMBOL."
SNAP
I THOUGHT I TOLD YOU TO STOP SAYING THAT!
TROMP TROMP TROMP TROMP TROMP!!
AH HA HA HA HA!
ENH, NATSUMI-CHAN CAN OUTRUN HER...
TO BE CONTINUED.

Chapter 37

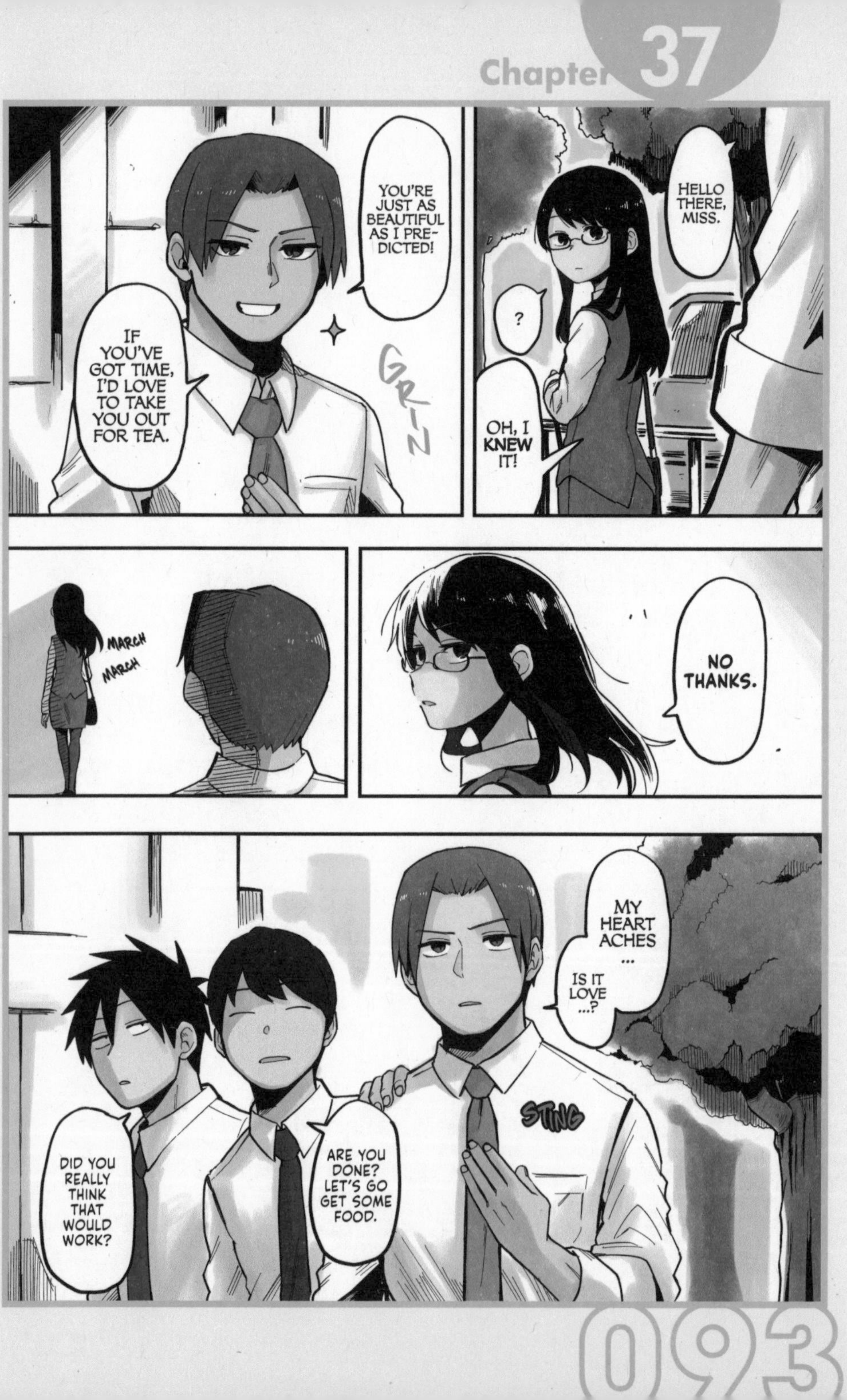
HELLO THERE, MISS.
?
OH, I KNEW IT!
YOU'RE JUST AS BEAUTIFUL AS I PREDICTED!
IF YOU'VE GOT TIME, I'D LOVE TO TAKE YOU OUT FOR TEA.
GRIN
NO THANKS.
MARCH
MARCH
MY HEART ACHES...
IS IT LOVE...?
STING
ARE YOU DONE? LET'S GO GET SOME FOOD.
DID YOU REALLY THINK THAT WOULD WORK?

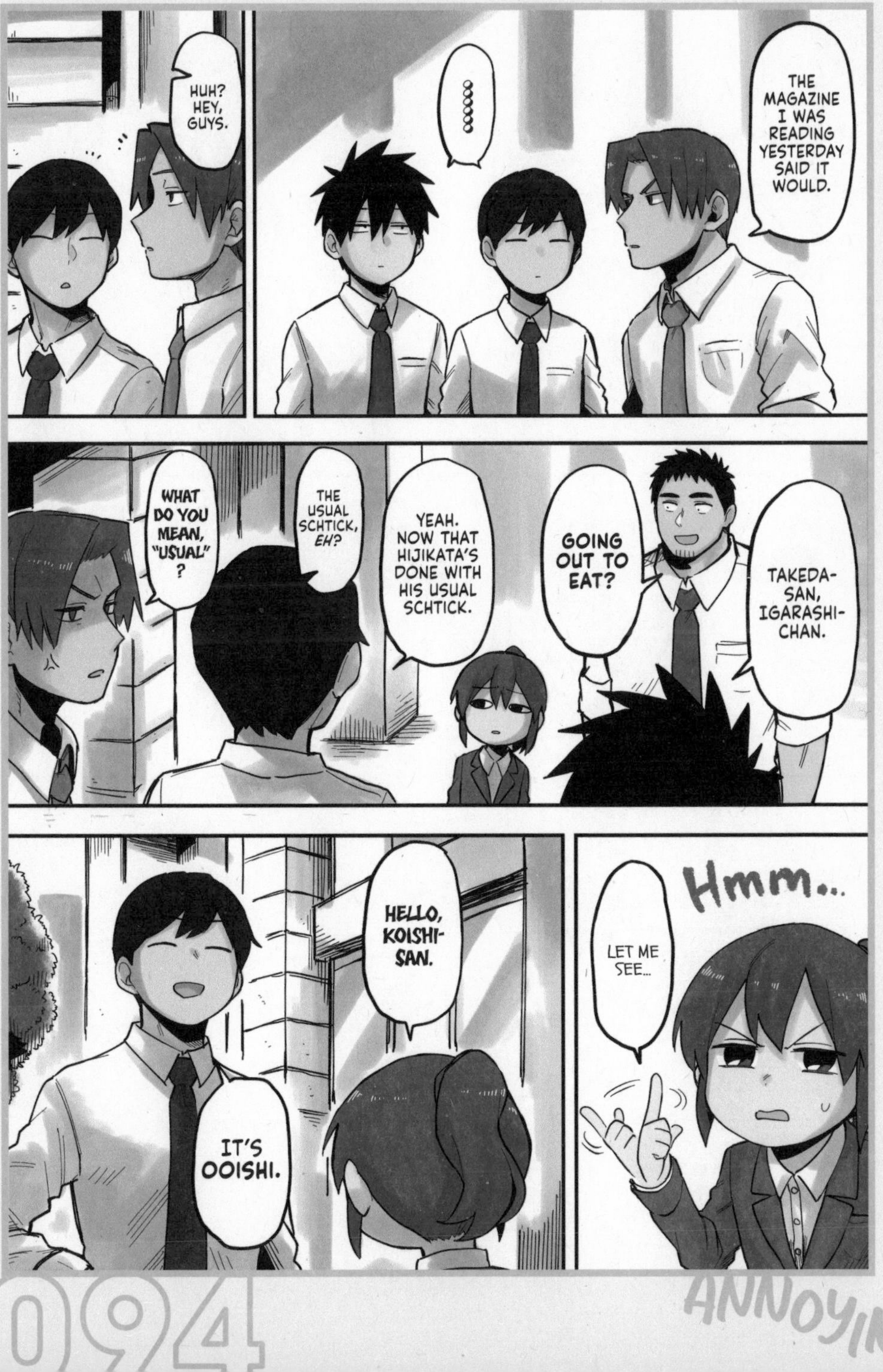
THE MAGAZINE I WAS READING YESTERDAY SAID IT WOULD.
......
HUH? HEY, GUYS.
TAKEDA-SAN, IGARASHI-CHAN.
GOING OUT TO EAT?
YEAH. NOW THAT HIJIKATA'S DONE WITH HIS USUAL SCHTICK.
THE USUAL SCHTICK, *EH?*
WHAT DO YOU MEAN, "USUAL"?
Hmm...
LET ME SEE...
HELLO, KOISHI-SAN.
IT'S OOISHI.

094

ANNOYING

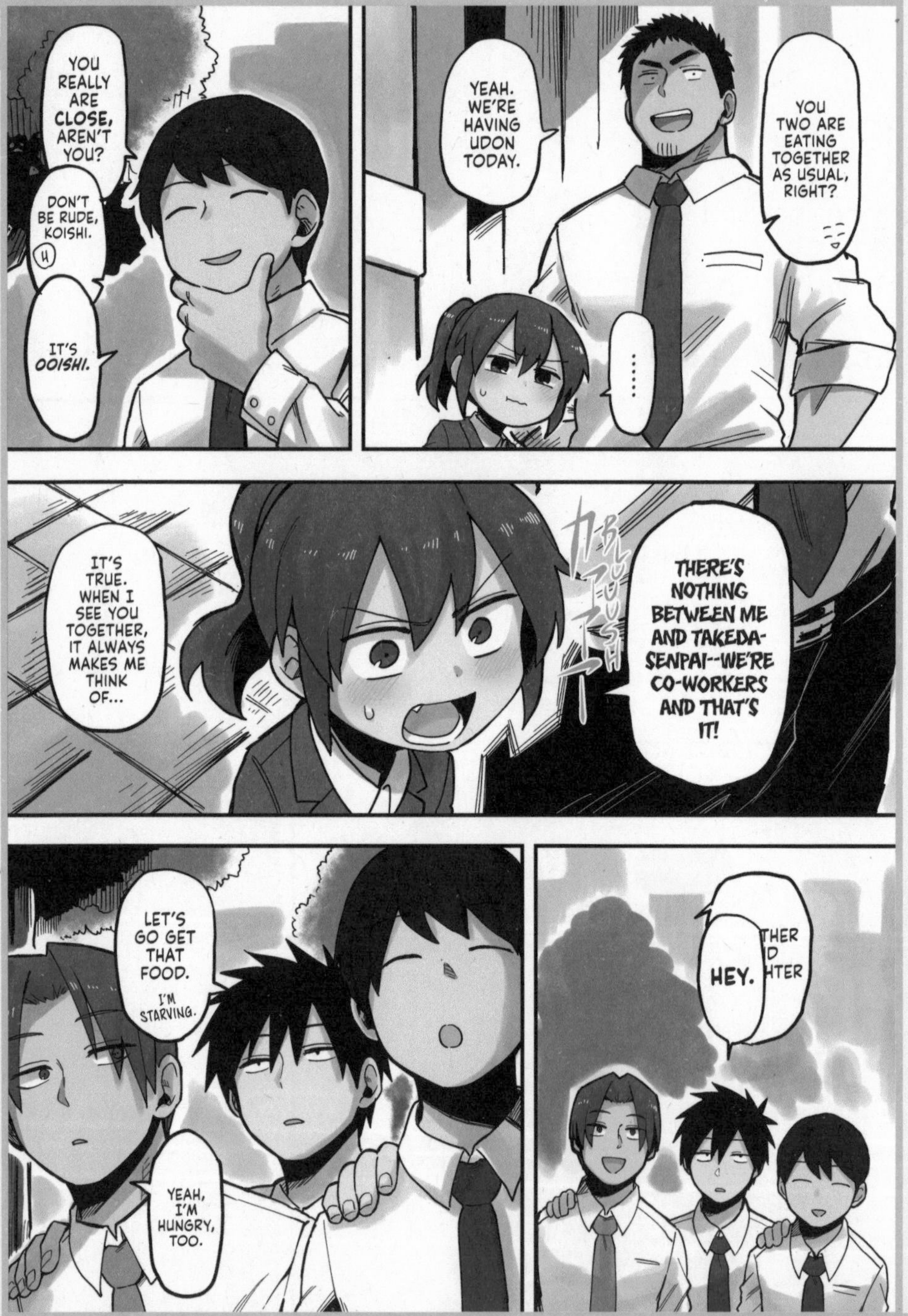
YOU TWO ARE EATING TOGETHER AS USUAL, RIGHT?
YEAH. WE'RE HAVING UDON TODAY.
......
YOU REALLY ARE CLOSE, AREN'T YOU?
DON'T BE RUDE, KOISHI.
IT'S OOISHI.
THERE'S NOTHING BETWEEN ME AND TAKEDA-SENPAI--WE'RE CO-WORKERS AND THAT'S IT!
BLUUSH
IT'S TRUE. WHEN I SEE YOU TOGETHER, IT ALWAYS MAKES ME THINK OF...
HEY.
LET'S GO GET THAT FOOD. I'M STARVING.
YEAH, I'M HUNGRY, TOO.

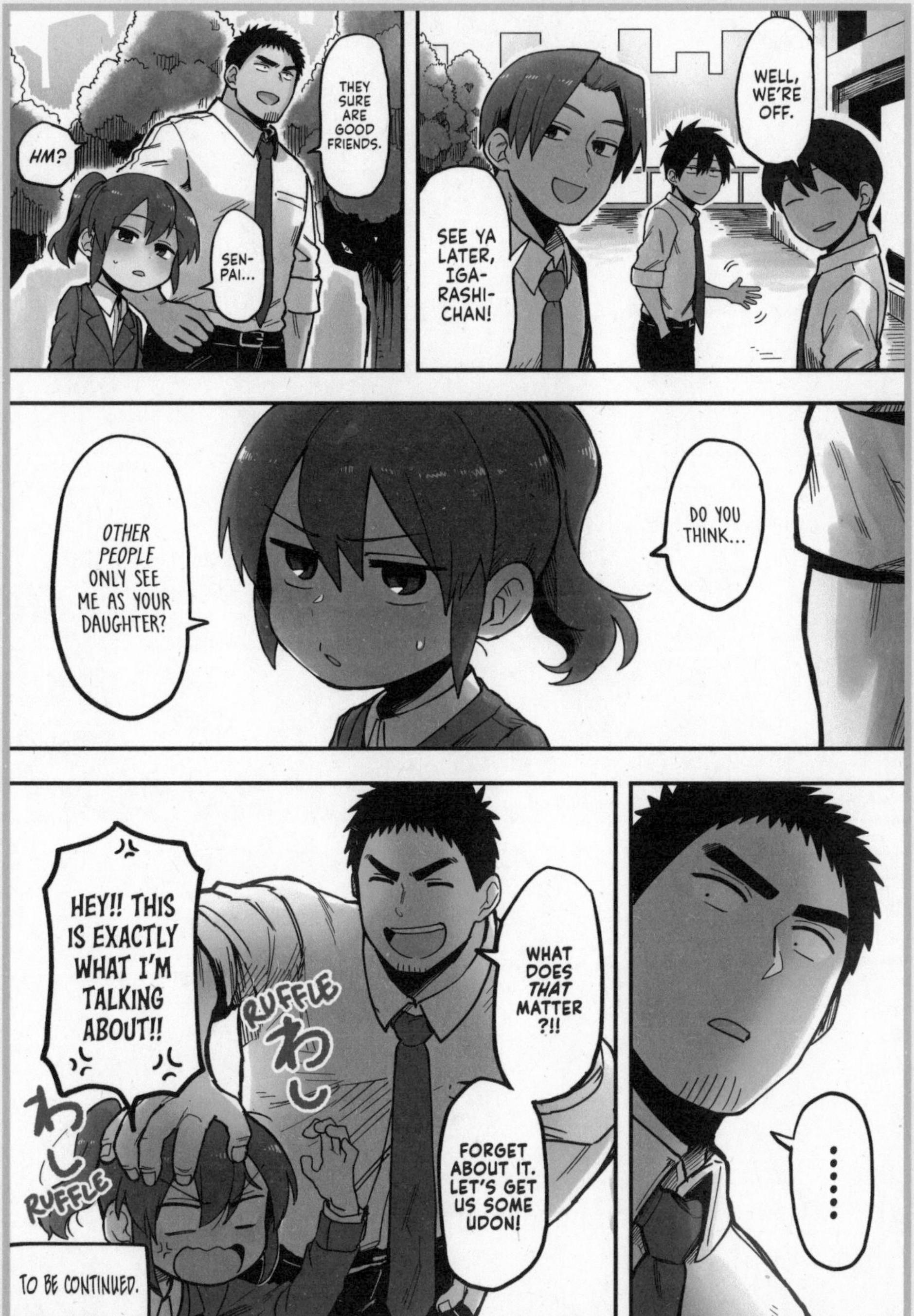
WELL, WE'RE OFF.
SEE YA LATER, IGA-RASHI-CHAN!
THEY SURE ARE GOOD FRIENDS.
HM?
SEN-PAI...
DO YOU THINK...
OTHER PEOPLE ONLY SEE ME AS YOUR DAUGHTER?
......
WHAT DOES *THAT* MATTER?!!
FORGET ABOUT IT. LET'S GET US SOME UDON!
RUFFLE わし
HEY!! THIS IS EXACTLY WHAT I'M TALKING ABOUT!!
わし RUFFLE
TO BE CONTINUED.

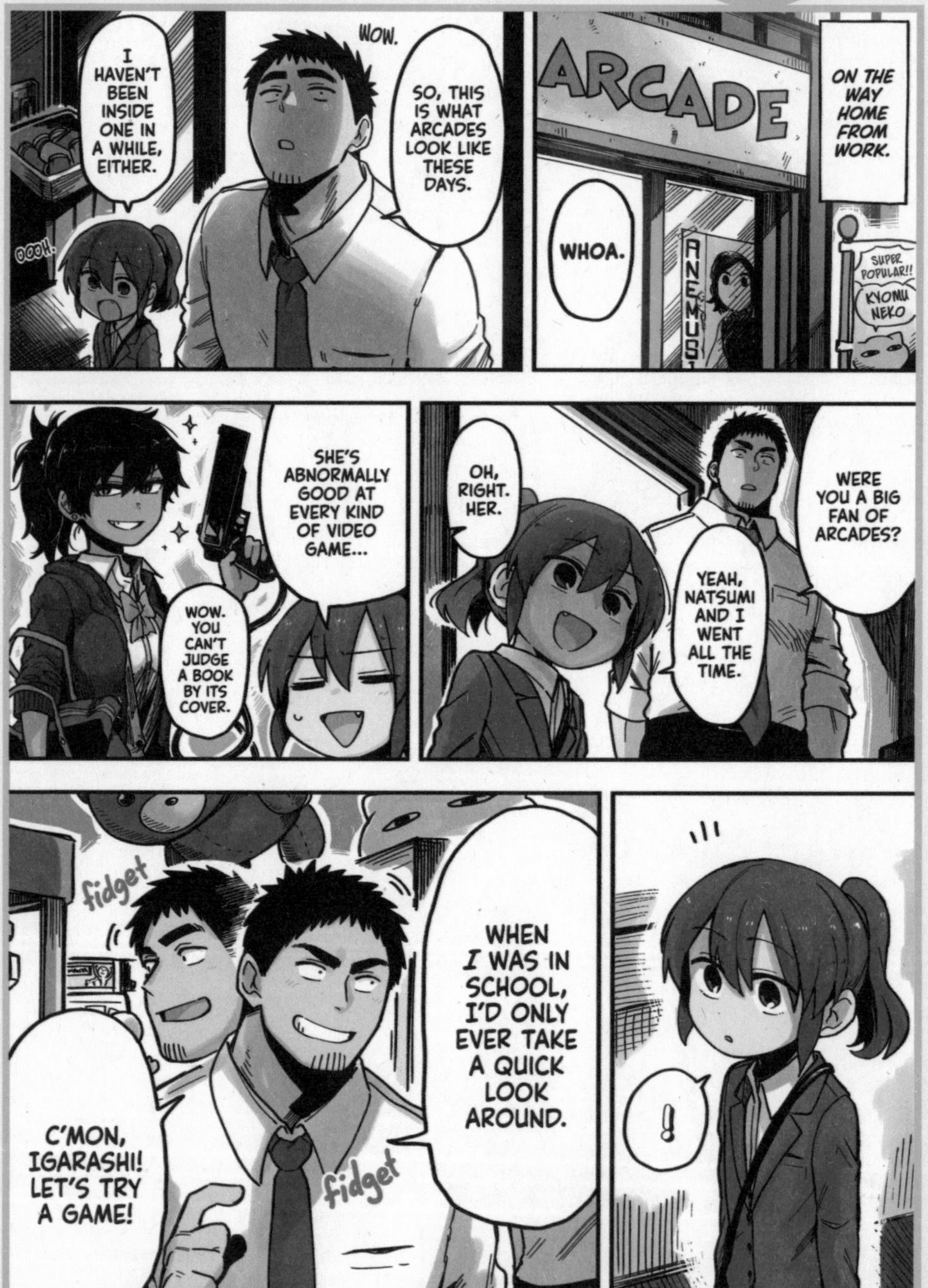
ARCADE
ON THE WAY HOME FROM WORK.
WHOA.
SUPER POPULAR!!
KYOMU NEKO
WOW.
SO, THIS IS WHAT ARCADES LOOK LIKE THESE DAYS.
I HAVEN'T BEEN INSIDE ONE IN A WHILE, EITHER.
OOOH.
WERE YOU A BIG FAN OF ARCADES?
YEAH, NATSUMI AND I WENT ALL THE TIME.
OH, RIGHT. HER.
SHE'S ABNORMALLY GOOD AT EVERY KIND OF VIDEO GAME...
WOW. YOU CAN'T JUDGE A BOOK BY ITS COVER.
!
WHEN *I* WAS IN SCHOOL, I'D ONLY EVER TAKE A QUICK LOOK AROUND.
fidget
fidget
C'MON, IGARASHI! LET'S TRY A GAME!

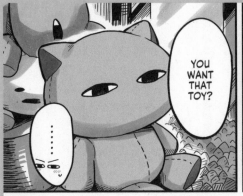

YOU WANT THAT TOY?

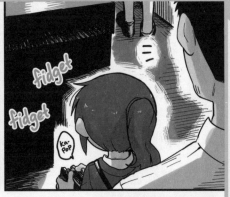

fidget
fidget

ka-pop

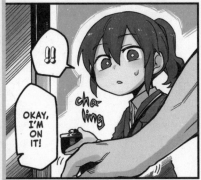

OKAY, I'M ON IT!

cha-ling

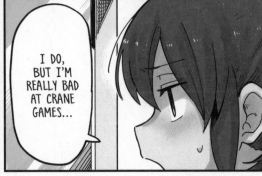

I DO, BUT I'M REALLY BAD AT CRANE GAMES...

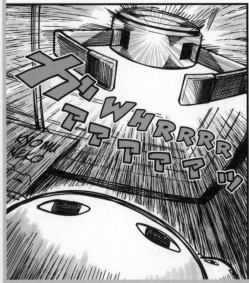

WHRRRRR

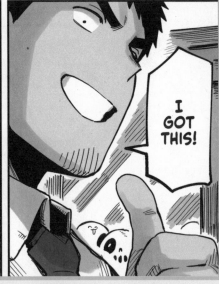

I GOT THIS!

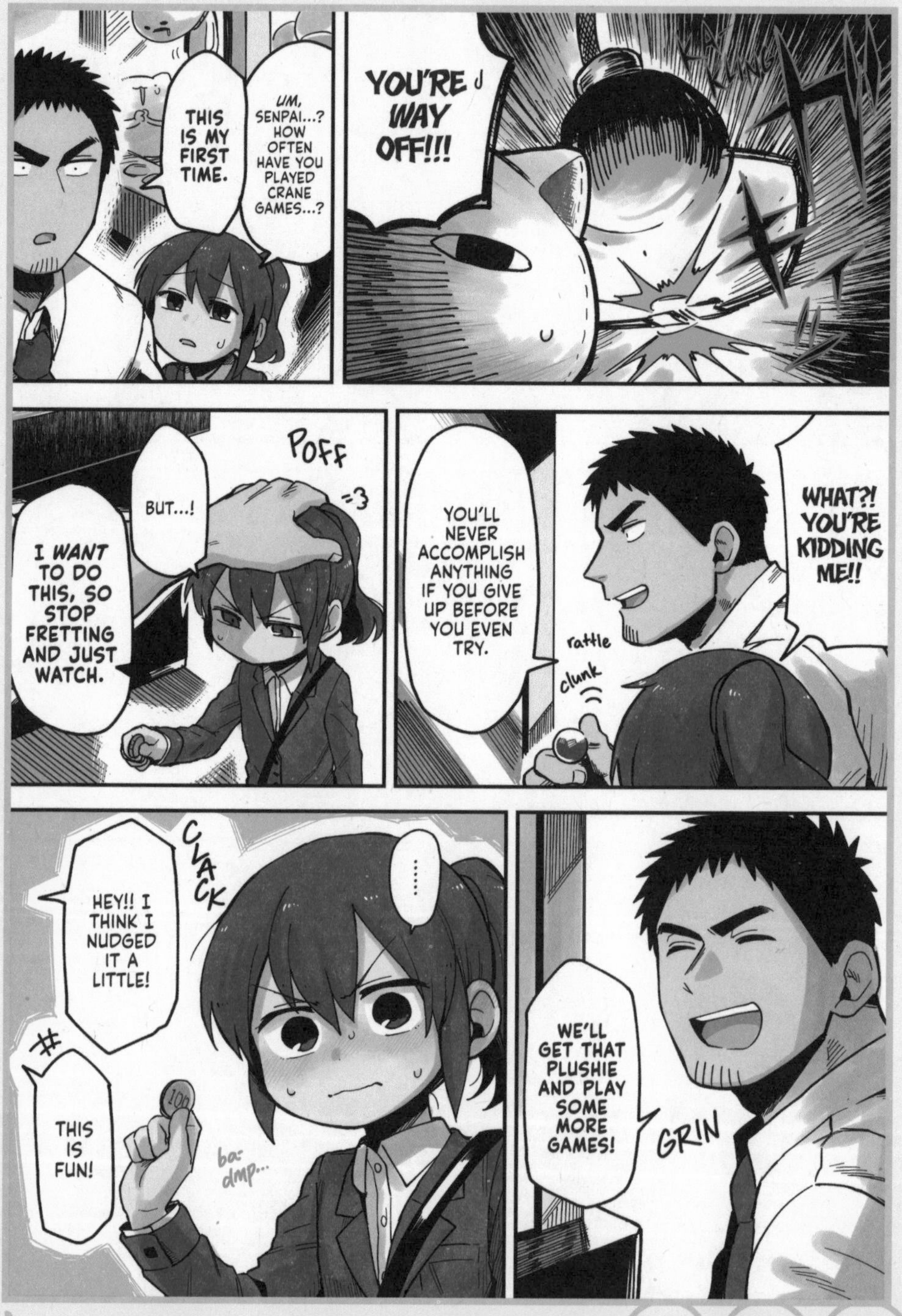
YOU'RE WAY OFF!!!
UM, SENPAI...? HOW OFTEN HAVE YOU PLAYED CRANE GAMES...?
THIS IS MY FIRST TIME.
WHAT?! YOU'RE KIDDING ME!!
YOU'LL NEVER ACCOMPLISH ANYTHING IF YOU GIVE UP BEFORE YOU EVEN TRY.
rattle
clunk
POFF
BUT...!
I WANT TO DO THIS, SO STOP FRETTING AND JUST WATCH.
WE'LL GET THAT PLUSHIE AND PLAY SOME MORE GAMES!
GRIN
......
CLACK
HEY!! I THINK I NUDGED IT A LITTLE!
THIS IS FUN!
ba-dmp...

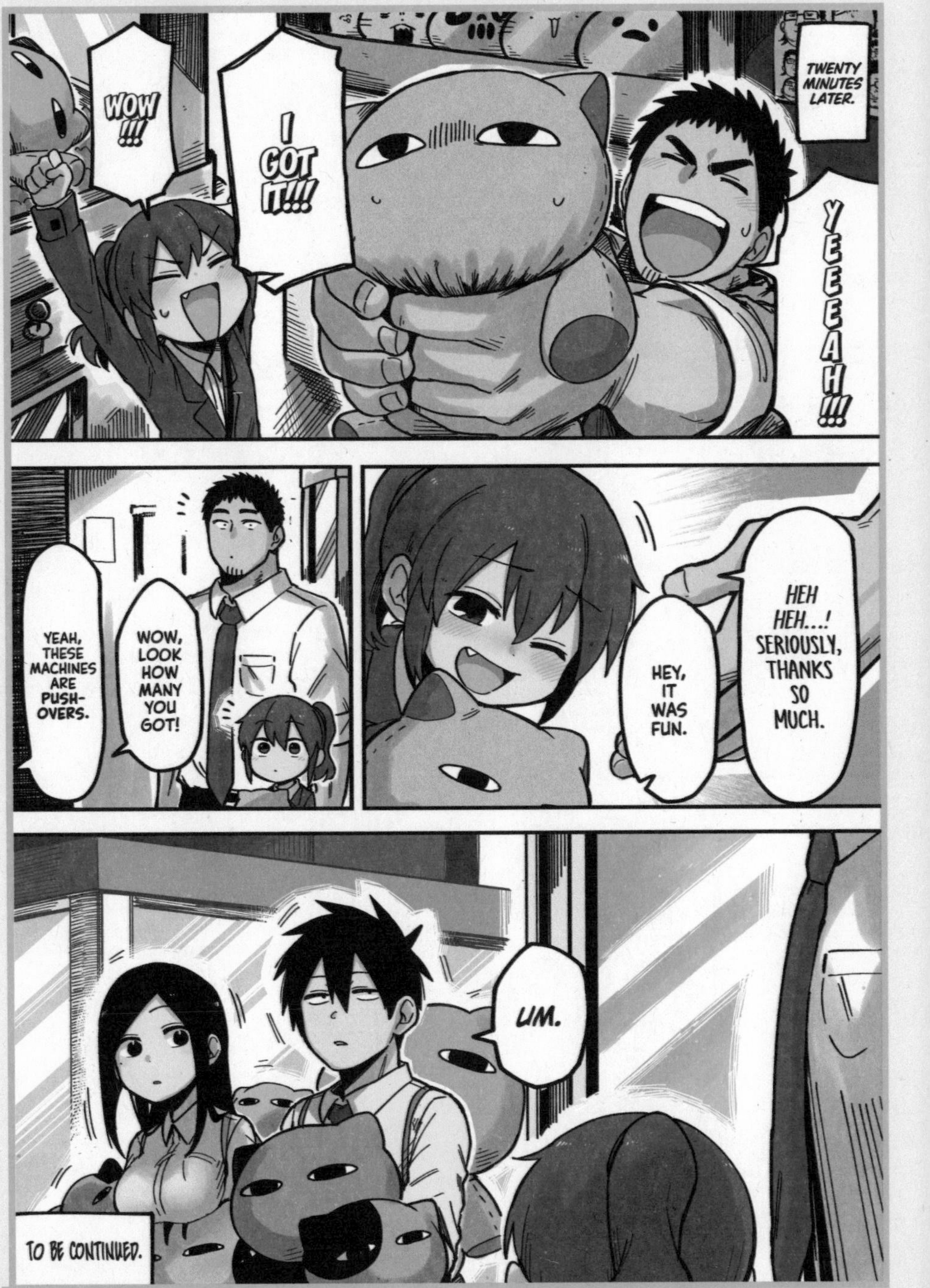
TWENTY MINUTES LATER.
YEEEEAH!!!
I GOT IT!!!
WOW!!!
HEH HEH...! SERIOUSLY, THANKS SO MUCH.
HEY, IT WAS FUN.
WOW, LOOK HOW MANY YOU GOT!
YEAH, THESE MACHINES ARE PUSH-OVERS.
UM.
TO BE CONTINUED.

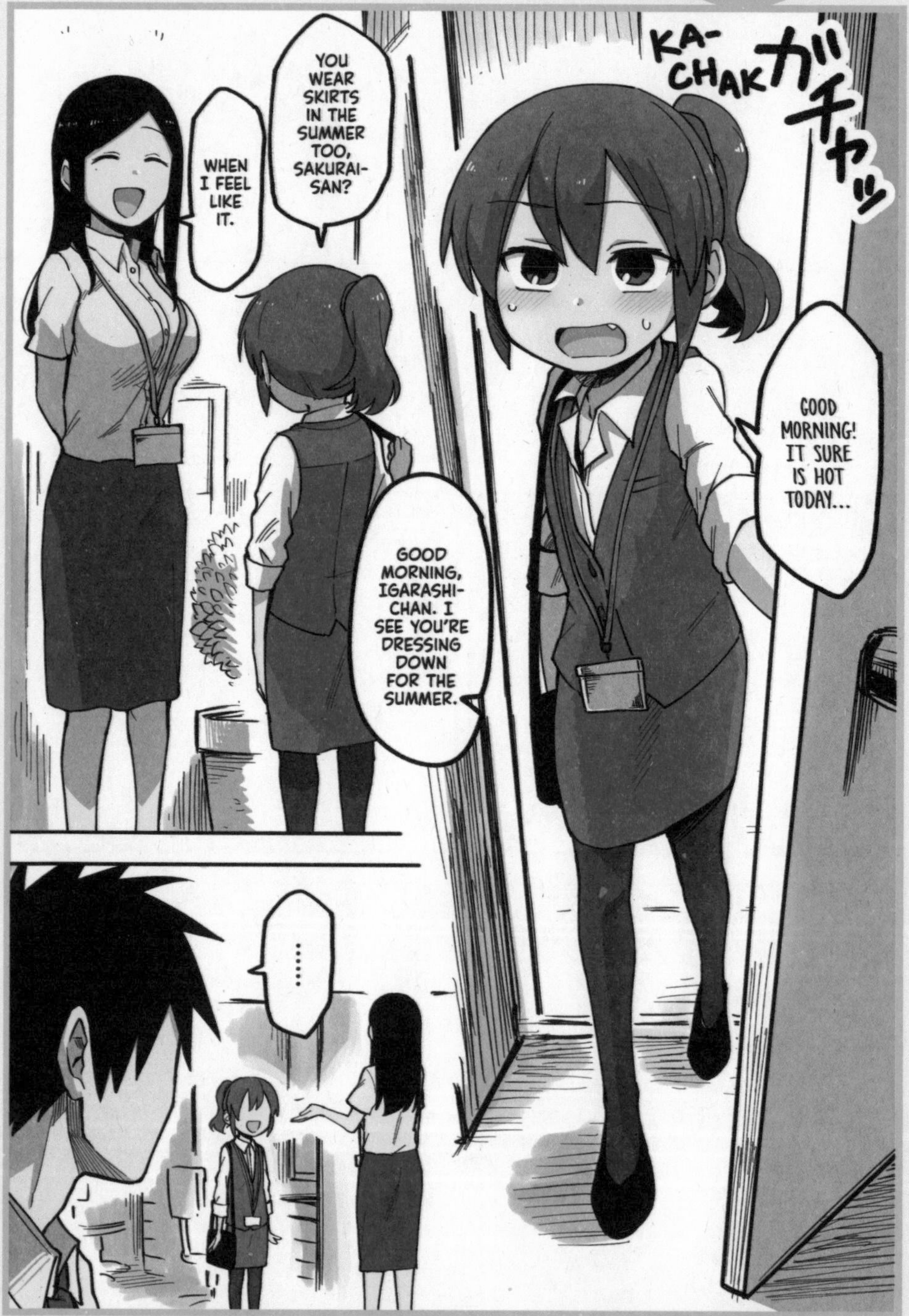
KA-CHAK
ガチャッ
GOOD MORNING! IT SURE IS HOT TODAY...
GOOD MORNING, IGARASHI-CHAN. I SEE YOU'RE DRESSING DOWN FOR THE SUMMER.
YOU WEAR SKIRTS IN THE SUMMER TOO, SAKURAI-SAN?
WHEN I FEEL LIKE IT.
......

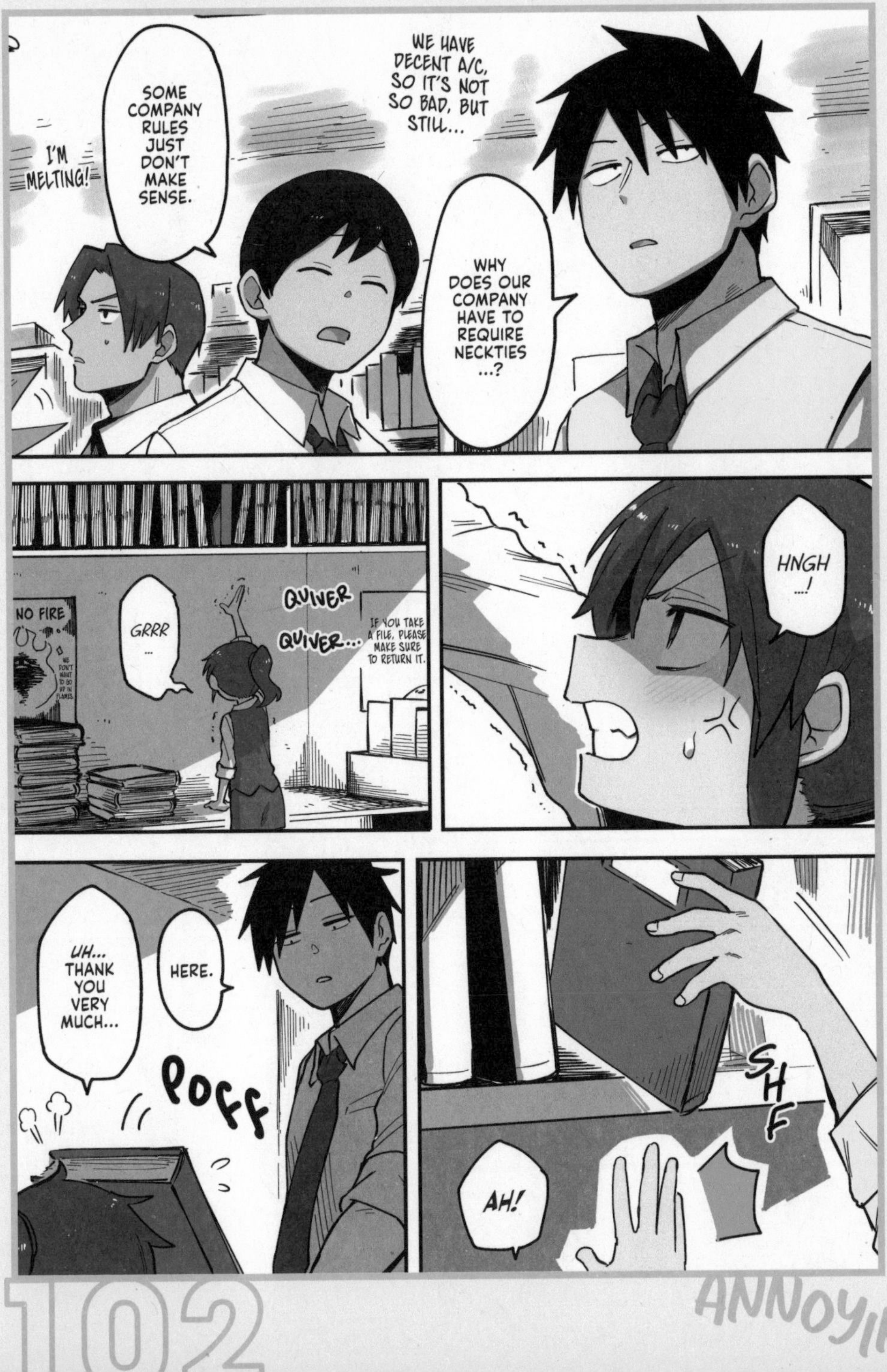

WHY DOES OUR COMPANY HAVE TO REQUIRE NECKTIES ...?
WE HAVE DECENT A/C, SO IT'S NOT SO BAD, BUT STILL...
SOME COMPANY RULES JUST DON'T MAKE SENSE.
I'M MELTING!
HNGH ...!
QUIVER
QUIVER...
IF YOU TAKE A FILE, PLEASE MAKE SURE TO RETURN IT.
GRRR ...
NO FIRE
WE DON'T WANT TO GO UP IN FLAMES.
SHF
AH!
HERE.
UH... THANK YOU VERY MUCH...
POFF

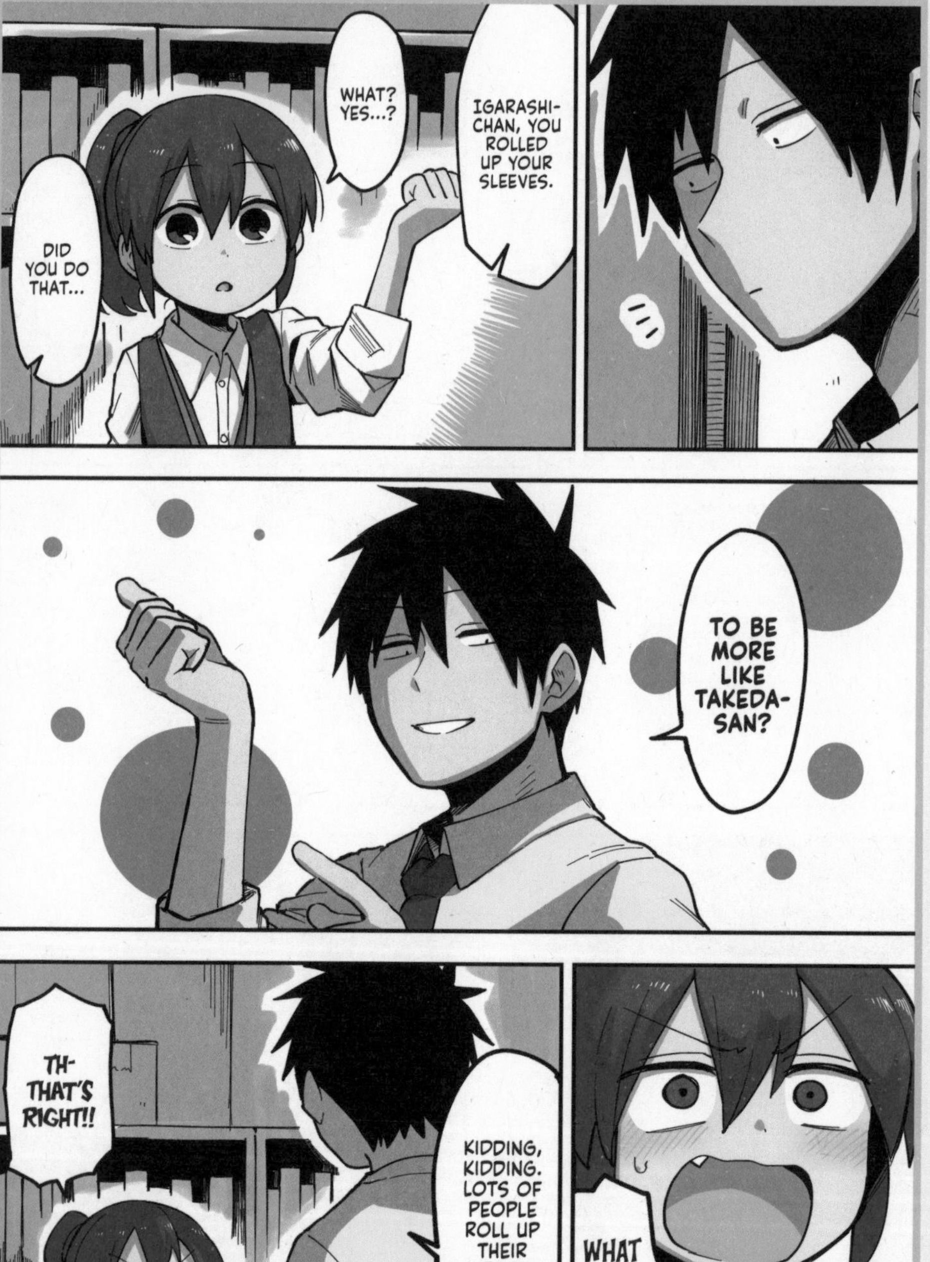
IGARASHI-CHAN, YOU ROLLED UP YOUR SLEEVES.
WHAT? YES...?
DID YOU DO THAT...
TO BE MORE LIKE TAKEDA-SAN?
WHAT ?!
KIDDING, KIDDING. LOTS OF PEOPLE ROLL UP THEIR SLEEVES.
TH-THAT'S RIGHT!!

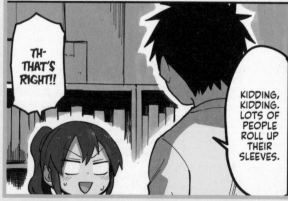

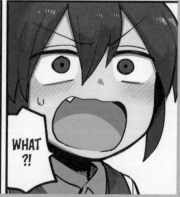

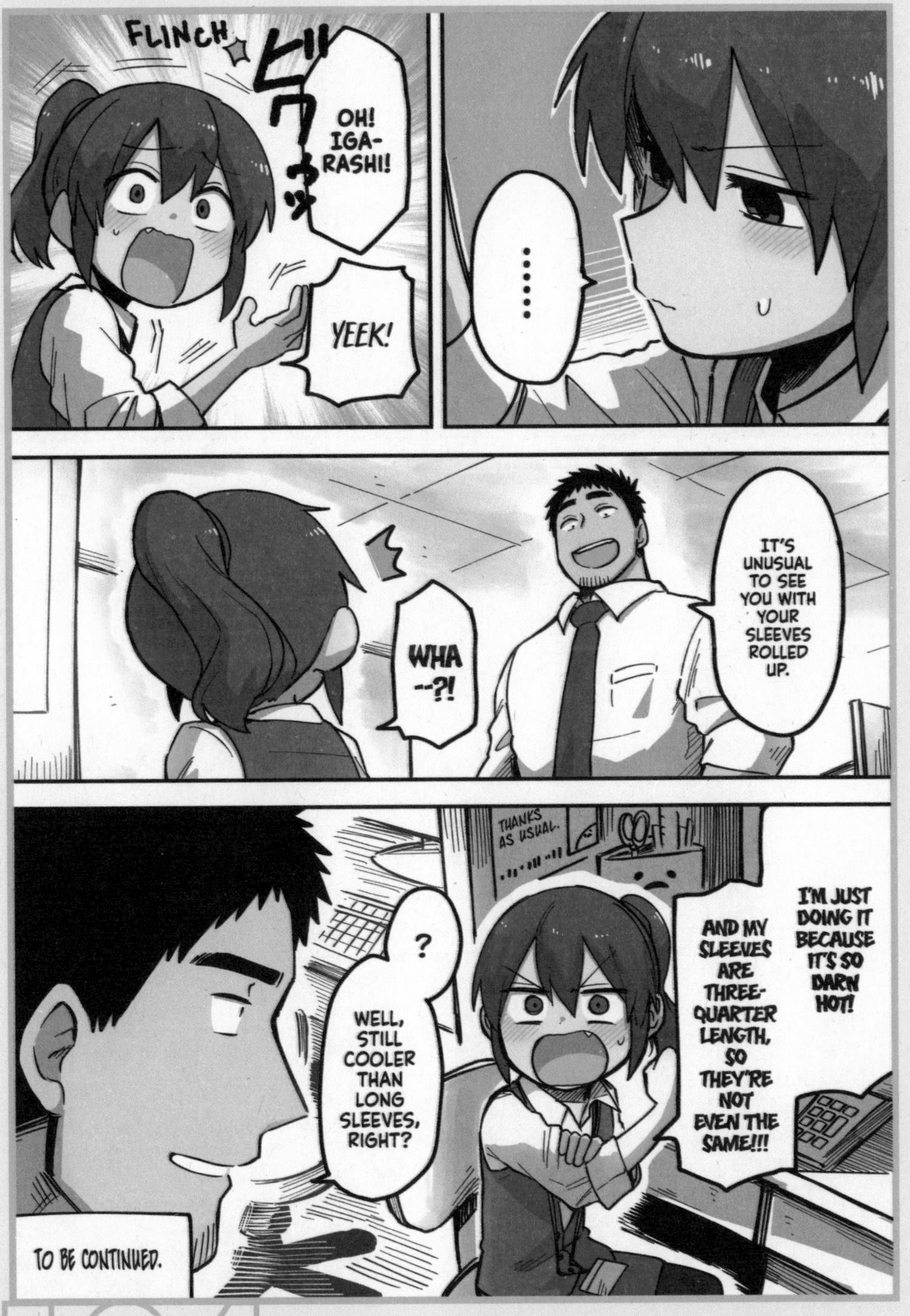
……
OH! IGA-RASHI!
ビクッ
FLINCH
YEEK!
IT'S UNUSUAL TO SEE YOU WITH YOUR SLEEVES ROLLED UP.
WHA--?!
I'M JUST DOING IT BECAUSE IT'S SO DARN HOT!
AND MY SLEEVES ARE THREE-QUARTER LENGTH, SO THEY'RE NOT EVEN THE SAME!!!
THANKS AS USUAL.
?
WELL, STILL COOLER THAN LONG SLEEVES, RIGHT?
TO BE CONTINUED.

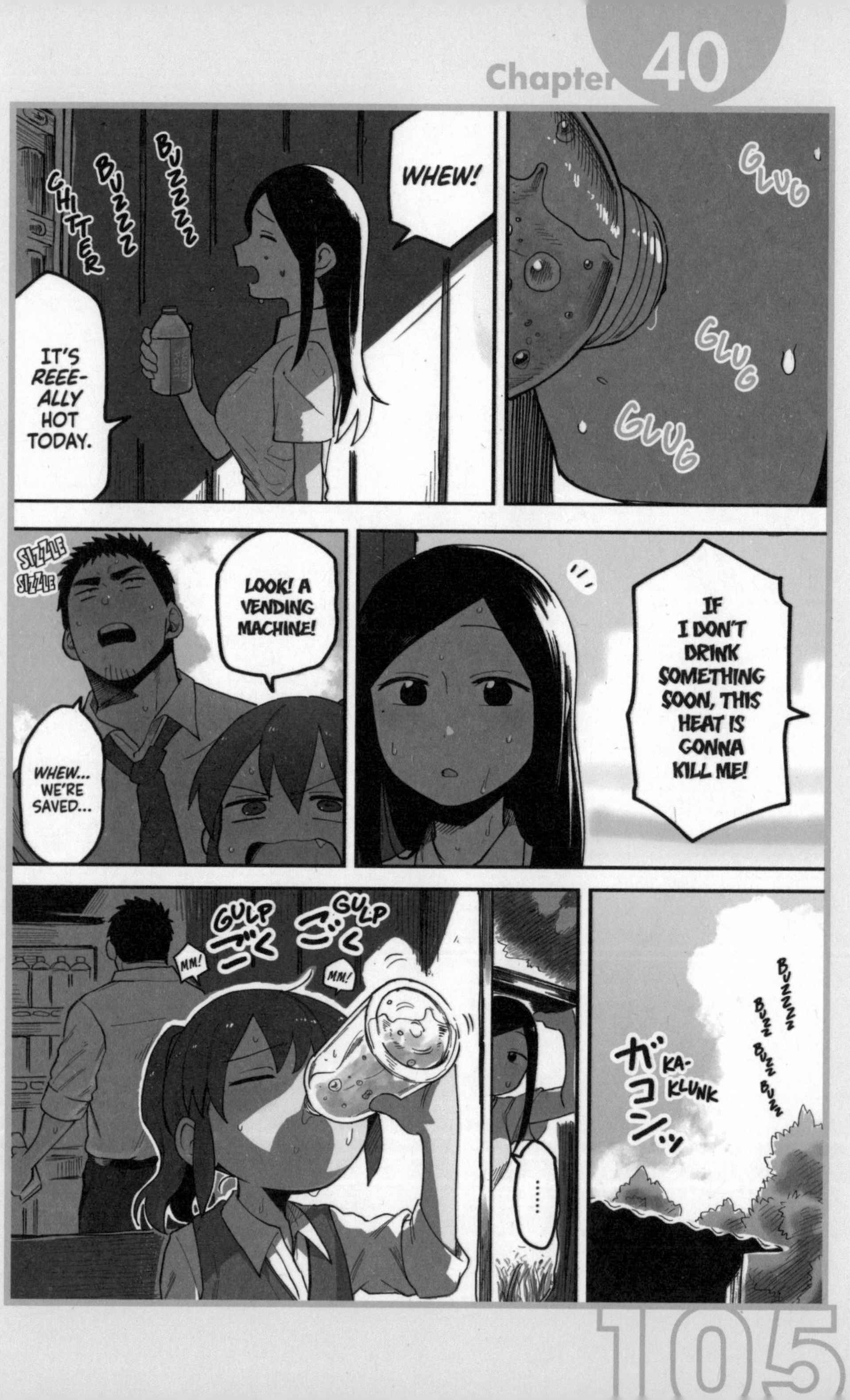
GLUG
GLUG
GLUG
WHEW!
BUZZZZ
BUZZZ
CHITTER
IT'S REEE-ALLY HOT TODAY.
IF I DON'T DRINK SOMETHING SOON, THIS HEAT IS GONNA KILL ME!
LOOK! A VENDING MACHINE!
SIZZLE
SIZZLE
WHEW... WE'RE SAVED...
BUZZZZ
BUZZ BUZZ BUZZ
ガコンッ
KA-KLUNK
......
GULP
ごく
GULP
ごく
MM!
MM!

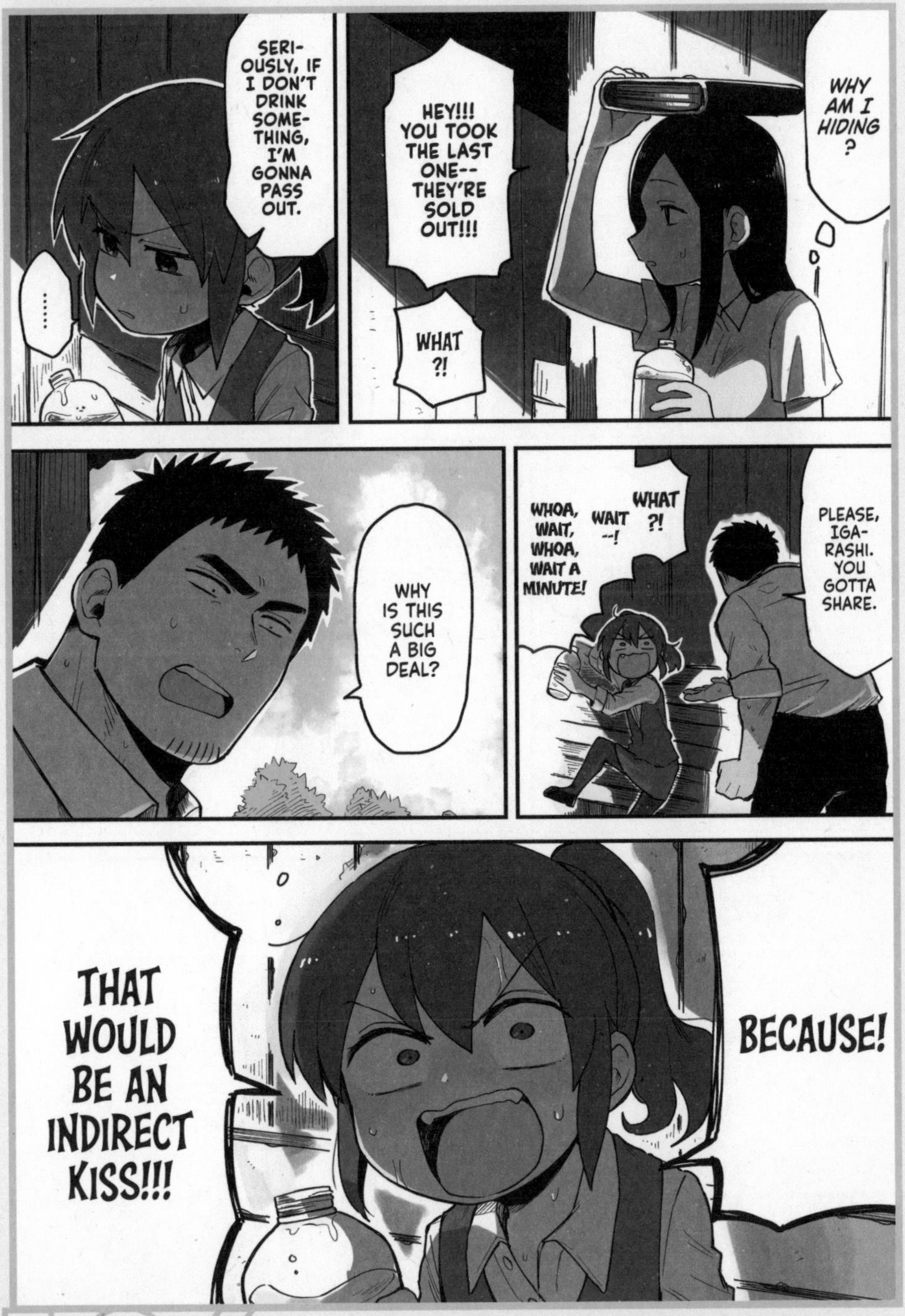
WHY AM I HIDING?
HEY!!! YOU TOOK THE LAST ONE--THEY'RE SOLD OUT!!!
WHAT?!
SERIOUSLY, IF I DON'T DRINK SOMETHING, I'M GONNA PASS OUT.
......
PLEASE, IGARASHI. YOU GOTTA SHARE.
WHAT?!
WAIT--!
WHOA, WAIT, WHOA, WAIT A MINUTE!
WHY IS THIS SUCH A BIG DEAL?
BECAUSE!
THAT WOULD BE AN INDIRECT KISS!!!

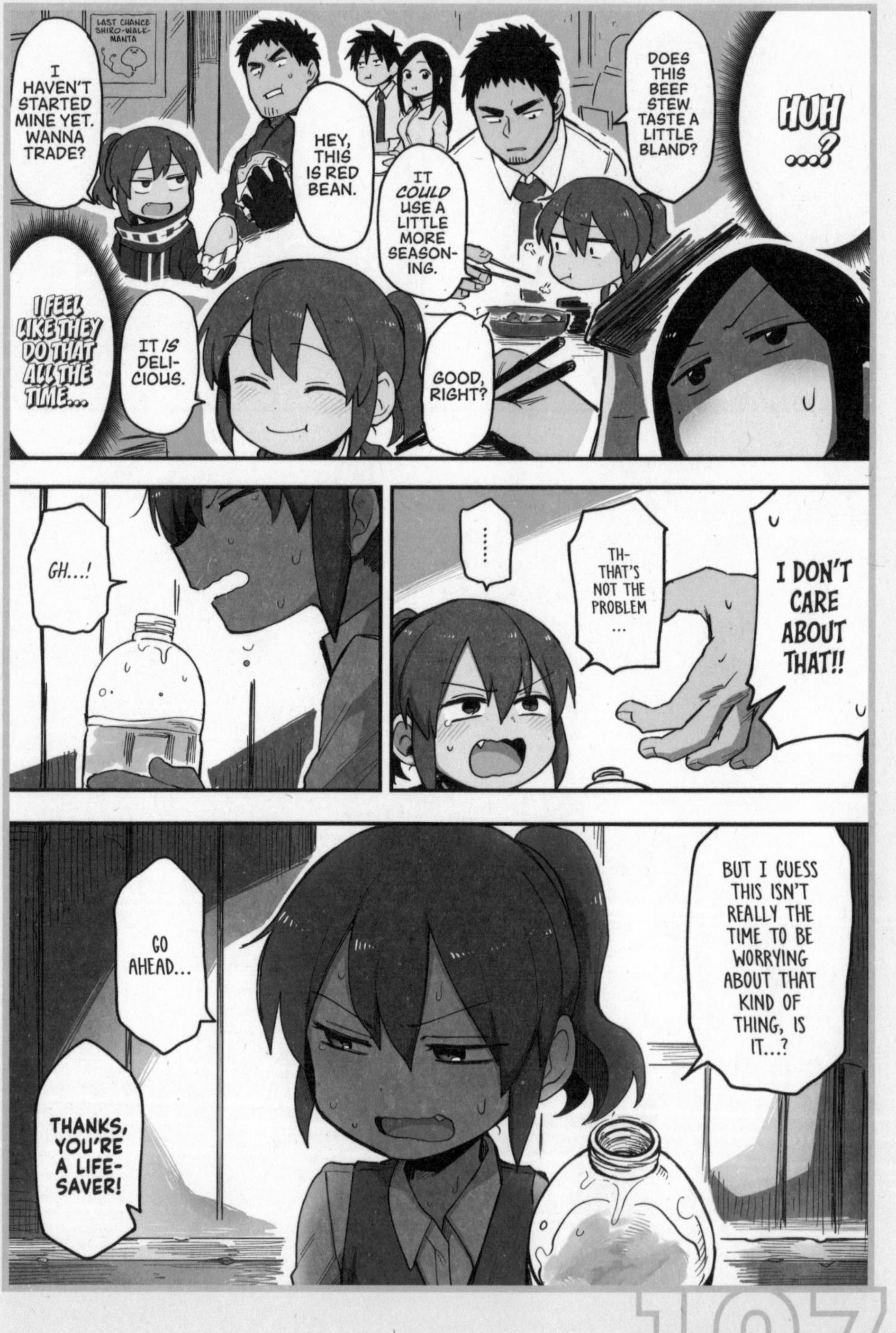
HUH ...?
DOES THIS BEEF STEW TASTE A LITTLE BLAND?
IT COULD USE A LITTLE MORE SEASON-ING.
HEY, THIS IS RED BEAN.
I HAVEN'T STARTED MINE YET. WANNA TRADE?
LAST CHANCE SHIRO-WALK-MANTA
GOOD, RIGHT?
IT IS DELI-CIOUS.
I FEEL LIKE THEY DO THAT ALL THE TIME...
I DON'T CARE ABOUT THAT!!
TH-THAT'S NOT THE PROBLEM ...
......
GH...!
BUT I GUESS THIS ISN'T REALLY THE TIME TO BE WORRYING ABOUT THAT KIND OF THING, IS IT...?
GO AHEAD...
THANKS, YOU'RE A LIFE-SAVER!

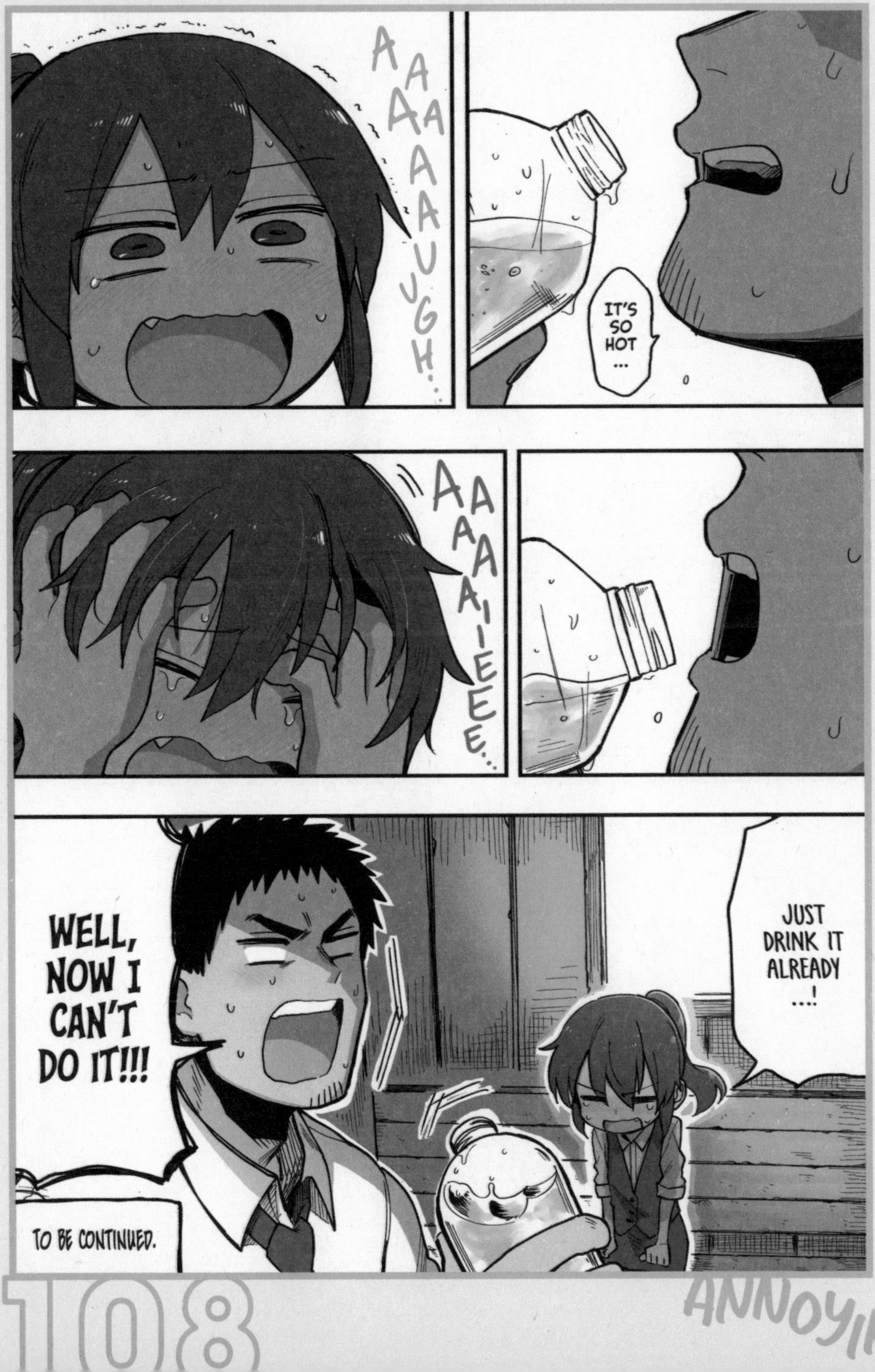
IT'S SO HOT ...
AAAAAAAUGH...
AAAAAAIEEEEE...
JUST DRINK IT ALREADY ...!
WELL, NOW I CAN'T DO IT!!!
TO BE CONTINUED.

P. 94, panel 5 - Koishi/Ooishi
Koishi means "little stone," and *Ooishi* means "big stone."
In other words, Igarashi is calling him small.

P. 97, panel 2 - Kyomu Neko
Kyomu means "nothingness" or "nihility," and *neko* means "cat,"
so Kyomu Neko is a nihilist cat.

P. 101, panel 3 - Dressing down for summer
The Japanese government started a campaign in 2005,
called Cool Biz, that introduced a more liberal dress code
for the summer to reduce air conditioning use.

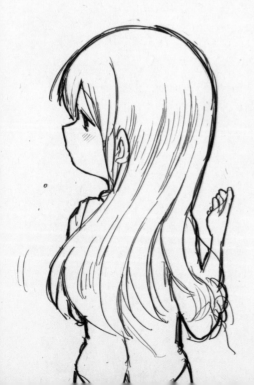

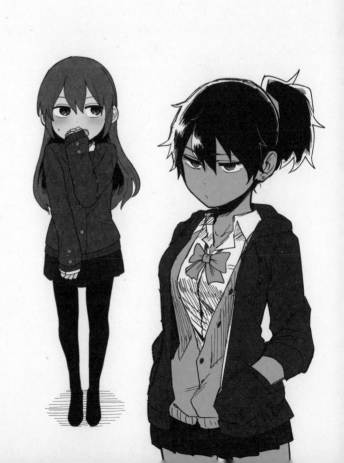

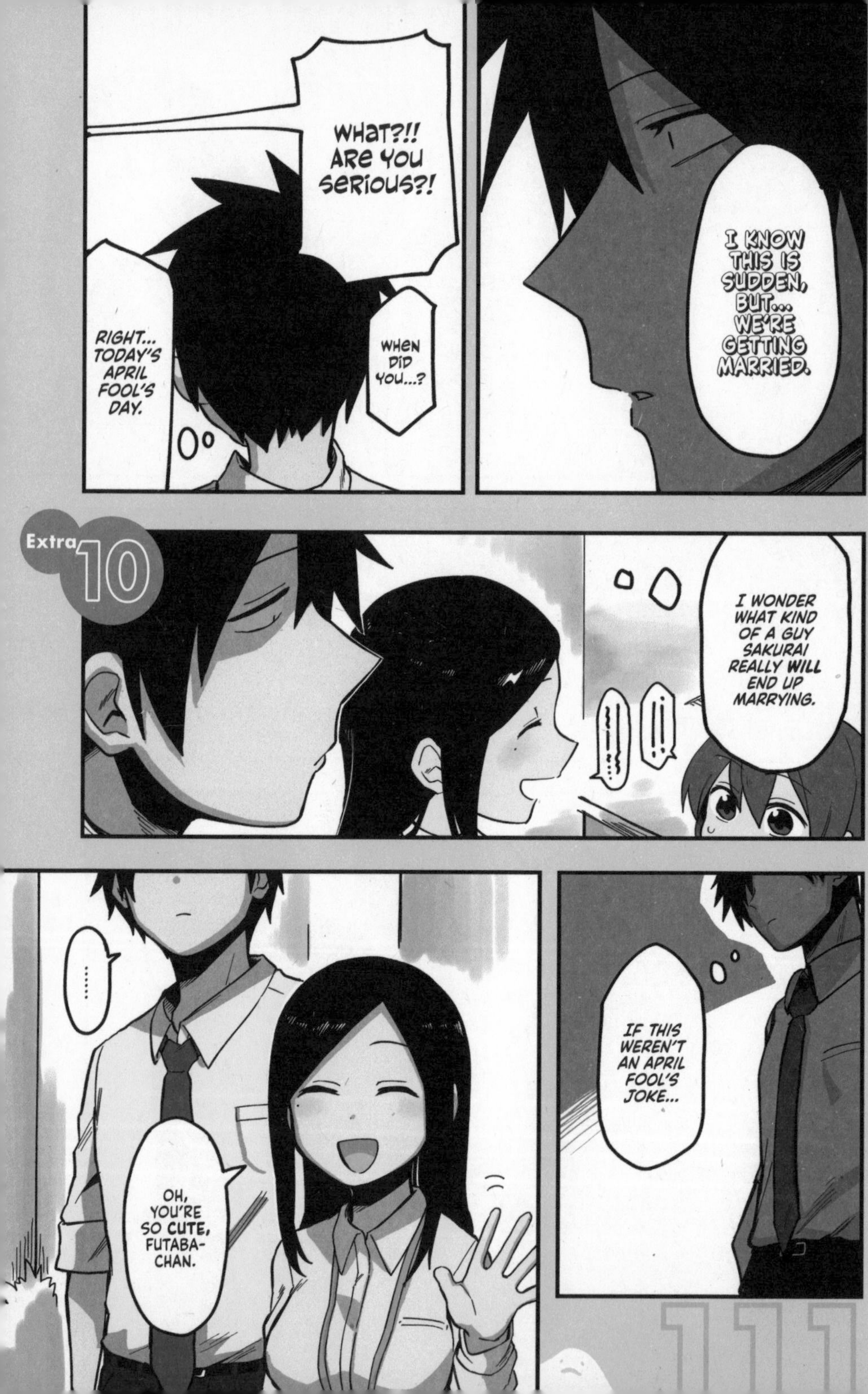
I KNOW THIS IS SUDDEN, BUT... WE'RE GETTING MARRIED.
WHAT?!! ARE YOU SERIOUS?!
WHEN DID YOU...?
RIGHT... TODAY'S APRIL FOOL'S DAY.
Extra 10
I WONDER WHAT KIND OF A GUY SAKURAI REALLY WILL END UP MARRYING.
IF THIS WEREN'T AN APRIL FOOL'S JOKE...
......
OH, YOU'RE SO CUTE, FUTABA-CHAN.

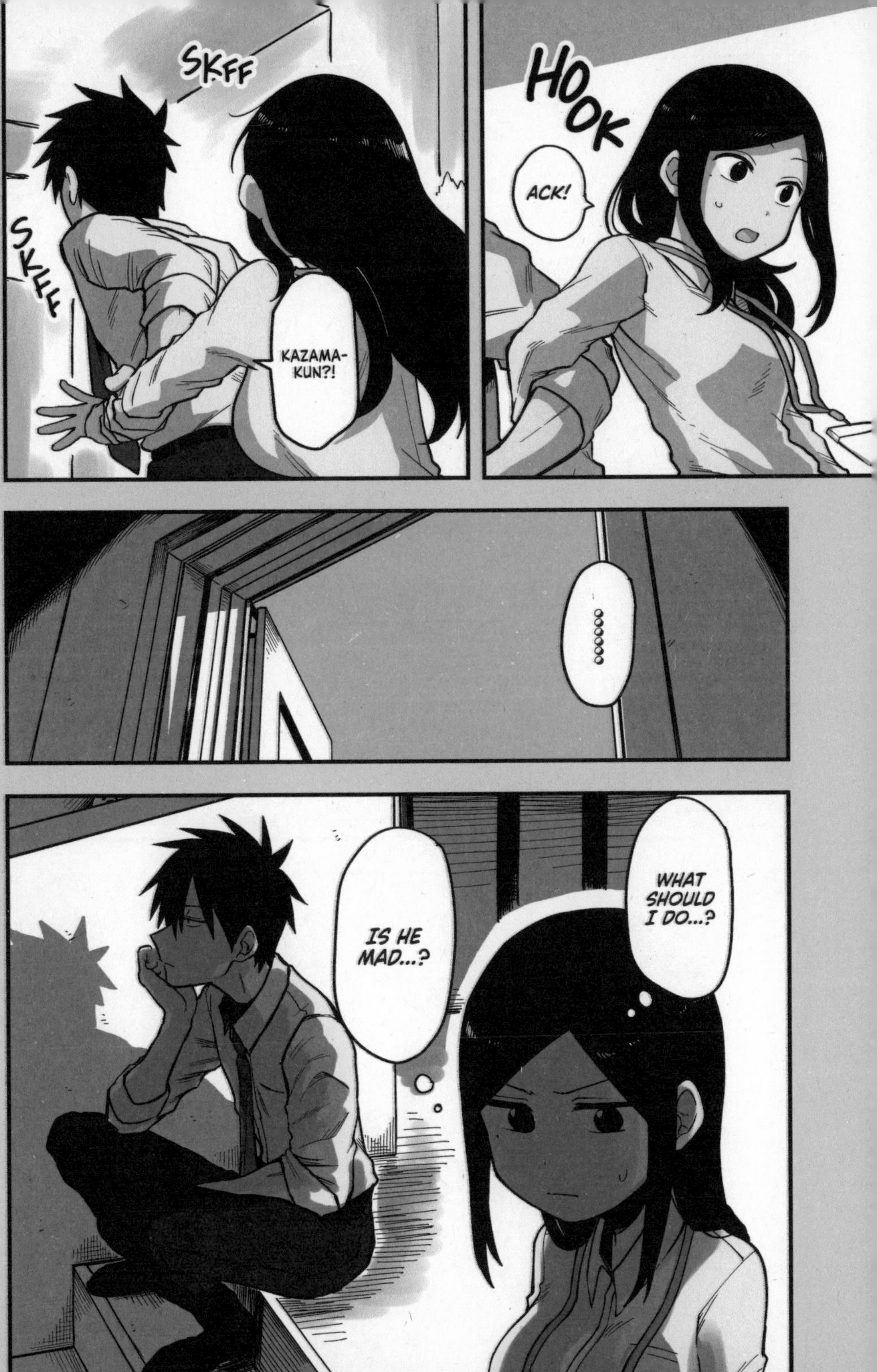
HOOK
ACK!
SKFF
SKFF
KAZAMA-KUN?!
......
WHAT SHOULD I DO...?
IS HE MAD...?

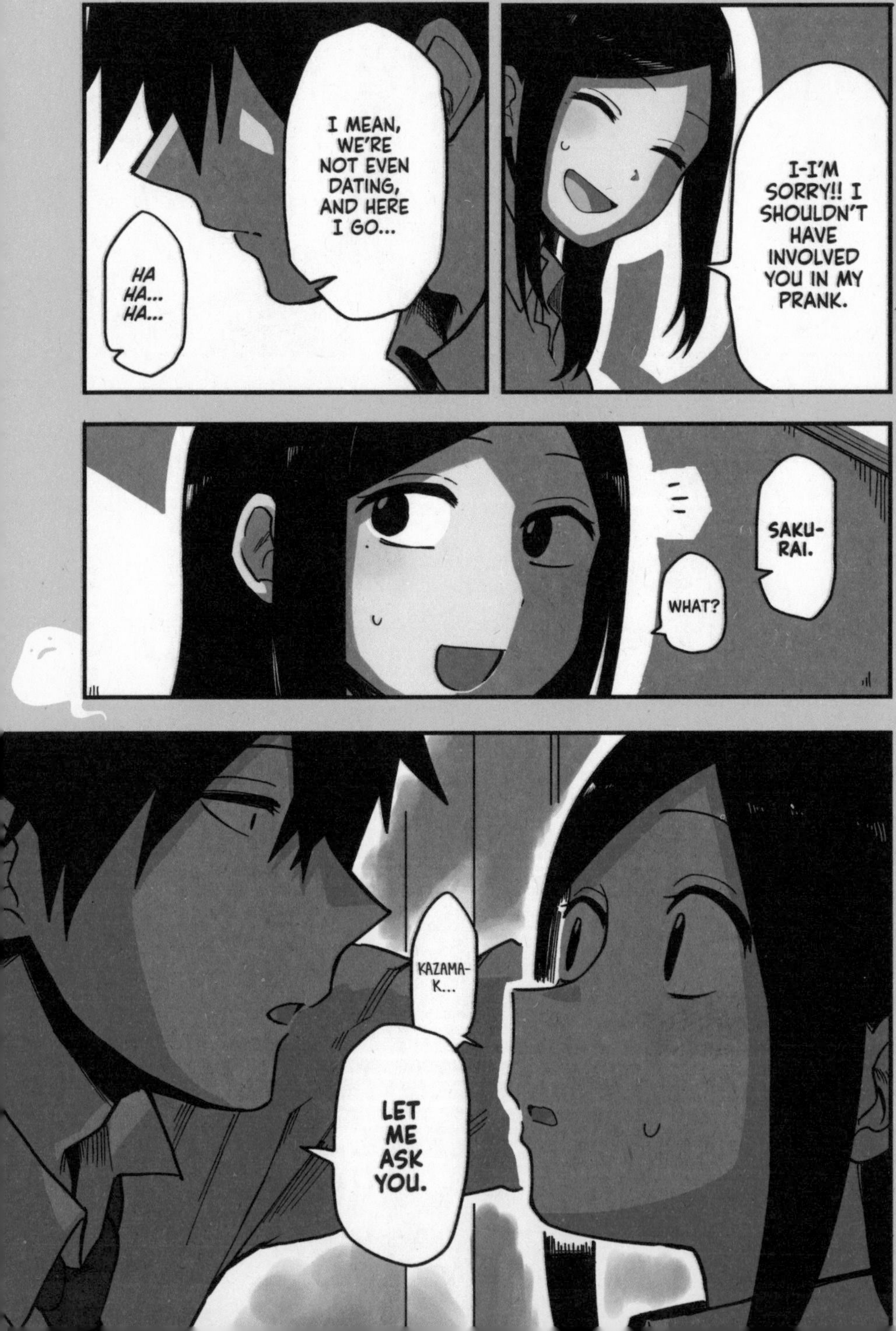
I-I'M SORRY!! I SHOULDN'T HAVE INVOLVED YOU IN MY PRANK.
I MEAN, WE'RE NOT EVEN DATING, AND HERE I GO...
HA HA... HA...
SAKU-RAI.
WHAT?
KAZAMA-K...
LET ME ASK YOU.

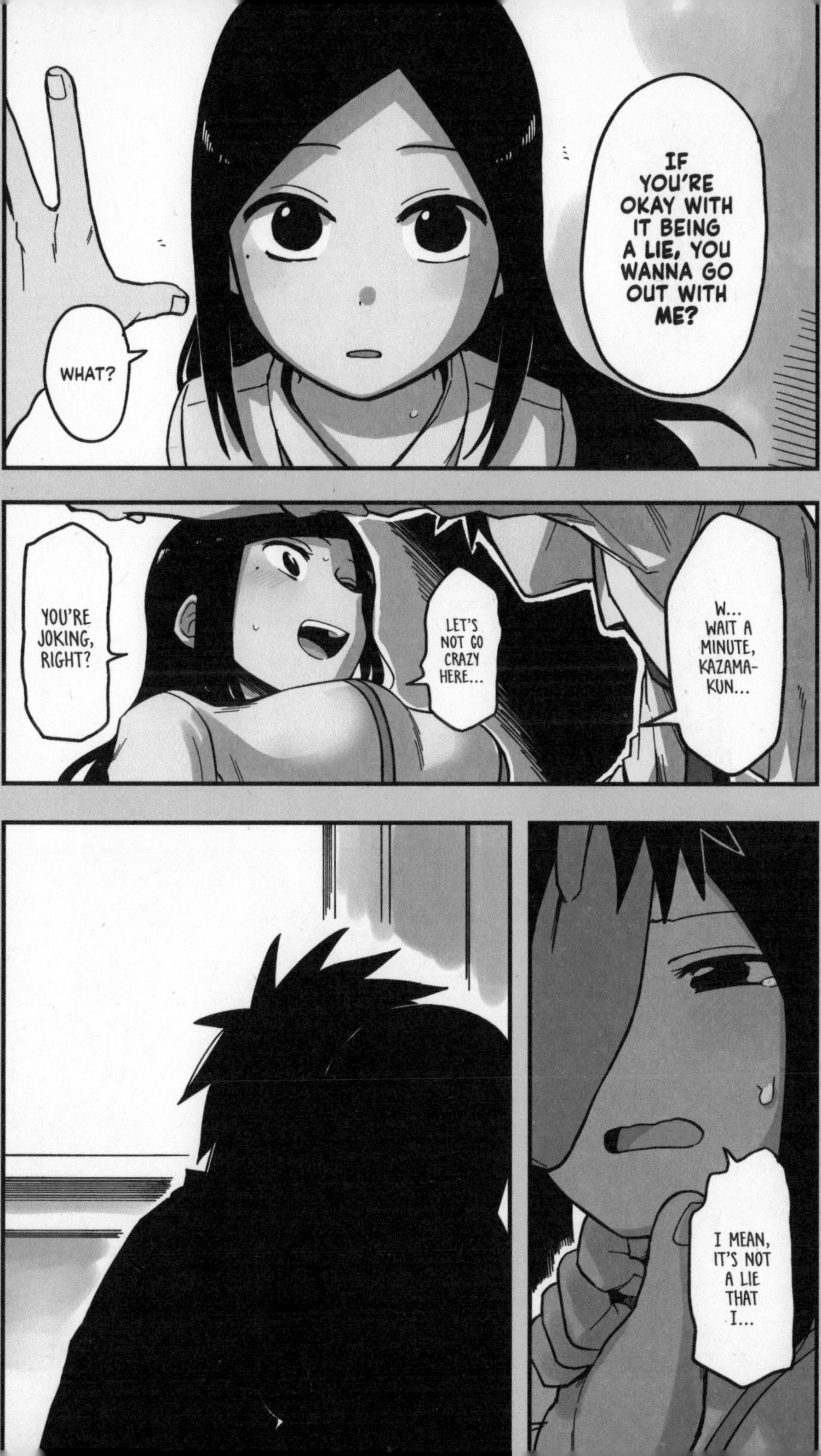
IF YOU'RE OKAY WITH IT BEING A LIE, YOU WANNA GO OUT WITH ME?
WHAT?
W... WAIT A MINUTE, KAZAMA-KUN...
LET'S NOT GO CRAZY HERE...
YOU'RE JOKING, RIGHT?
I MEAN, IT'S NOT A LIE THAT I...

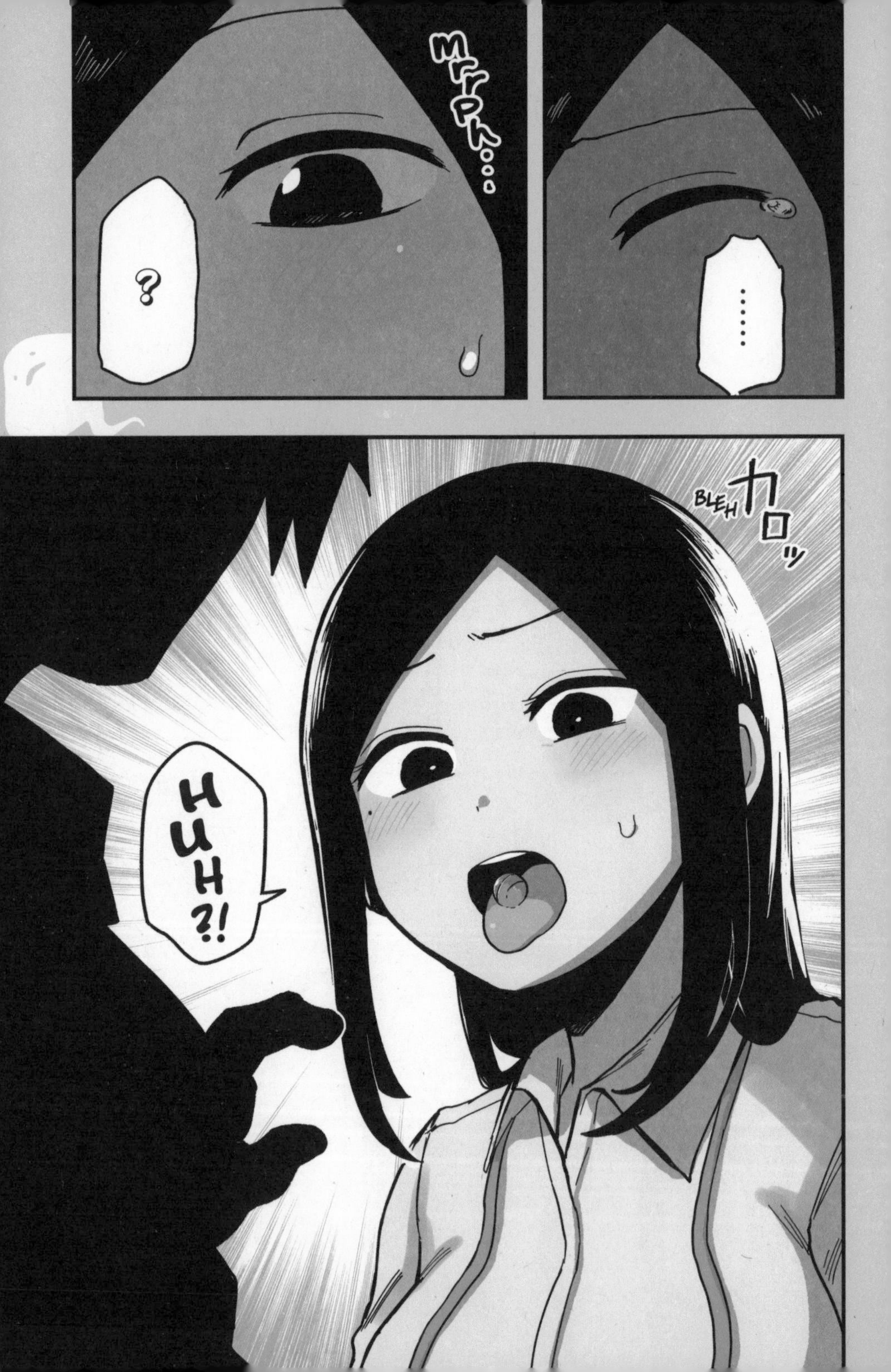
......
Mrrph...
?
BLEH
カロッ
HUH?!

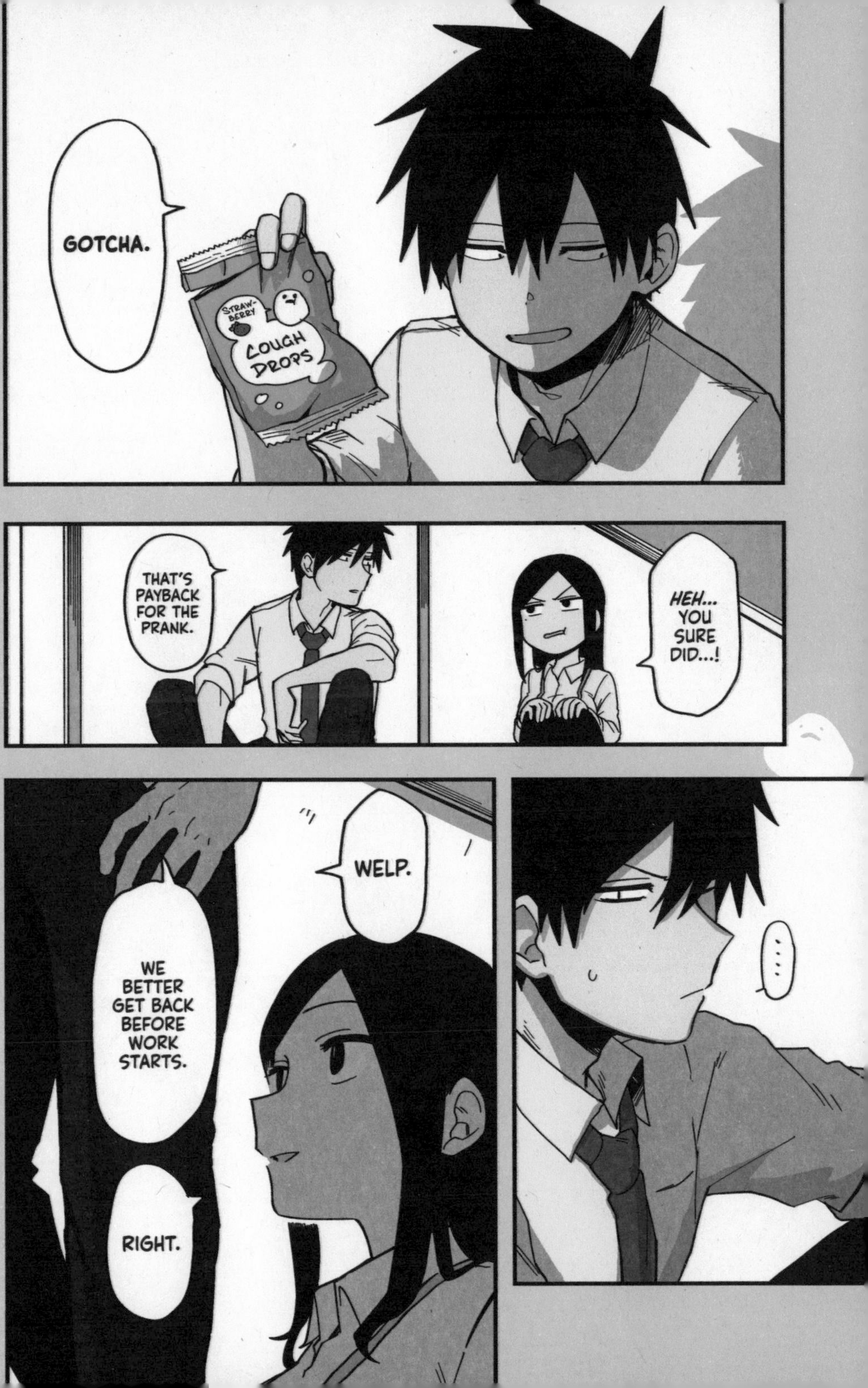
GOTCHA.
STRAW-BERRY
COUGH DROPS
HEH... YOU SURE DID...!
THAT'S PAYBACK FOR THE PRANK.
....
WELP.
WE BETTER GET BACK BEFORE WORK STARTS.
RIGHT.

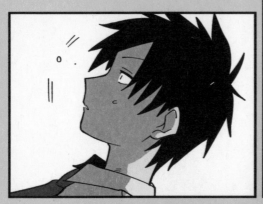

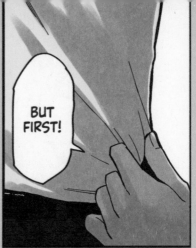

BUT FIRST!

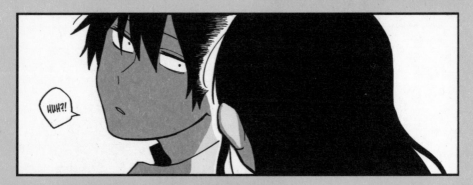

HUH?!

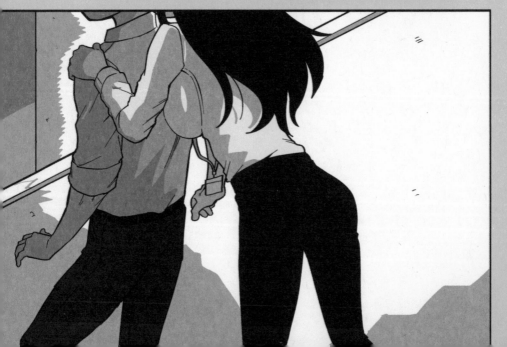

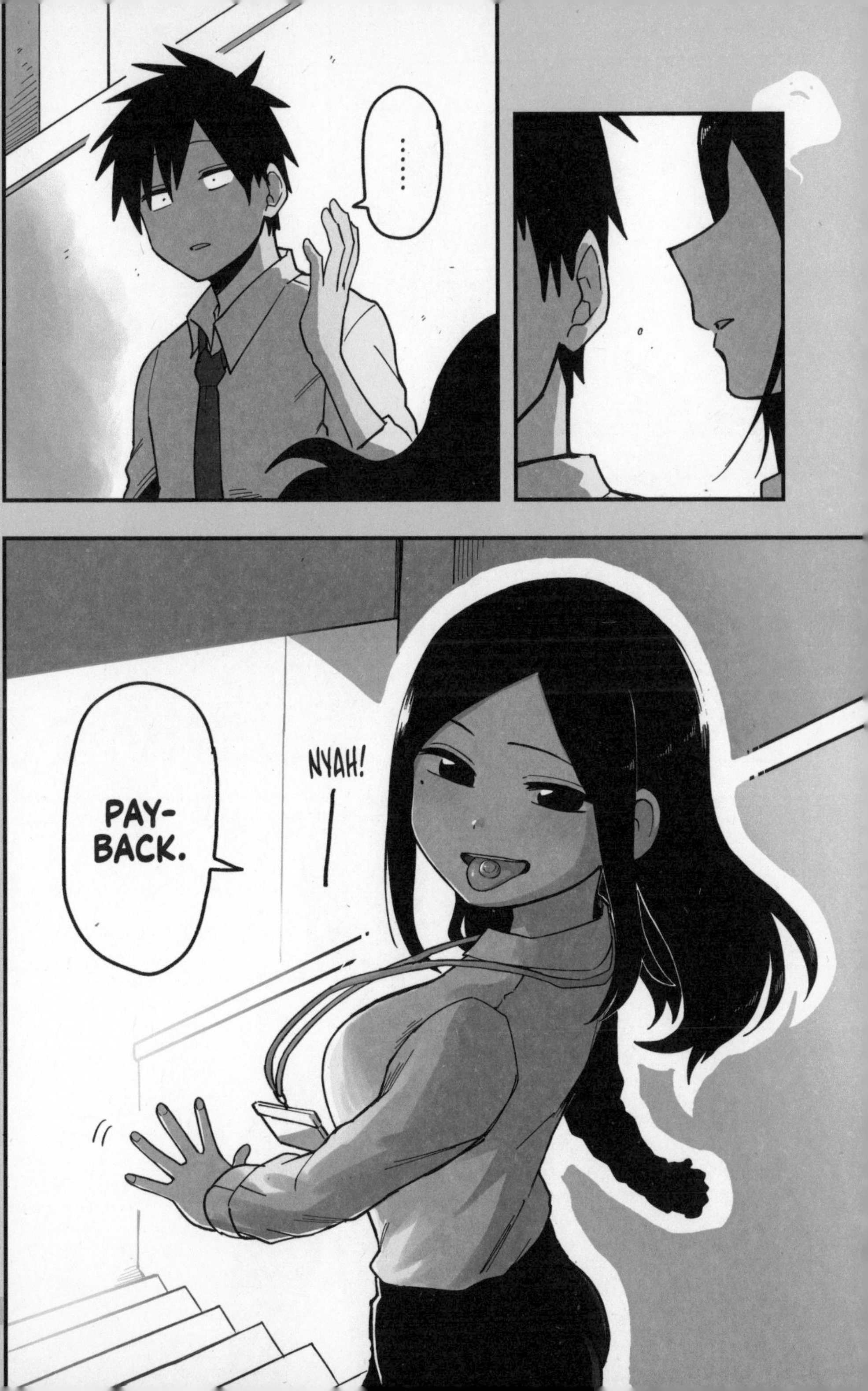
......
NYAH!
PAY-BACK.

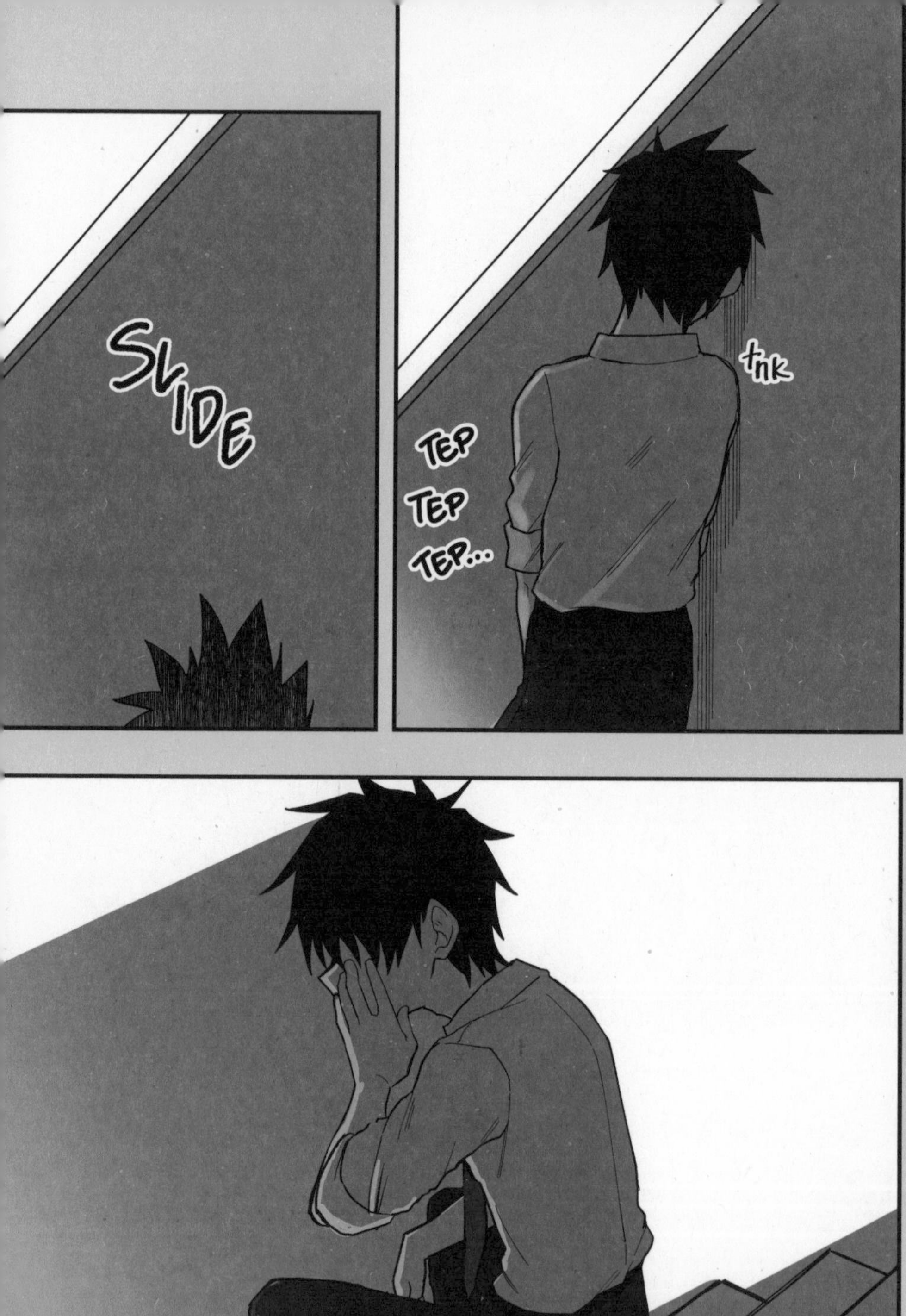
tnk
TEP
TEP
TEP...
SLIDE

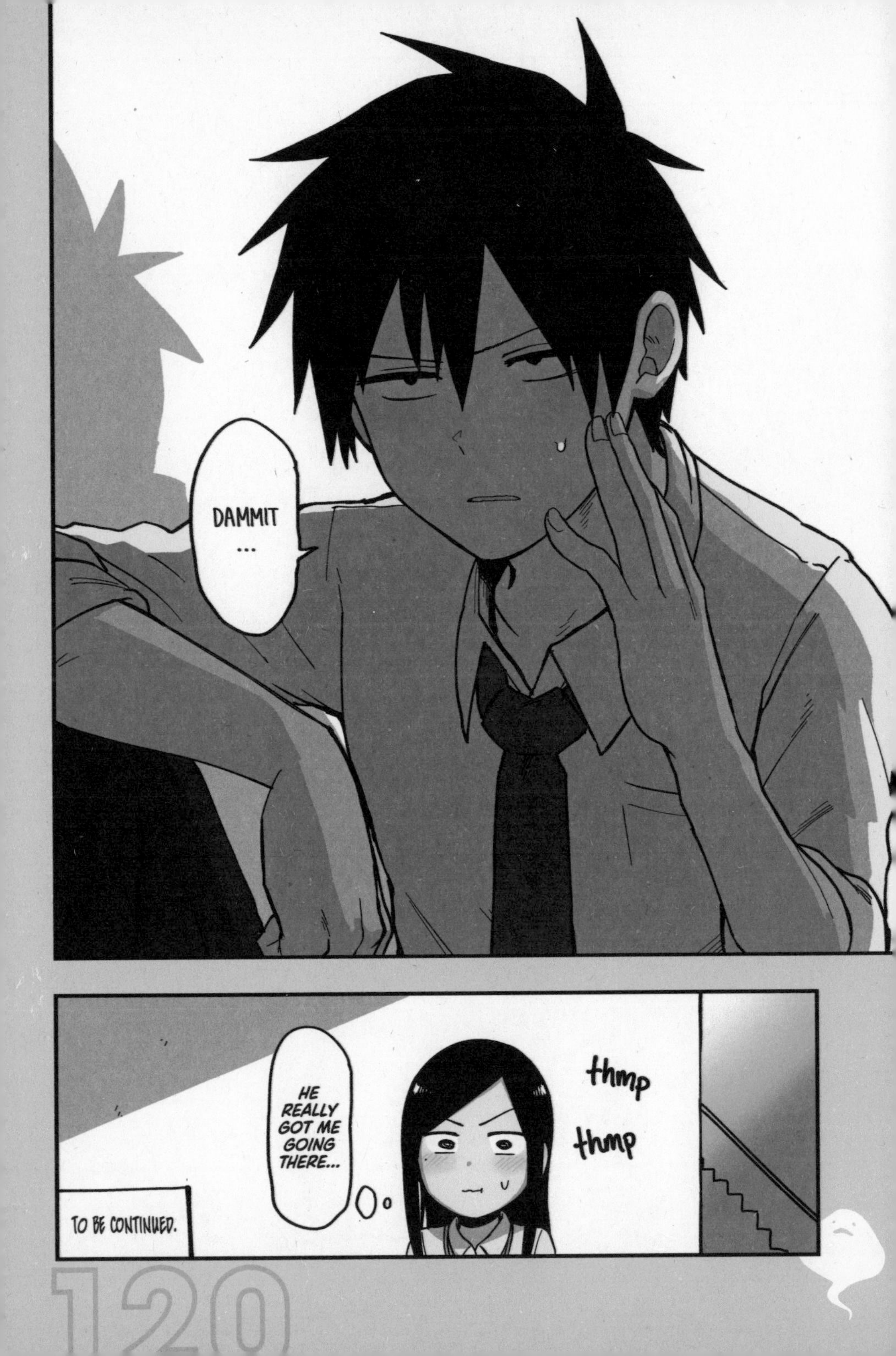
DAMMIT ...
thmp
thmp
HE REALLY GOT ME GOING THERE...
TO BE CONTINUED.

120

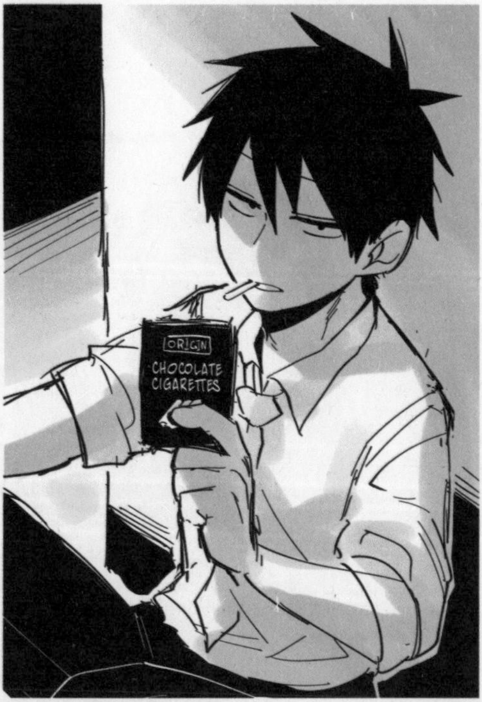
ORIGIN
CHOCOLATE CIGARETTES

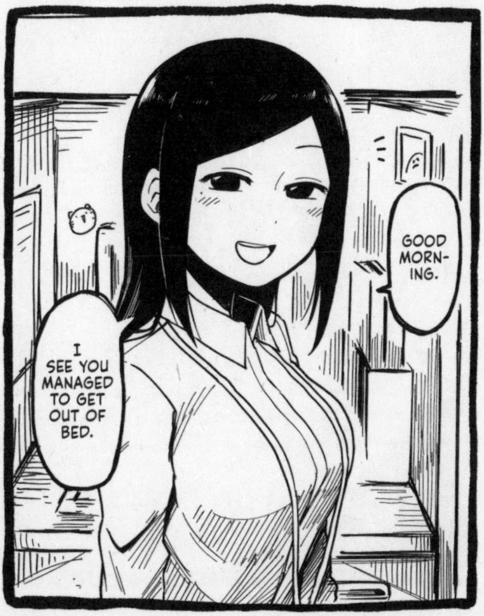
GOOD MORNING.
I SEE YOU MANAGED TO GET OUT OF BED.

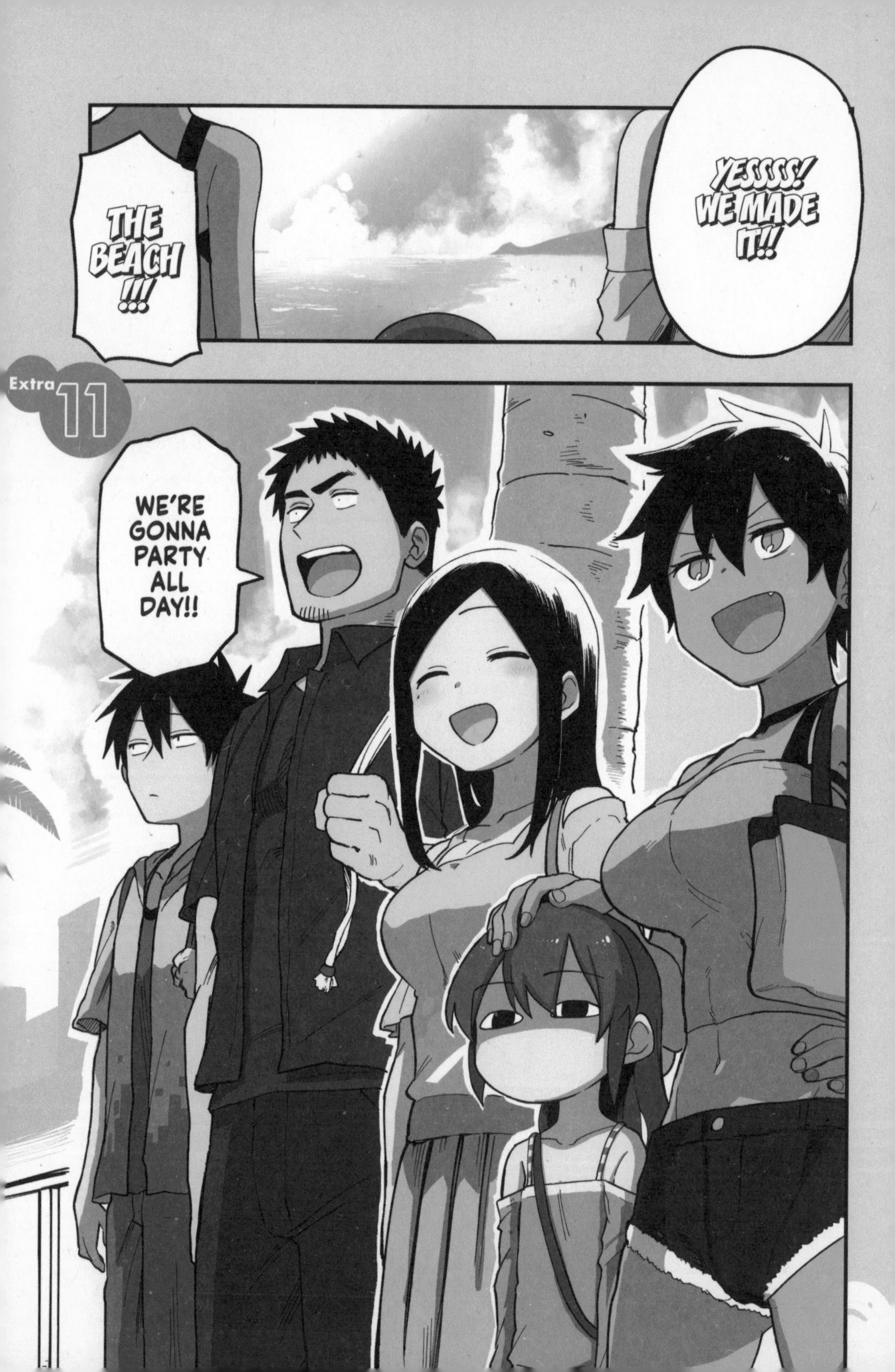
YESSSS! WE MADE IT!!
THE BEACH!!!
Extra 11
WE'RE GONNA PARTY ALL DAY!!

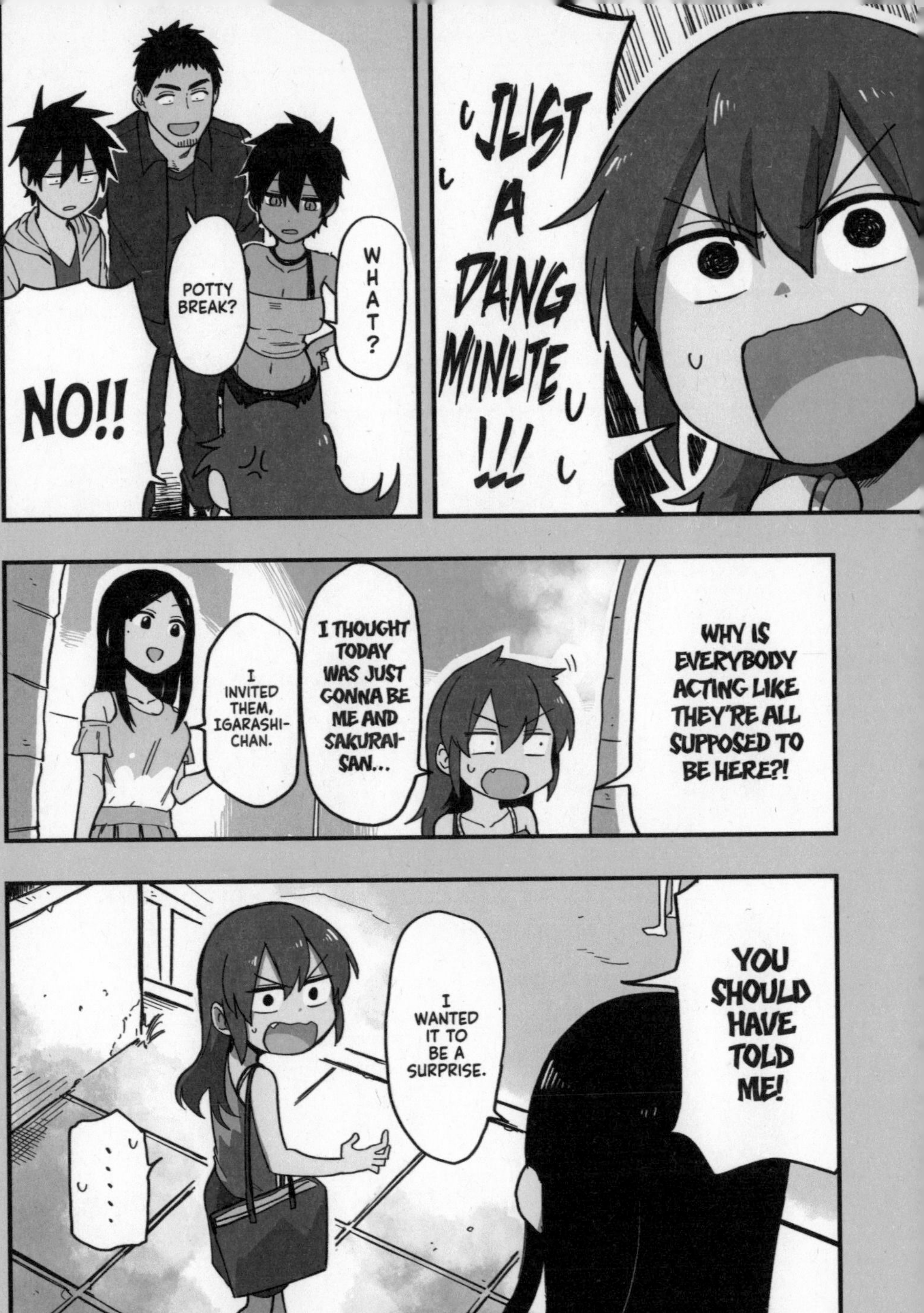

JUST A DANG MINUTE!!!
WHAT?
POTTY BREAK?
NO!!
WHY IS EVERYBODY ACTING LIKE THEY'RE ALL SUPPOSED TO BE HERE?!
I THOUGHT TODAY WAS JUST GONNA BE ME AND SAKURAI-SAN...
I INVITED THEM, IGARASHI-CHAN.
YOU SHOULD HAVE TOLD ME!
I WANTED IT TO BE A SURPRISE.
......

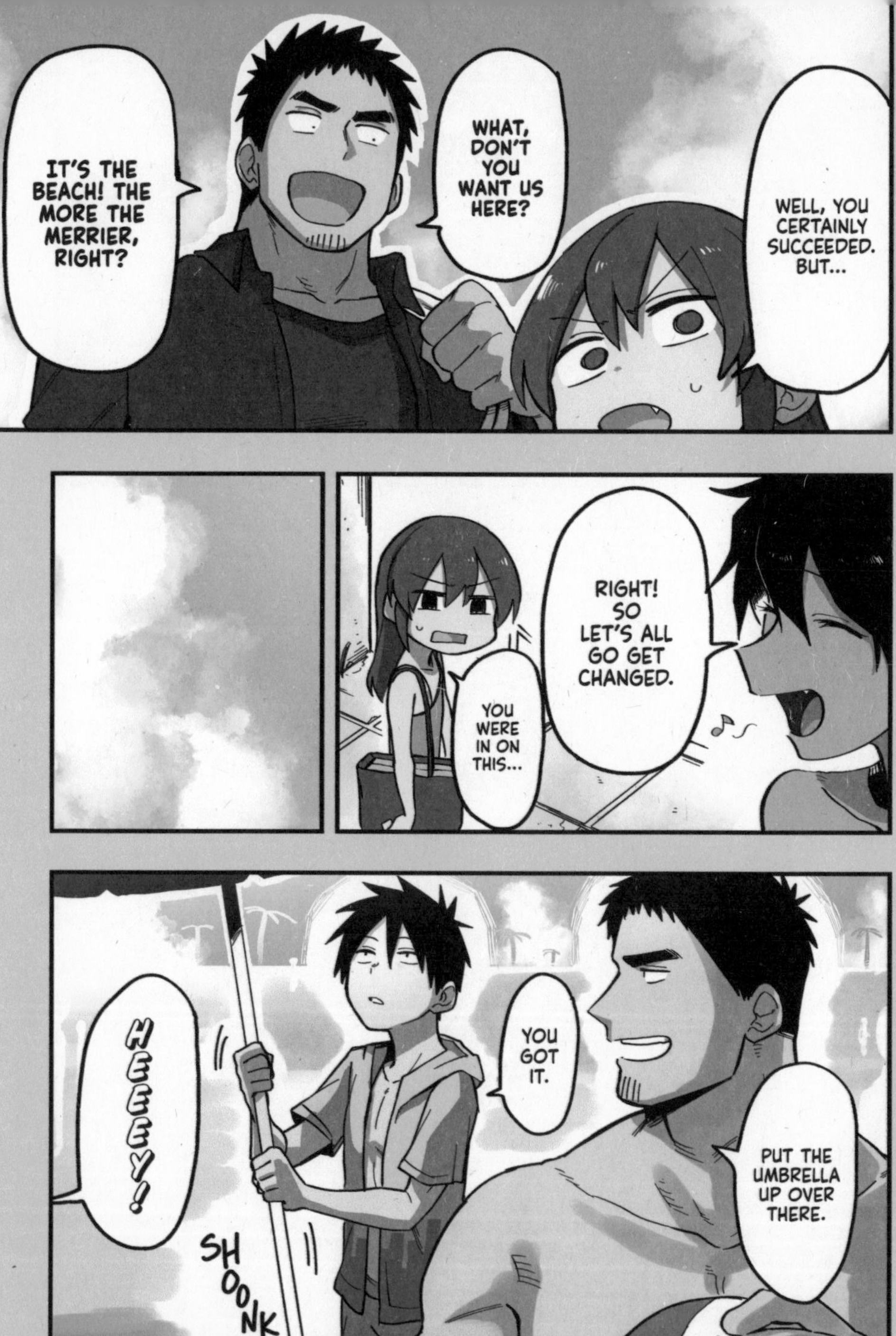
WELL, YOU CERTAINLY SUCCEEDED. BUT...
WHAT, DON'T YOU WANT US HERE?
IT'S THE BEACH! THE MORE THE MERRIER, RIGHT?
RIGHT! SO LET'S ALL GO GET CHANGED.
YOU WERE IN ON THIS...
PUT THE UMBRELLA UP OVER THERE.
YOU GOT IT.
HEEEEY!
SHOONK

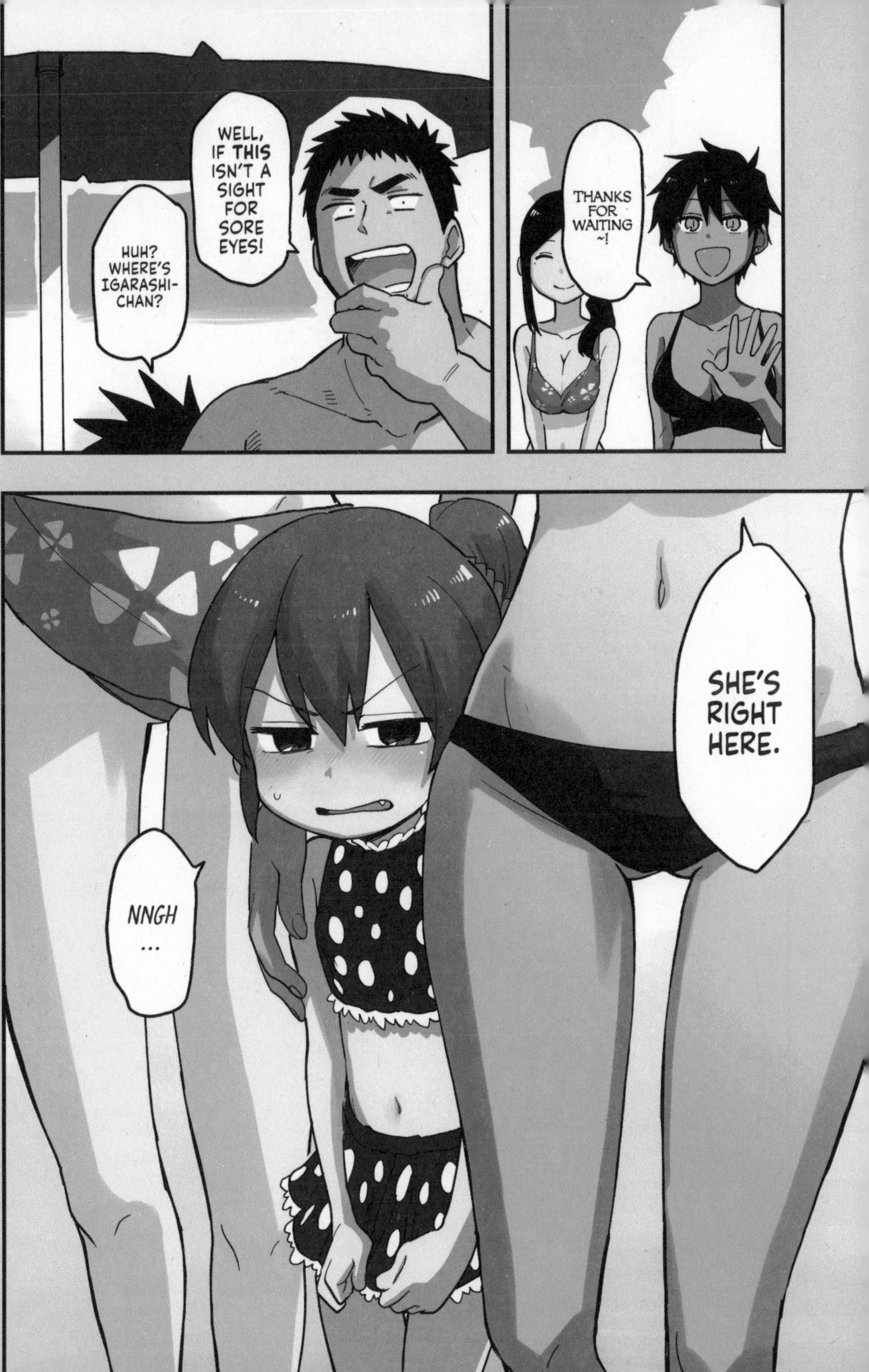
THANKS FOR WAITING ~!
WELL, IF THIS ISN'T A SIGHT FOR SORE EYES!
HUH? WHERE'S IGARASHI-CHAN?
SHE'S RIGHT HERE.
NNGH ...

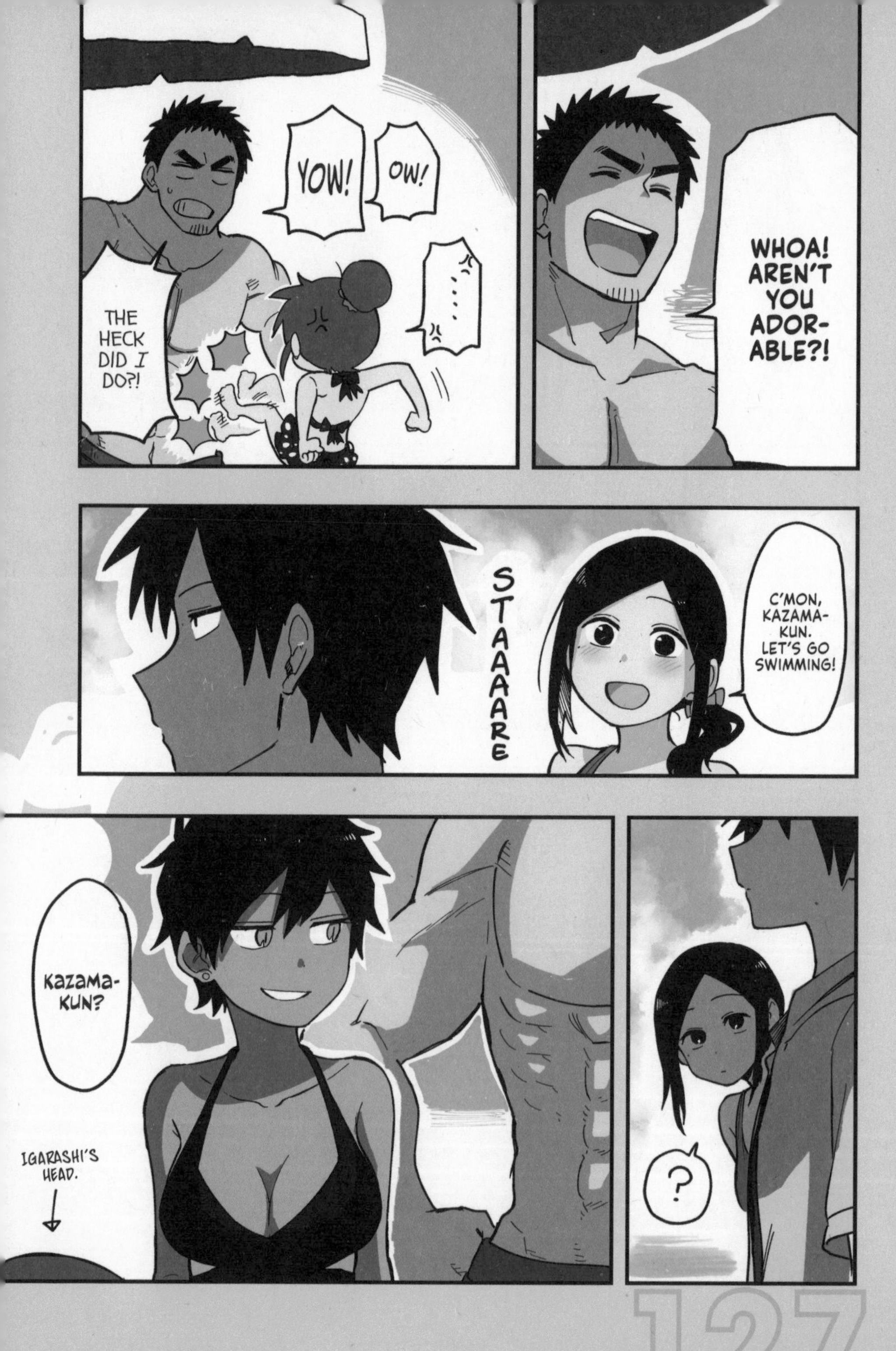
WHOA! AREN'T YOU ADORABLE?!
OW!
YOW!
……
THE HECK DID I DO?!
C'MON, KAZAMA-KUN. LET'S GO SWIMMING!
STAAAARE
?
KAZAMA-KUN?
IGARASHI'S HEAD.

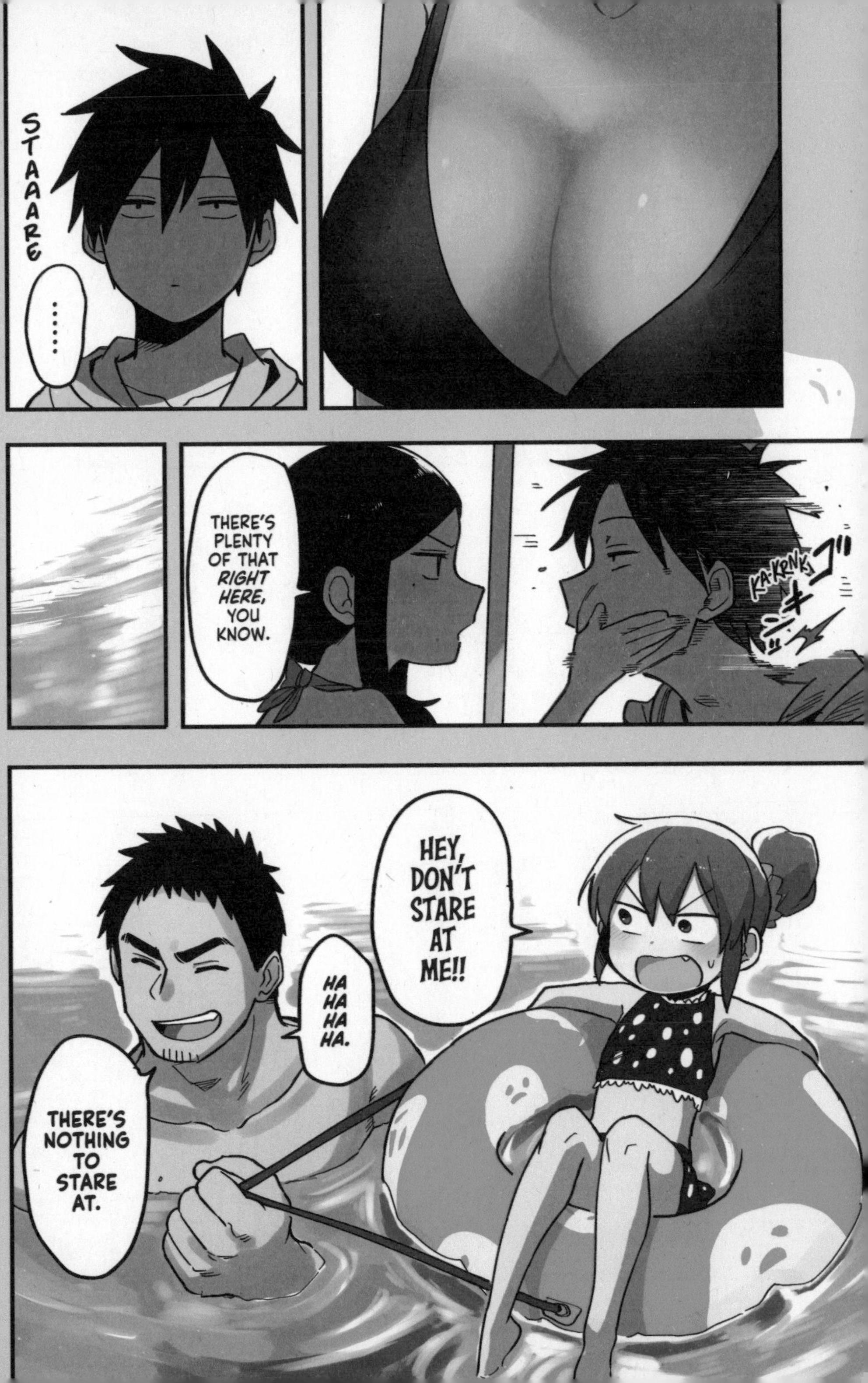
STAAAARE
......
KA-KRNK!
THERE'S PLENTY OF THAT *RIGHT HERE*, YOU KNOW.
HEY, DON'T STARE AT ME!!
HA HA HA HA HA.
THERE'S NOTHING TO STARE AT.

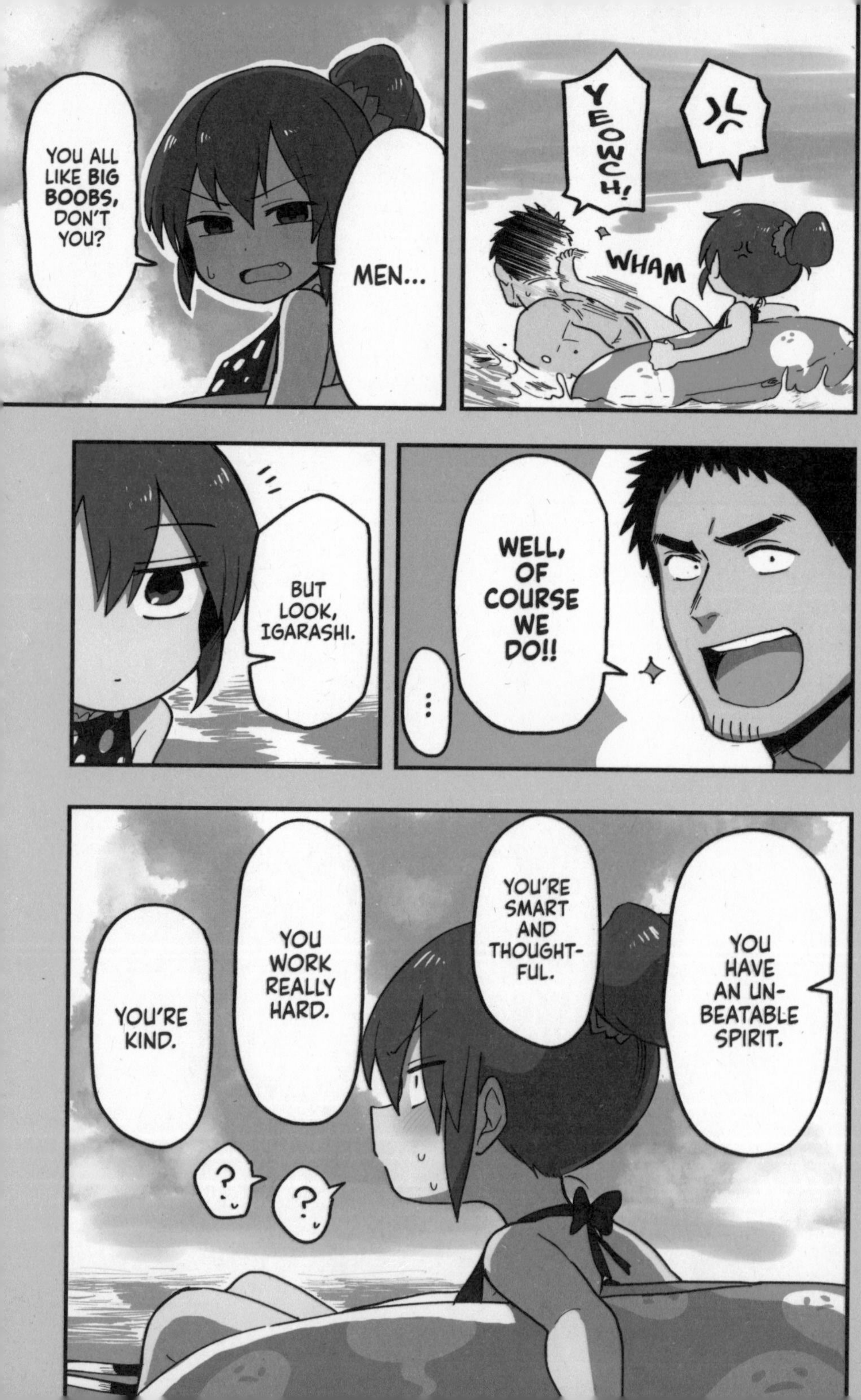
YEOWCH!
WHAM
MEN...
YOU ALL LIKE BIG BOOBS, DON'T YOU?
WELL, OF COURSE WE DO!!
...
BUT LOOK, IGARASHI.
YOU HAVE AN UN-BEATABLE SPIRIT.
YOU'RE SMART AND THOUGHT-FUL.
YOU WORK REALLY HARD.
YOU'RE KIND.
?
?

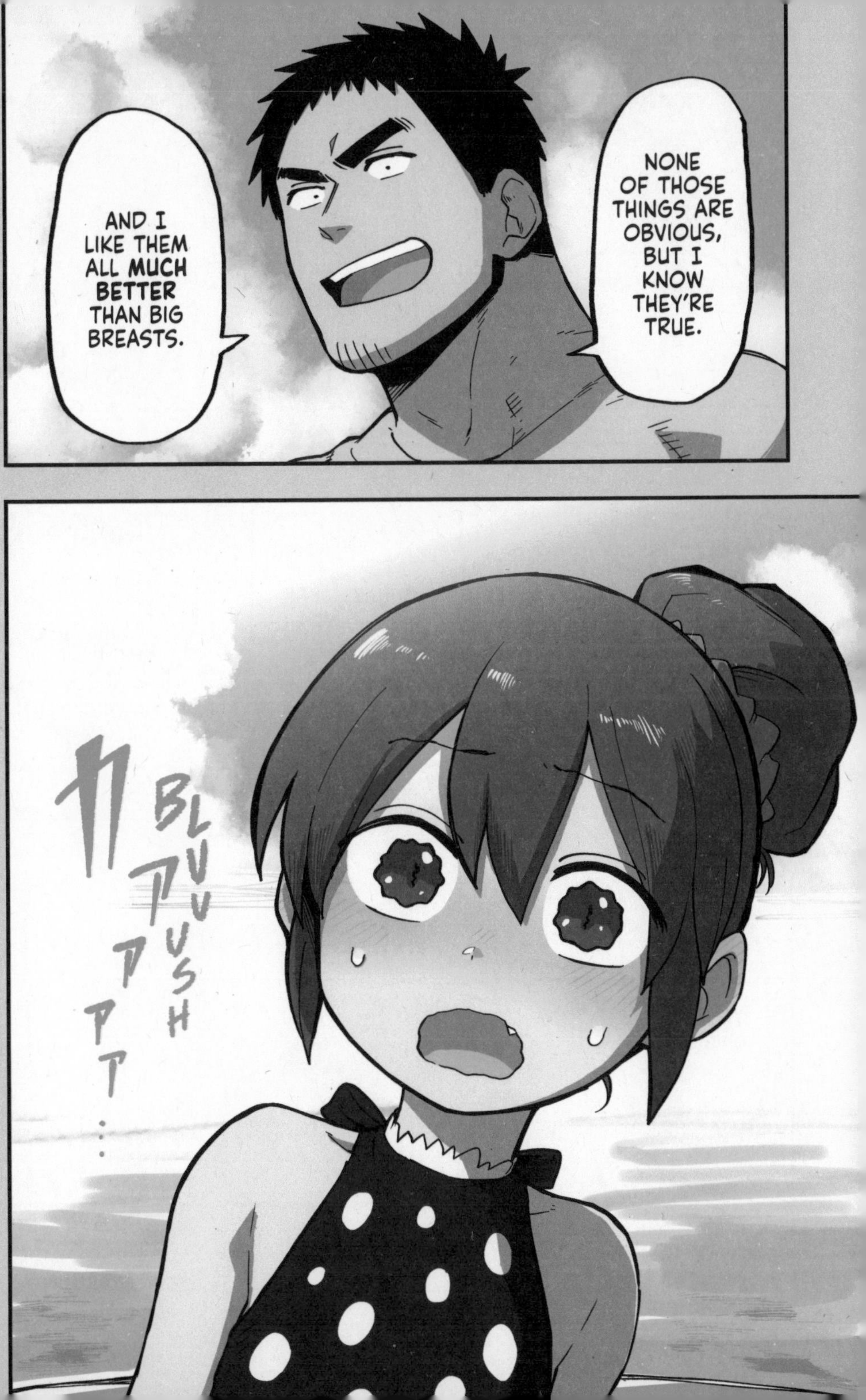
NONE OF THOSE THINGS ARE OBVIOUS, BUT I KNOW THEY'RE TRUE.
AND I LIKE THEM ALL **MUCH BETTER** THAN BIG BREASTS.
カァァァ…
BLUUUSH

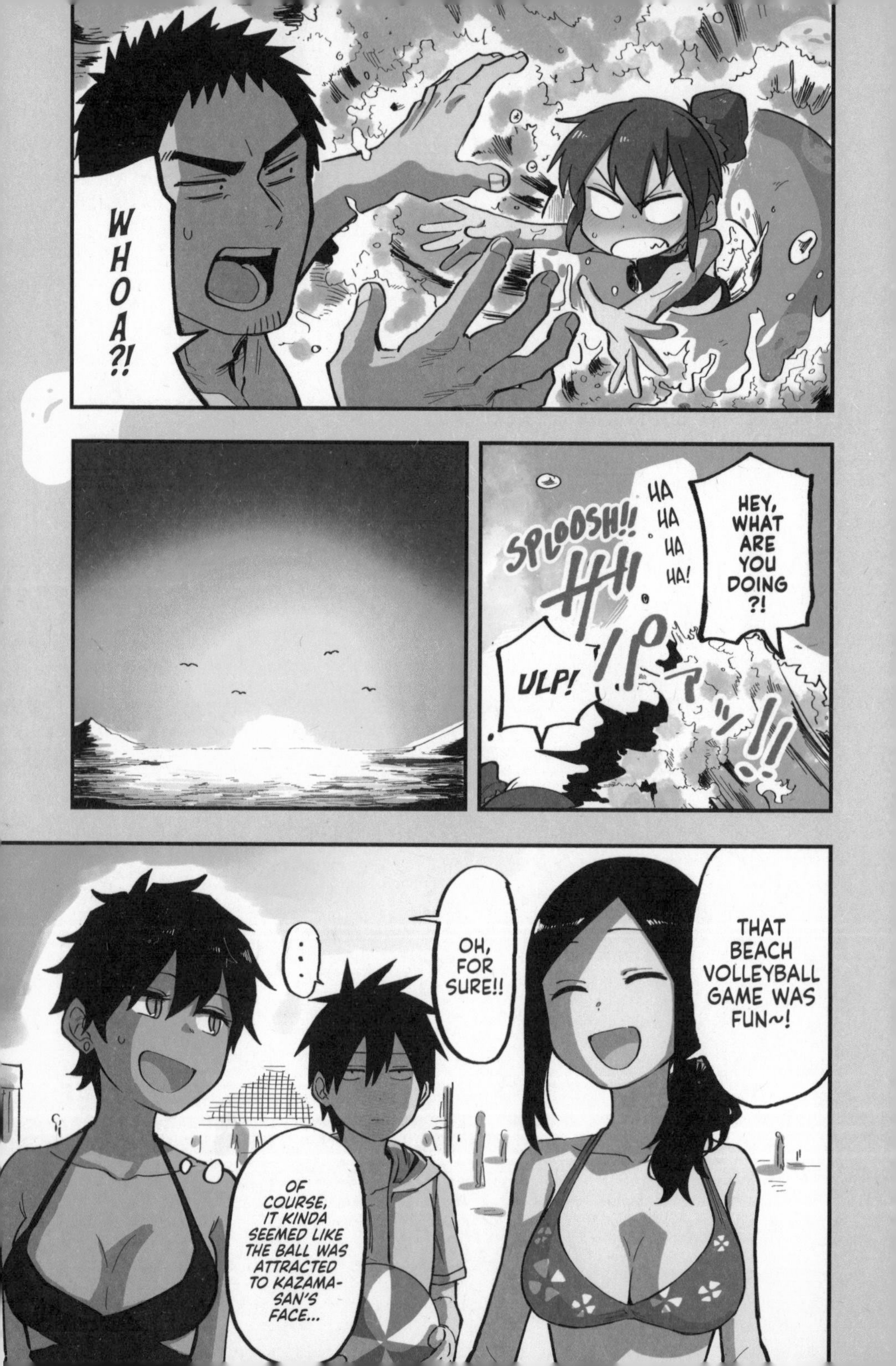
WHOA?!
HEY, WHAT ARE YOU DOING?!
HA HA HA HA!
SPLOOSH!!
ULP!
THAT BEACH VOLLEYBALL GAME WAS FUN~!
OH, FOR SURE!!
...
OF COURSE, IT KINDA SEEMED LIKE THE BALL WAS ATTRACTED TO KAZAMA-SAN'S FACE...

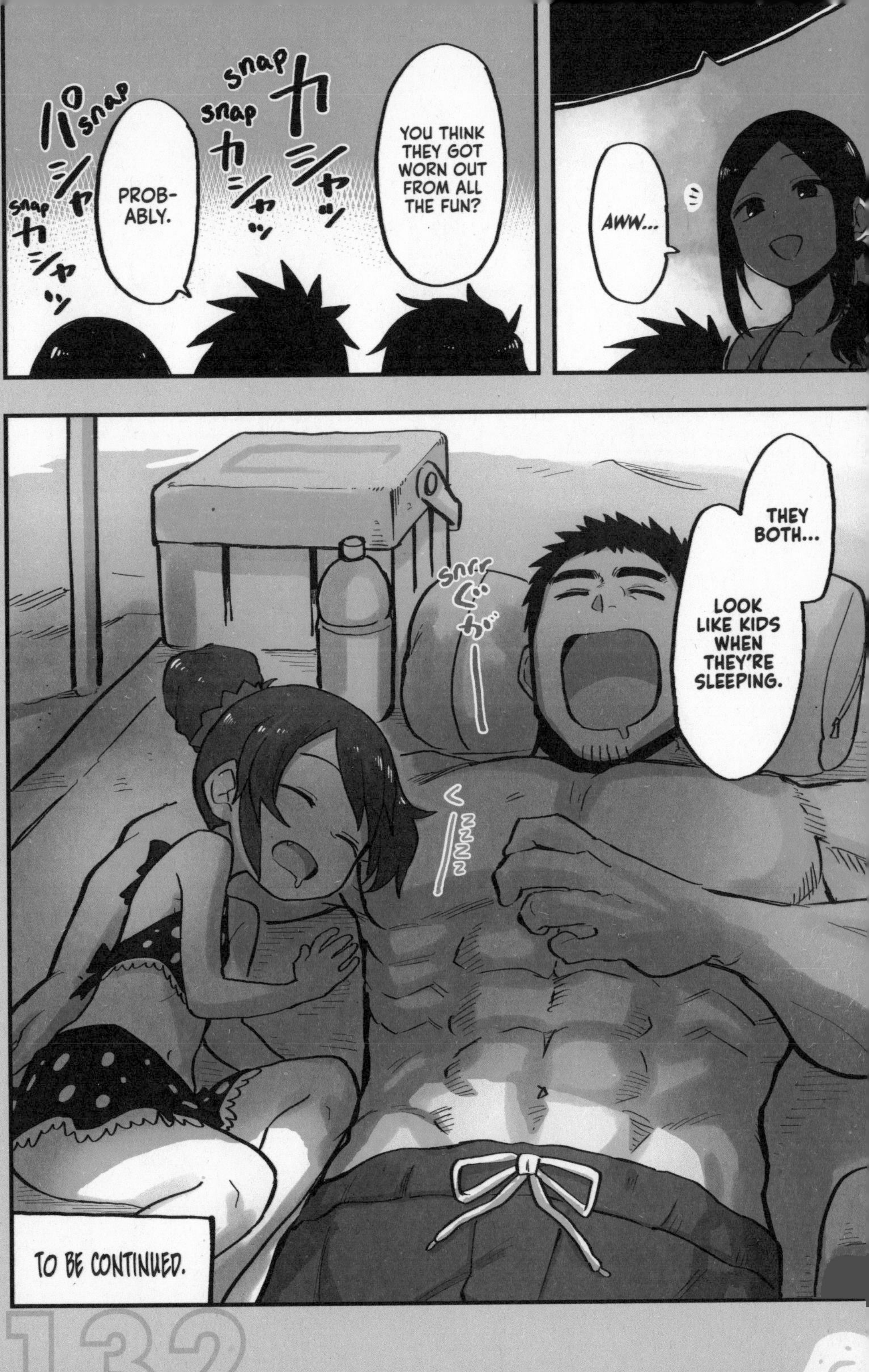
AWW...
YOU THINK THEY GOT WORN OUT FROM ALL THE FUN?
snap カシャッ
snap カシャッ
PROBABLY.
パsnap シャ
snap カシャッ
THEY BOTH...
LOOK LIKE KIDS WHEN THEY'RE SLEEPING.
Snrr ぐが――
く――zzzz
TO BE CONTINUED.

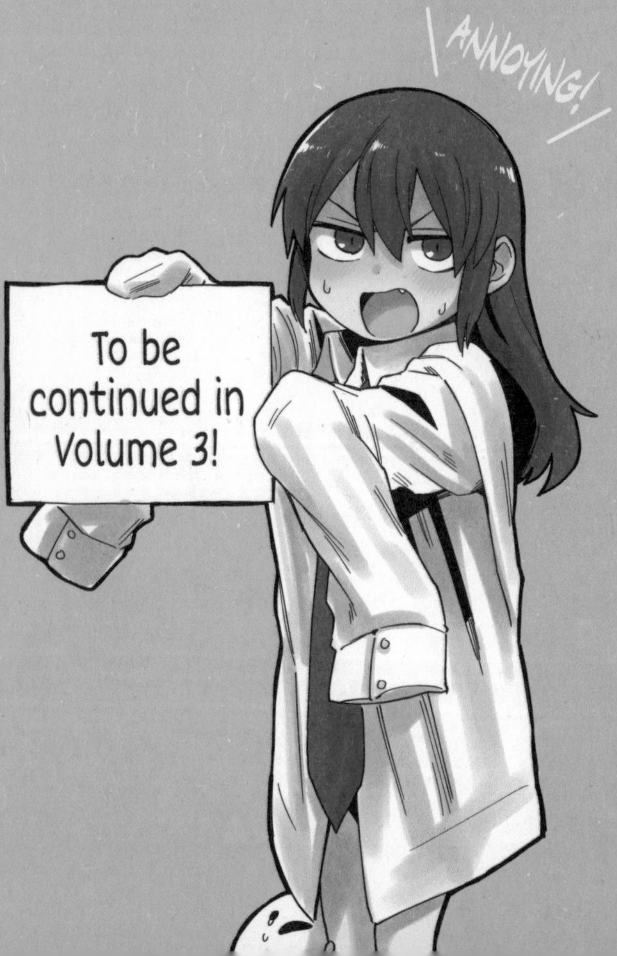
ANNOYING!
To be continued in Volume 3!

Afterword

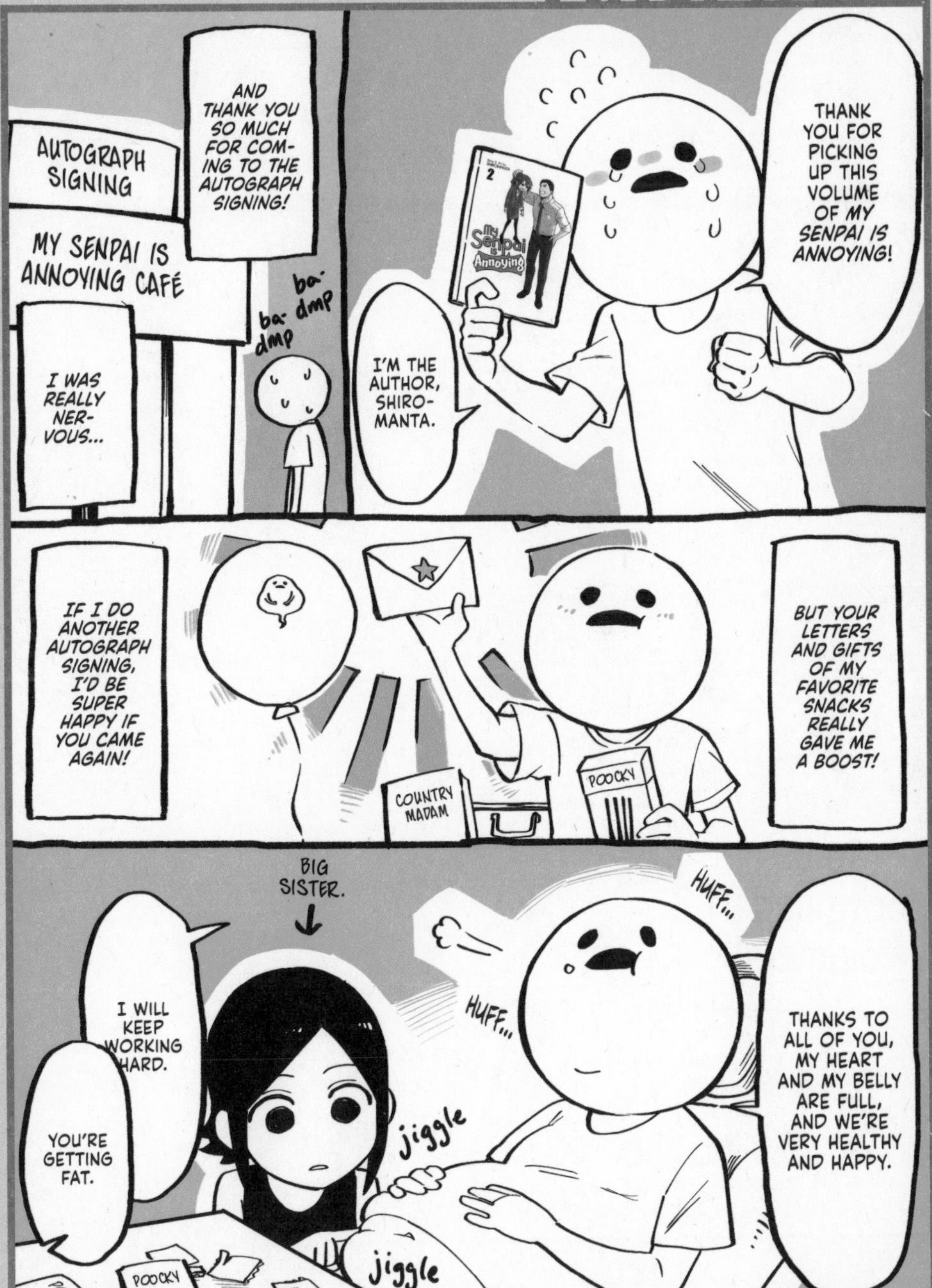
THANK YOU FOR PICKING UP THIS VOLUME OF MY SENPAI IS ANNOYING!
My Senpai is Annoying
2
I'M THE AUTHOR, SHIROMANTA.
AND THANK YOU SO MUCH FOR COMING TO THE AUTOGRAPH SIGNING!
AUTOGRAPH SIGNING
MY SENPAI IS ANNOYING CAFÉ
ba-dmp
ba-dmp
I WAS REALLY NERVOUS...
BUT YOUR LETTERS AND GIFTS OF MY FAVORITE SNACKS REALLY GAVE ME A BOOST!
POOCKY
COUNTRY MADAM
IF I DO ANOTHER AUTOGRAPH SIGNING, I'D BE SUPER HAPPY IF YOU CAME AGAIN!
THANKS TO ALL OF YOU, MY HEART AND MY BELLY ARE FULL, AND WE'RE VERY HEALTHY AND HAPPY.
HUFF...
HUFF...
BIG SISTER.
I WILL KEEP WORKING HARD.
jiggle
jiggle
YOU'RE GETTING FAT.
POOCKY
POOCKY
COUNTRY MADAM

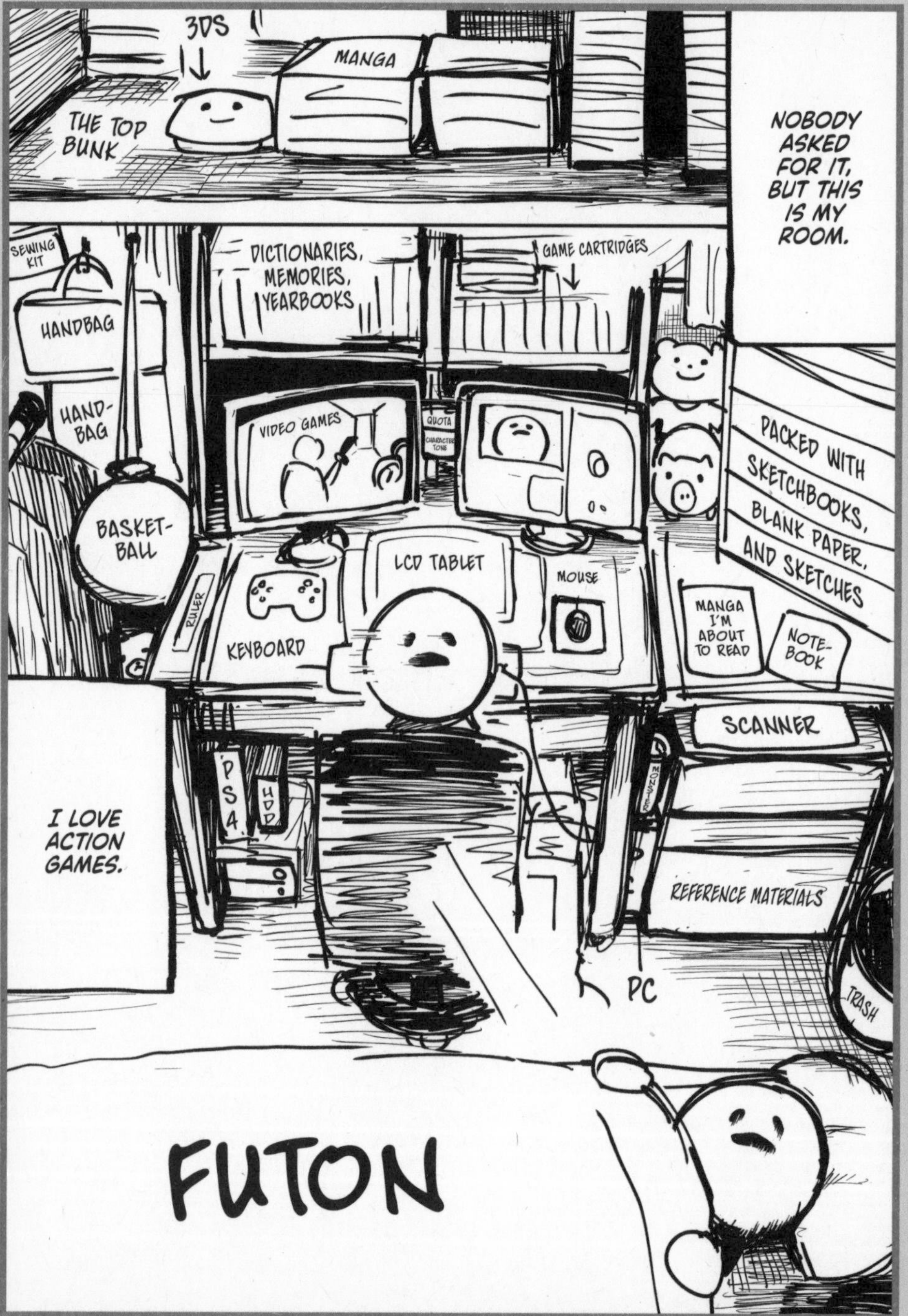
NOBODY ASKED FOR IT, BUT THIS IS MY ROOM.
MANGA
3DS
THE TOP BUNK
GAME CARTRIDGES
DICTIONARIES, MEMORIES, YEARBOOKS
SEWING KIT
HANDBAG
PACKED WITH SKETCHBOOKS, BLANK PAPER, AND SKETCHES
QUOTA
CHARACTER TONE
VIDEO GAMES
HAND-BAG
BASKET-BALL
NOTE-BOOK
MANGA I'M ABOUT TO READ
MOUSE
LCD TABLET
KEYBOARD
RULER
SCANNER
REFERENCE MATERIALS
PS4
HDD
I LOVE ACTION GAMES.
TRASH
PC
FUTON

しろまんた

SHIROMANTA

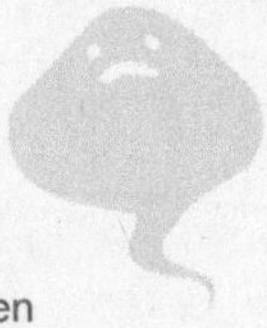

The hot days went on so long this summer that I got heatstroke. When you get sick, you can't doodle, play games, or draw manga, so everyone take good care of yourselves!
My diet was a success.

My Senpai is Annoying

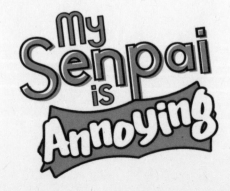

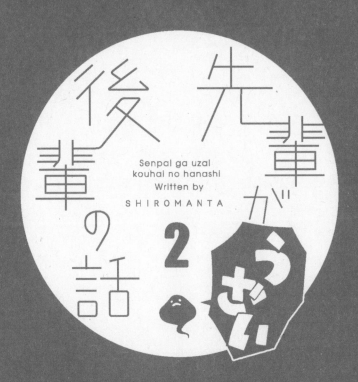

Senpai ga uzai
kouhai no hanashi
Written by
SHIROMANTA

2

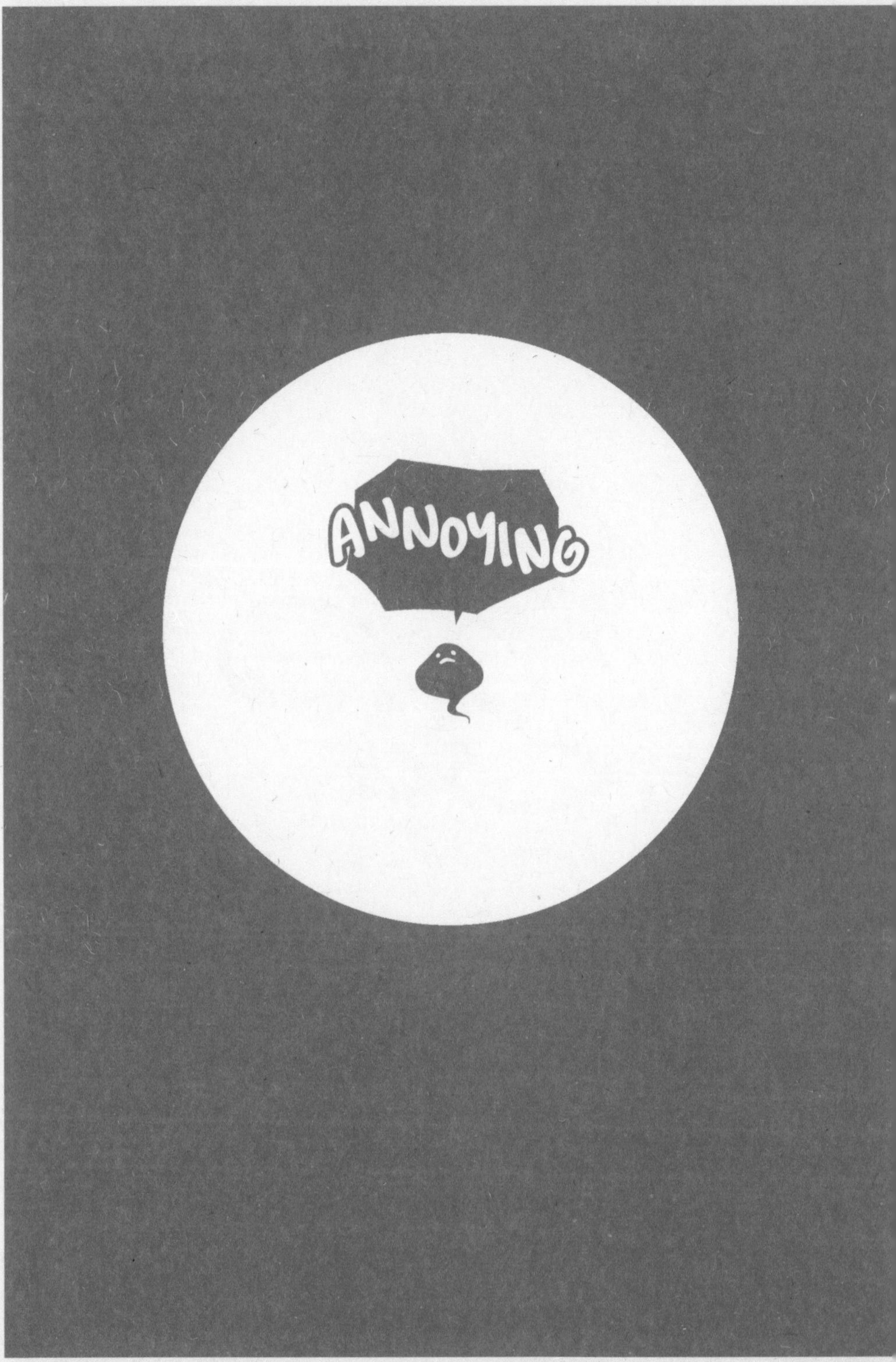
ANNOYING

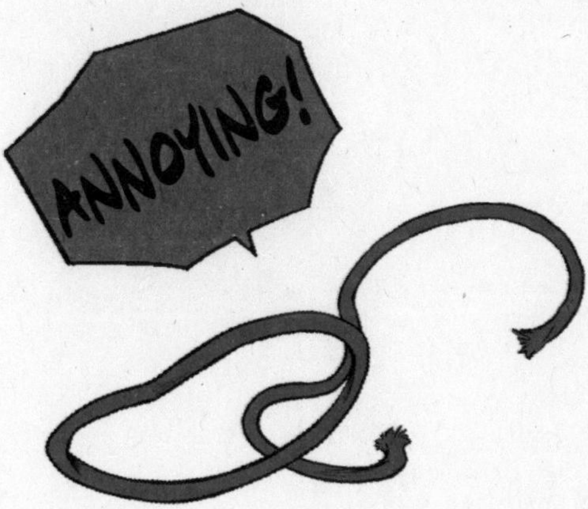
ANNOYING!

ANNOYING

My Senpai is Annoying

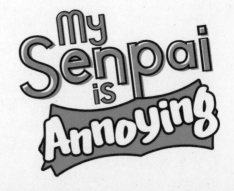

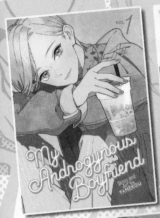
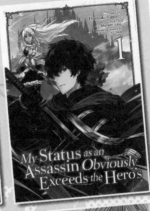
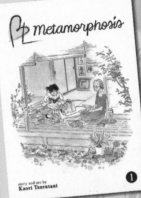
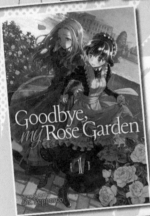
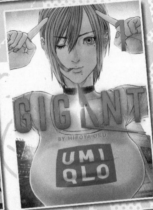
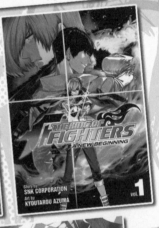
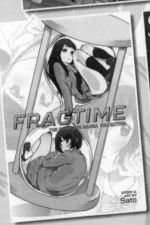
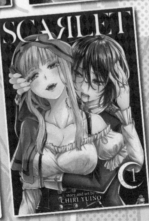
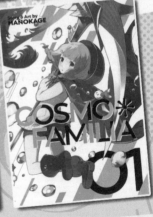

SEVEN SEAS ENTERTAINMENT PRESENTS

My Senpai is Annoying

story & art by SHIROMANTA

TRANSLATION
Alethea & Athena Nibley

LETTERING AND RETOUCH
Lys Blakeslee

COVER DESIGN
Nicky Lim

PROOFREADER
Stephanie Cohen

EDITOR
Shanti Whitesides

PREPRESS TECHNICIAN
Rhiannon Rasmussen-Silverstein

PRODUCTION MANAGER
Lissa Pattillo

MANAGING EDITOR
Julie Davis

ASSOCIATE PUBLISHER
Adam Arnold

PUBLISHER
Jason DeAngelis

MY SENPAI IS ANNOYING VOLUME 2
© Shiromanta 2018
First published in Japan in 2018 by ICHIJINSHA Inc., Tokyo.
English translation rights arranged with Kodansha Ltd., Tokyo, Japan.

Seven Seas press and purchase enquiries can be sent to Marketing Manager Lianne Sentar at press@gomanga.com. Information regarding the distribution and purchase of digital editions is available from Digital Manager CK Russell at digital@gomanga.com.

Seven Seas and the Seven Seas logo are trademarks of Seven Seas Entertainment. All rights reserved.

ISBN: 978-1-64505-536-5

Printed in Canada

First Printing: September 2020

10 9 8 7 6 5 4 3 2 1

FOLLOW US ONLINE: www.sevenseasentertainment.com

READING DIRECTIONS

This book reads from *right to left*, Japanese style. If this is your first time reading manga, you start reading from the top right panel on each page and take it from there. If you get lost, just follow the numbered diagram here. It may seem backwards at first, but you'll get the hang of it! Have fun!!

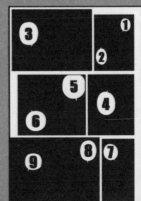